P9-CJP-059

WISE WOMEN

POSTSCRIPT

WISE WOMEN
Folk and Fairy Tales
from around the World

Retold and Edited by

Suzanne I. Barchers

Illustrated by
Leann Mullineaux

1990
LIBRARIES UNLIMITED, INC.
Englewood, Colorado

Copyright © 1990 Suzanne I. Barchers
All Rights Reserved
Printed in the United States of America

No part of this publication may be reproduced, stored in a
retrieval system, or transmitted, in any form or by any means,
electronic, mechanical, photocopying, recording, or otherwise, without the prior written permission of the publisher.

LIBRARIES UNLIMITED, INC.
P.O. Box 6633
Englewood, CO 80155-6633

Library of Congress Cataloging-in-Publication Data

Barchers, Suzanne I.
    Wise women : folk and fairy tales from around the world / retold
and edited by Suzanne I. Barchers ; illustrated by Leann Mullineaux.
    xiv, 324 p. 17x25 cm.
    ISBN 0-87287-816-3
    1. Women--Folklore.   I. Mullineaux, Leann.   II. Title.
GR740.B3   1990
398.2'082--dc20
                                                    90-38395
                                                       CIP

Wise Women: Folk and Fairy Tales from around the World
is dedicated to Miles Olson and Virginia Westerberg
in appreciation for their inspiration and guidance.

CONTENTS

Maidens: Clever and True

Attendants: Ingenious and Loyal

Wives and Mothers: Devoted and Cunning

Mature Women: Bold and Wise

PREFACE

Women have always played key roles in the folk and fairy tales of the world. However, their images often have been tainted by their popular characterizations as passive heroines in need of rescue ("Sleeping Beauty" and "Snow White"), as insipid victims ("Little Red Riding Hood" and "Rapunzel"), or as willful, spoiled princesses ("The Frog Princess" and "The Princess on the Glass Hill").

Marcia Lieberman discusses the profound influence fairy tales have had, stating, "Millions of women must surely have formed their psycho-sexual self-concepts, and their ideas of what they could or could not accomplish, what sort of behavior would be rewarded, and of the nature of the reward itself, in part from their favorite fairy tales."[1] What little girl could resist the power of the "happily ever after" theme with its promise of beauty, wealth, and a romantic rescue by a prince? Lieberman points out that some might consider the passivity of heroines an archetypal female behavior, but critics of such tales are more likely to consider them as powerful training manuals for girls.

Often contrasted against the pretty and passive heroine is the truly powerful adult female who is vain, jealous, proud, or evil. She is Hansel and Gretel's stepmother who places a higher priority on her own full stomach than on the lives of the children; she is Cinderella's stepsister who resorts to cutting off a toe or heel to attract a prince; she is the king's mother who tries to kill her grandchildren in Perrault's "The Sleeping Beauty in the Wood." Not only is she aggressive and commanding, she is usually ugly. "It is a psychological truth that as children, and as women, girls fear homeliness ... and this fear is a major source of anxiety, diffidence, and convictions of inadequacy and inferiority among women."[2]

---

[1]Marcia R. Lieberman, " 'Some Day My Prince Will Come': Female Acculturation through the Fairy Tale," *College English* 34 (December 1972): 385.

[2]Ibid.

Feminists might conclude that today's children should not be exposed to the stereotypes of traditional folk and fairy tales. But diligent searching of the literature demonstrates that though limited in number there are traditional tales worthy of reading and hearing. In an initial study of over 2,000 folk and fairy tales only 67 different tales were found to have female heroes who showed intelligence, perseverance, or bravery. After further review of another 2,000 tales, the total rose to 100 different tales with female heroes. It is from this set of tales that *Wise Women* has been drawn.

These are not tales of females thrust into traditionally male roles. They are not contrived, although "The Little Old Woman Who Went to the North Wind" may seem like a role reversal because a more commonly found later variant features her son in the heroic role as he travels to the North Wind. These tales include daughters, sisters, maidens, attendants, wives, mothers, and mature women who are clever, courageous, loyal, wise, and bold. Although some of the tales by necessity include some characters who provide negative portrayals of women, such as an evil stepmother or jealous sister, the tales were selected carefully to represent the best of the heroic women. Some of them are repeatedly heroic, as in "Princess Sivatra," while Gretel is included because of only one fleeting moment of heroism. Occasionally the female hero receives magical help, as in "Kumba and Kambili," but generally most are heroic for their ingenuity and resourcefulness.

Though attention has been given to the negative effect of the images of passive women in fairy tales, there is no mention in the literature of the possible negative consequences of the traditional role required of men to rescue, slay dragons, or pursue quests. Though the focus of *Wise Women* is on heroic females, this is not a collection of stories of male victims. Certainly Tam Lin and the Beast are in danger, relying upon the love of a woman to rescue them. And some of the men are ridiculous, as in "The Foolish Husbands"; a few are evil, as in "Bolster"; and some are spineless, as is the father in "Hansel and Gretel." But there are more who are as equally devoted or enterprising as the women in the tales.

These men and women provide a balance seldom found in traditional collections of folk and fairy tales. They are for readers of all ages who love the traditional form of the folk and fairy tale.

ACKNOWLEDGMENTS

Grateful acknowledgment is made for permission to use the following copyrighted tales: "The Grateful Prince" and "The Lute Player" from *The Violet Fairy Book*, edited by Andrew Lang, published by Dover Publications, Inc., 1966; "Beauty and the Beast," "The Master-Maid," "East of the Sun and West of the Moon," and "The Forty Thieves" from *The Blue Fairy Book*, edited by Andrew Lang, published by Dover Publications, Inc., 1965; "Catherine and Her Destiny," "King Lindorm," "The Snow Queen," "The Water of Life," and the "Wounded Lion" from *The Pink Fairy Book*, by Andrew Lang, published by Dover Publications, Inc., 1967; "The Girl and the Road Agent," "How Toodie Fixed Old Grunt," and "What Candy Ashcraft Done" from *The Devil's Pretty Daughter*, by Vance Randolph, © 1955, published by Columbia University Press, used by permission; "Rachel Found the Gold" from *Sticks in the Knapsack and Other Ozark Tales*, edited by Vance Randolph, © 1958, by permission of the estate of Vance Randolph; "How Kate Got a Husband," "The Poppet Caught a Thief," and "The Woman and the Robber" from *Who Blowed Up the Church House?—and Other Ozark Folk Tales*, edited by Vance Randolph, © 1952, by permission of the estate of Vance Randolph; "The Basil Plant" and "The Little Orphan Girl" from *Folktales of Chile* by Yolando Pino-Saavedra, © 1967 by the University of Chicago, all rights reserved; "St. David's Flood" from *Folktales of England*, by Katherine Briggs and Ruth Tongue, © 1965 by the University of Chicago, all rights reserved; "The Twelve Months," edited by Georgios A. Megas, © 1970 by the University of Chicago, all rights reserved; "The Wild Goose Lake" from *Folktales of China*, edited by Wolfram Eberhard, © 1965; "The Legend of Tchi-Niu," "Ubazakura," and "Stone Patience and Knife Patience" from *Fairy Tales of the Orient*, selected by Pearl S. Buck, © 1965 by Pearl S. Buck and Lyle Kenyon Engel, reprinted by permission of Harold Ober Associates Incorporated; "One More Child" from *The Beautiful Blue Jay and Other Tales of India* by John W. Spellman, © 1967 by John W. Spellman, used by permission.

Grateful acknowledgment is made for permission to use the following copyrighted tales as the source for retelling: "The Creature in the Forest" (for "Martha, the Holy Woman"), "The Terrible Lion-Man" (for "Kumba and Kambili"), and "The Saving of Tam Lin" (for "Janet and Tam Lin") from *Great Myths and Legends*, The 1984 Childcraft Annual, © 1984 by World Book, Inc.

All other tales were retold from a variety of sources. Many are from a combination of sources and variants, or both. Some minor liberties were taken with some retellings; for example, references to physical characteristics were omitted if they were unnecessary to the story. "The Snow Queen" by Hans Christian Andersen is a literary tale, as opposed to a tale recorded from oral sources.

D·A·U·G·H·T·E·R·S

Clever and Courageous

THE PEASANT'S CLEVER DAUGHTER
(Germany and Italy)

here once was a peasant who had only a small house and a daughter. One day his daughter suggested that he ask the king for a piece of land to farm. The king saw how poor they were and granted their request, giving them a small piece of grassland to clear.

The peasant and his daughter were spading the field when they found a mortar of pure gold. "Listen," said the father, "the king was kind enough to give us this field. Why don't we give him this mortar in return?"

"But father, if we give him a mortar and no pestle, he'll want a pestle as well. We should just keep quiet."

But the father wouldn't listen. He took the mortar to the king, telling him that he had found it in his field and asking the king to accept it as a gift.

The king took the mortar, asking the peasant if he had found anything else.

"No," answered the peasant.

"What about the pestle?" asked the king. "There must be a pestle as well. Bring me the pestle!"

The peasant told him that there was no pestle, but the king wouldn't listen. He threw the peasant into prison, telling him that he would stay there until he produced the pestle.

When the servants brought him his bread and water, they heard him sighing, "Oh, if I had only listened to my daughter. If I had only listened to my daughter." He would not eat or drink, but only sighed, "Oh, if I had only listened to my daughter."

The servants told the king about how the peasant kept sighing, "Oh, if I had only listened to my daughter," and about how he would not eat or drink. The king had the servants bring the peasant and he asked him why he kept sighing.

"Oh, if I had only listened to my daughter."

"What did she tell you?" asked the king.

"She told me not to give you the mortar, for you would only want the pestle as well."

The king responded, "Well, if your daughter is so clever, tell her I want to see her."

Soon she came before the king, who said that since she was so clever he had a riddle for her to solve and that if she solved it he would marry her. She answered that of course she would solve it.

"Here is the riddle. Come to me not clothed, not naked, not riding, not walking, not on the road, not off the road. If you can do that, I will marry you."

She went home and took off all her clothes and wrapped a big fishnet around her so she was not naked. Then she hired a donkey and tied the fishnet to its tail. The donkey dragged her along, neither walking nor riding. As he dragged her along the wagon tracks, she touched her big toes to the ground so that she was neither on the road nor off it. When she came to the king he said that she had truly solved the riddle and fulfilled all his requirements. He let her father out of prison, married her, and put her in charge of all his royal possessions.

Some years later the king was inspecting his troops, and some peasants who were selling wood stopped their wagons outside the palace. Some of the wagons were drawn by oxen and some were drawn by horses. One of the peasants had three horses and one of them had a foal that ran off and lay down between two oxen that were harnessed to another peasant's wagon. The two peasants began to fight because each one wanted to keep the foal. The argument was brought before the king, and he decided that since the foal had lain between the oxen it must stay with the oxen.

The other peasant left, weeping over the loss of his foal, but as he had heard that the queen was kindhearted and of common heritage, he decided to appeal to her for help.

The queen said, "If you promise to keep this a secret, I will tell you what to do. Tomorrow morning, when the king goes out to inspect his troops, take a fishnet, stand in the middle of the road, and pretend that you are fishing. Shake out the net now and then as if it were full and go on fishing." And she told him what to say when the king questioned him.

The next morning the peasant stood fishing on dry land. The king saw him and sent his orderly to ask the peasant what he was doing. He told the orderly he was fishing and when the orderly asked him how he could possibly fish with no water, the peasant replied, "There is just as much chance of my catching a fish on dry land as there is an ox having a foal."

The orderly took the peasant's answer to the king and the king summoned the peasant. "You did not think of this alone. Where did you get help?" The peasant insisted he thought of it himself. So they beat him until he confessed that the queen had helped him.

When the king went to his wife, he said, "Why have you been untrue? I won't have you for my wife any longer. Go back to the peasant life you came from." However, he gave her one last request, permission to take with her the best and dearest farewell gift she could think of.

"Yes, my dear husband," she said, "if that is your command, I will obey it." She threw her arms around him, kissed him, and asked him to have a farewell drink with her. She sent for a strong sleeping potion, adding it to the drink, and while the king took a big swallow, she only sipped a little. When he was sleeping soundly, she called a servant and wrapped a fine white sheet around the king. The servant carried him to a carriage that was waiting at the door and she took him home to her bed in her little house.

He slept through the next day and night, and when he finally woke up, he looked around and said, "Where am I?" He called for his servants, but no one came.

At last his wife came to his bedside and said, "Dear king and husband, you told me to take what was best and dearest with me. Nothing is better or dearer to me than you. So I took you with me."

The king's eyes filled with tears. "Dearest wife, never again shall we part." He took her back to the royal palace and married her again. I think they are still together even now.

THE YOUNG HEAD OF THE FAMILY
(China)

There once was an old Chinese gentleman who had three sons. Two were married, but his youngest had not yet found a bride. The man's household was generally happy until the two daughters-in-law left to visit their mother. One day he was contemplating how he might stop their visits when he thought of a plan.

The next time they asked to leave to visit their mother he said, "You may go this time, but upon your return you must bring me two things. If my request is not fulfilled you will not be allowed to visit your mother again."

"Of course, father. Just tell us what you want," said the daughters-in-law.

"You must bring me some wind wrapped in paper," he said to the one daughter-in-law. And to the other he said, "You must bring me some fire wrapped in paper."

The girls were puzzled about these requests, but they were so anxious to see their mother they did not worry about fulfilling them. Their visit was pleasant, passing quickly. Suddenly it was time to return and they realized they had not given any thought to the old man's request.

Yet, leave they must, and as they walked along the road their dejection was obvious to all who passed them. They wondered aloud how they could return empty-handed and were overheard by a young girl on a buffalo. She asked them to tell her their story, and they explained that they could never return to visit their mother if they went to their home without wind and fire wrapped in paper.

"Your task is an easy one," the girl said. "Bring the old man a fan and a lantern and he will be satisfied."

The daughters-in-law were delighted that their problems were solved, and they thanked the young girl before continuing on their way.

When they arrived, the old man was dismayed that they had answered his riddles. He insisted they tell him how they had solved them and they told him about meeting the young girl who was so clever.

"Such a shrewd girl must be a part of my family. She shall marry my son," declared the old man. He sent out messengers who searched the countryside for the girl on the buffalo. When they found her, he sent word that she should come to meet his family.

When she arrived, he proposed that she should marry his youngest son. As all marriages customarily were arranged and she did not find the youngest son displeasing, she accepted. She soon proved her intelligence by her efficient management of the household.

The old man was exceedingly pleased with his life. His contentment was so great that he had a sign reading "No Sorrow" placed over his gate. Shortly after this, a mandarin passing by the house saw the sign and became curious about the person who had the audacity to proclaim his happiness to all who passed. He decided to confront the residents and punish them for their impudence. But it was the clever daughter-in-law who came out to meet him.

"For your impertinence at proclaiming this to be a house of no sorrow, you must weave me a cloth as long as this road," the mandarin commanded.

"Of course, your Excellency," the young girl answered. "I will be pleased to honor your command when you have found the two ends of the road and measured how many feet long the cloth must be."

The mandarin was at a loss. The cleverness of her answer had him baffled. He said to the girl, "Perhaps instead your fine shall be the amount of oil there is in the sea."

"Of course, your Excellency," agreed the young girl once again. "Tell me the number of gallons in the sea and I will begin to press the oil from the beans."

Again the mandarin was silenced. He thought for a moment and decided it would be difficult to best this clever girl. He stooped and picked up a nearby pigeon.

"You are quick with your thinking. I have decided not to fine you after all. But I have another question for you. Tell me if I intend to squeeze this pigeon to death or let it fly free."

The girl bowed to the mandarin and said, "Your Excellency, I am only a mere woman, whereas you are a highly regarded mandarin. You must be able to tell me when I have one of my feet inside the threshold and one of them outside whether I intend to go in or come out."

Once again the mandarin was silenced. The young girl bowed again and said, "If your Excellency cannot answer my riddle, you should not expect me to answer your riddle."

"You are correct," the mandarin said. "It is now clear to me why this is a house of no sorrow."

The mandarin resumed his journey, and the young girl resumed her excellent management of the household.

THE GIRL AND THE ROAD AGENT
(United States, Ozarks)

One time there was a man that didn't do no work, as he just loaned out money at big interest. He didn't trust nobody but his own daughter, and she was a big stout girl about sixteen years old. Some folks over east of town had paid off their mortgage, and the girl was a-carrying the money home to her pappy. It was small bills and silver, in a little paper sack.

She was walking along tending to her own business, when here come a road agent all dressed up. He says, "Howdy," and then all of a sudden he jumped off'n his horse and grabbed her from behind. Most of her dress was tore off right now, but she kicked the fellow in the belly and yelled like a steam engine. When she seen he was getting the best of her, the girl tore the poke and scattered silver dollars all over the place. The road agent dropped her like a hot potater and begun to pick up the money. The girl just laid still for a minute, and then she jumped on his big horse and away she went. The road agent run and hollered and fired his pistol, but he didn't hit nothing.

When the girl got home the old man says what on earth do you mean, riding around the country half-naked? And whose horse is that, and where is the money for the mortgage? She told him what happened, and they looked in the saddlebags. And what do you think? Them saddlebags was plumb full of gold and silver! Finally her pappy says, "Are you hurt?" and she told him no. So then the old man says, "Daughter, you have done a fine day's work, because there is ten times as much money in the saddlebags as you had in the paper poke. And we got a good horse besides, with a fine saddle and bridle to boot."

And that's the way it was, too. Because if a fellow is a road agent he can't go hollering to the law, or else the sheriff might want to know where he got all that gold and silver. And maybe there is a reward out for him besides. Also the girl would tell the jury how this man attacked her and tore her clothes off, so he'd be throwed in the jailhouse for seventy years' hard labor. It just goes to show that honesty pays off in the long run, like the old man says.

THE TALE OF THE OKI ISLANDS
(Japan)

There once was a girl named Tokoyo who was dearly loved by her father, Oribe Shima. Oribe was a samurai, a soldier of great nobility. But he and his daughter had been separated when the emperor banished him after a misunderstanding. The emperor had suffered from ill health for many years and often acted in haste because of his discomfort. Oribe had been sent to the Oki Islands, a desolate set of islands off the coast of Japan. There Oribe passed lonely days, wondering what Tokoyo was doing and dreaming of his former life.

Tokoyo was an exceptionally brave girl. Her many years spent diving for oysters had made her strong and courageous. She decided she would no longer be separated from her father and sold nearly all her belongings so that she could go to him.

She arrived at the village of Akasaki and looked longingly across the sea to the distant islands where her father was exiled. She asked many fishermen to take her to the islands, but no one dared risk the anger of the emperor.

But Tokoyo would not be dissuaded. After buying a bit of food, she waited for nightfall. Then she stole down to the edge of the water and cut loose a small sailboat. All through the night and the next day she sailed across the sea until she arrived on the shore of one of the islands. Darkness was closing in and she fell exhausted to the ground where she slept through the night.

The next morning she started walking along the shore. She asked a fisherman about her father and he cautioned her to never mention his name aloud or she would risk further retribution. Heeding his advice, she wandered from village to village, listening to the people's conversations, hoping to learn about her father. No one spoke of him.

After many days she came to a shrine high above the water where she prayed to Buddha for help. It was evening and she dozed for some time, only to be awakened by the sound of a young girl's weeping. She looked around her and saw a priest praying over a lovely young girl who was dressed in a white robe. The priest led the sobbing girl to the high rocks and continued his prayers. Tokoyo crept up behind them and just as the priest was about to push the girl over the rocks and into the sea below, Tokoyo grabbed her and pulled her back onto the rocks.

13

The priest was astounded at her actions and told her why he had been about to sacrifice the young girl.

"The Oki Islands are plagued by an evil sea god who demands the sacrifice of a young girl each year. If we disobey him, he becomes enraged. His storms cause the death of many of our fishermen. Thus we must sacrifice one to save the lives of many."

Tokoyo answered, "Please let me take her place. I have come to these islands to find my father who was banished by the emperor. I have not been able to reach him and without him my life is empty. I have written a letter to him. If you would be so kind as to deliver it I will die in peace."

Tokoyo knelt and prayed for courage. She put on the white robe the girl had worn, and she also placed her jeweled dagger between her teeth. While the girl and the priest watched, Tokoyo bowed low to them and then dived into the sea. Her body disappeared beneath the waves.

Tokoyo's years of diving gave her confidence. She descended deeper and deeper into the sea. As she reached the bottom she saw a huge cave covered with glittering shells. She took her dagger in her hand and swam into the cave, stopping quickly at the sight of a man. Looking more closely she realized it was a statue of the emperor who had banished her father. Working quickly, she removed the statue and began swimming back to the entrance of the cave.

Suddenly Tokoyo was startled by the sight of a huge scaly monster that had red eyes, many legs, and a long ridged tail. The beast was so big that it wallowed in the heavy sea. Having the advantage of speed, Tokoyo swam quickly forward and thrust her dagger into one eye. Pulling it out, she watched as the evil sea god floundered in the water, thrashing with pain, searching for refuge in its cave entrance. Wasting no time, Tokoyo swam forward again and stabbed the monster in the heart. In a matter of seconds, the creature drifted to the sea's floor, dying a painful death.

Tokoyo wanted to prove to the people of the island that they no longer needed to fear the sea god. Gasping with the last of her breath, she dragged the monster's body as she swam to the surface.

Only a few minutes had passed since Tokoyo had dived into the sea, so the priest and the young girl were still on the rocky cliffs above Tokoyo. Seeing her struggling with the statue and the body of the monster, they rushed down the rocks to help her. Once she had rested on the sand for a moment she told them of her brave adventure.

Tokoyo was then heralded by everyone on the island. Messengers were sent to the emperor whose health had miraculously improved. When he learned of the statue, he realized that an enemy had created his image, cursed it, and put it in the cave. By retrieving it, Tokoyo had broken the evil spell. He wasted no time in releasing Oribe from his exile.

Tokoyo and her father were reunited and they returned to their village and lands. Soon their lives were as before and they rejoiced daily in their togetherness. The people of Oki never forgot the bravery of Tokoyo, telling of her feats even today.

THE WILD GOOSE LAKE
(China)

t is reported that a man by the name of Chiao lived with his daughter in the village P'o-lo at the foot of Horse Ear Mountain. The girl's name was Sea Girl.

One year there was such a great drought that the people could not live on the products of the fields. Sea Girl and her father went up to Horse Ear Mountain to cut bamboo to make brooms to sell. One day, after Sea Girl had cut a great deal of bamboo, she suddenly saw a shiny lake. The lake was absolutely clear; not a single fallen leaf was on the water. Whenever a leaf fell from any of the trees surrounding the lake, a big wild goose came and carried it away. This was called Wild Goose Lake.

Sea Girl was very glad she had found the lake, and quickly carried her bamboo home. The next day she took an ax and tried to see whether she could make an outlet from the lake to get water for the drought-stricken people. For half a day she walked around the lake. She saw that the lake was surrounded by big mountains, forests, and rocks, but in one place there was a stone gate. She worked a long time on it, but could not open it. This troubled her very much, and she sat down under a tree and tried to decide what she should do. All of a sudden a wild goose came and said to her, "Sea Girl, Sea Girl, you need a golden key to open Wild Goose Lake." Where could she find a golden key? Before she could ask, the goose was gone. Sea Girl walked along the shore until she came to a cypress forest. In the forest were three parrots, whom she asked, "Parrots, parrots, where can I find the golden key?"

The parrots answered her, "Sea Girl, Sea Girl, first you have to find the third daughter of the dragon king." Sea Girl continued to walk along the lake, searching for the dragon king's third daughter. When she came to a pine grove, she saw a peacock sitting on a tree and asked him, "Peacock, peacock, where can I find the dragon king's third daughter?" The peacock told her, "Sea Girl, Sea Girl, you will find her in the canyon of the southern mountain."

Then the peacock flew to the south and alighted in a cinnamon tree. Sea Girl followed the peacock, but when she came to the cinnamon tree she did not see the dragon king's third daughter. Again the peacock on the tree said to her, "Sea Girl, Sea Girl, the third daughter loves songs. If you sing the songs the folk sing, she will come forth." And then the peacock flew away.

Sea Girl began to sing. The first day she sang about the snowflakes on the mountains, but the dragon king's third daughter did not appear. The second day Sea Girl sang about the green grass in the lake, but still the third daughter did not come. On the third day Sea Girl sang about the blossoming flowers on the hills, until the sun disappeared behind the mountains.

Then the third daughter of the dragon king came out of the lake. The dragon king had made a rule that the people of his palace were not allowed to come into the human world without permission. But the third daughter loved folksongs so much that on the third day she could no longer contain herself and secretly came out of the water. Sea Girl sang even better than she herself and so she greatly admired her.

She asked Sea Girl, "Whose daughter are you? Where do you live? Why do you come to sing here every day?"

Sea Girl answered, "My name is Sea Girl. I live in P'o-lo village at the foot of Horse Ear Mountain. I am searching for the golden key to release the water of Wild Goose Lake to help the drought-stricken people."

The good-hearted third daughter told her, "The golden key is in the treasury of the dragon king, and a big eagle is guarding it. The eagle would kill anybody, except the king himself, who dared to enter the treasury. Only when the king leaves the palace," she said, "is there any possibility of getting into the treasury."

Finally one day, when the dragon king had left, the third daughter took Sea Girl into the palace. Taking turns, they sang songs in front of the treasury. At first the old eagle was asleep and paid no attention to the singing. Soon he awoke and, touched by the music, opened his wings and came to see who was singing. At this moment Sea Girl quickly slipped into the treasury to look for the golden key.

In the treasury her eyes were dazzled. The room was full of gold, silver, and precious stones. If she had taken but one of the jewels, she would have been wealthy for a lifetime. But she thought only of the golden key, and did not care about gold, silver, and riches. She quickly searched through the whole treasury without finding the key. Then in her haste she happened to knock over a big wooden box. When the box fell to the floor, it opened with a bang and out fell a shiny golden key. She took the key and hurriedly left the treasury. When Sea Girl came out, the dragon king's daughter stopped singing and both girls went out to Wild Goose Lake. When the beautiful songs stopped, the old eagle returned to his accustomed place and went back to sleep.

Sea Girl took the golden key and knocked three times at the gate. It opened and the water streamed out. In minutes all the canals of P'o-lo village were overflowing with water. When the daughter of the dragon king saw that the rush of water would sweep away the whole harvest, she quickly said, "Sea Girl, Sea Girl, the harvest will be washed away." Sea Girl looked back and became frightened. She stopped the water with some straw curtains.

Who would have thought that straw curtains would be so strong that water would only trickle through the seams, after the stone gate was gone? The curtains are still there, but they have become stone curtains by now.

When the dragon king returned, he found that the key was gone and he knew that his third daughter had allowed it to be stolen. He banished his daughter from the palace, and so she went to live on earth with Sea Girl, and both sang together the whole day long. Later the women of all the surrounding villages came together each year on the twenty-second day of the seventh moon to sing songs.

STONE PATIENCE AND KNIFE PATIENCE
(Turkey)

O nce there was a poor woman who had only one daughter, and this poor woman used to go out and wash linen while her daughter remained at home sewing. One day the daughter was sitting by her favorite place at the window when a little bird flew onto her sewing table and said, "Oh, little damsel, poor little damsel! What shall be your fate!" Whereupon it flew away again.

From that hour the damsel's peace of mind was gone, and in the evening she told her mother what the bird had said.

"Close the door and the window," said her mother when she heard the story, "then sit at your work as usual."

So the next morning the daughter closed the door and the window and sat down to her work. All at once there came a *whirr-r-r-r!* and there was the little bird again on the sewing table saying, "Oh, little damsel, poor little damsel! What shall be your fate!" With that it flew away again. The damsel was more terrified than ever, but her mother comforted her again.

"Tomorrow," she said, "tightly close the door and the window and get into the cupboard. Light a candle there and go on with your work."

As soon as her mother departed with the dawn, the girl closed up everything, lit a candle, and locked herself in the cupboard with her sewing table.

Scarcely had she stitched two stitches when the bird stood before her again, saying, "Oh, little damsel, poor little damsel! What shall be your fate!" and *whirr-r-r-r!* it flew away again. The damsel was in such distress that she scarcely knew where she was. She threw her work aside and began tormenting herself about what this saying might mean. Her mother, too, could not get to the bottom of the matter, and she remained at home the next day so that she might see the bird—but the bird did not come again.

Their worry continued, nevertheless, and all the joy of their life was gone. They never stirred from the house but watched and waited, continually wondering whether the bird might come again. One day their neighbor's daughter came and asked the woman to let her daughter go with them.

"If she went for a little outing," they said, "she might forget her trouble."

The woman did not like to let her go, but they promised to take great care and not to lose sight of her, so at last she consented.

The damsels went into the fields then, and danced and sang until the day was almost over. On the way home they sat down by a well and began to drink from it. The poor woman's daughter also went to drink—when lo! a wall rose up between her and the other damsels, but such a wall as the human eye had never yet beheld. It was so high, no voice could get over it; and it was so hard, no person could get through it. Oh, how terrified the poor damsel was, and what weeping and wailing and despair there was among her friends! What would become of the poor girl, and what would become of her poor mother?

"I will not tell," said one of the girls, "for no one will believe us!"

"But what shall we say to her mother now that she has disappeared before our eyes?" cried another.

"It is your fault, it is your fault! It was you who asked her!"

"No, it was you!"

So they fell to blaming each other, looking all the time at the great wall. Meanwhile the mother was waiting. She stood at the door of the house and watched as the girls drew near. They came weeping, not daring to tell the poor woman what had happened. Yet they had to tell, and when she heard, the woman rushed to the great wall that surrounded her daughter. So she remained outside, and they both wept and wailed as long as either of them had a tear left to flow.

In the midst of this great weeping the daughter fell asleep, and when she woke up next morning she saw a great door beside the wall.

"Whatever may happen to me, even if I am to perish, I will open this door!"

So saying, she opened it. Beyond the door was a beautiful palace, the like of which is not to be seen even in dreams. This palace had a vast hall, and on the wall of this hall hung forty keys. The damsel took the keys and began opening the doors of all the rooms around her. The first few rooms were full of silver and the second suite full of gold, the third suite full of diamonds and the fourth full of emeralds. Each apartment was filled with treasures more precious than those of the rooms that preceded it, so that the damsel's eyes were almost blinded by such splendor.

At last she entered the fortieth room, and there, stretched out on the floor, was a handsome Bey, with a fan of pearls beside him, and upon his breast a piece of paper on which was written: "Whoever fans me for forty days, and prays all that time by my side, will find her fate!"

Now the damsel remembered the little bird. So it was by the side of this sleeper that she was to meet her fate! Taking up the fan, she sat down beside him. Day and night she fanned him, praying continuously, until the fortieth day was at hand. On the morning of this last day she peeped out the window and beheld a slave girl in front of the palace. She decided to call this girl and ask her to pray beside the Bey for a moment, while she herself took a little repose. Then she hastened away and had her bath. She adorned herself so that the Bey, when he awoke, might see his life's fate at her best and rejoice at the sight.

Meanwhile the slave girl had read the piece of paper, and then while the damsel was preparing herself to look her best, the young Bey awoke. He looked about him, and as soon as he saw the slave girl he embraced her and called her his wife.

The poor damsel, entering at this moment, could scarcely believe her own eyes, but the slave girl, who was jealous of her, said to the Bey, "I, a sultan's daughter, am not ashamed to go about just as I am, and this chit of a serving-maid dares to appear before me arrayed so finely!" She chased the damsel out of the room, and sent her to work in the kitchen. The Bey was surprised, but could not say a word, for the slave girl was his bride, while it appeared that the other damsel was only a kitchen wench.

Now the Feast of Bairam was approaching, and, as is the custom at such times, the Bey gave gifts to those of his household. So he went to his bride and asked her what she would like on the Feast of Bairam. The girl replied that she wished for a garment that had never been sewn by a needle, nor been cut by scissors. Then he went down to the kitchen and asked the damsel what she would like.

"The stone-of-patience has a yellow color, and the knife-of-patience has a brown handle. Bring them both to me," said the damsel.

The Bey went on his way then and got his bride her garment, but the stone-of-patience and the knife-of-patience he could not find. What was he to do? He could not return without the gifts. So he boarded his ship to search in other countries.

The ship had only got halfway to its destination when suddenly it stopped short, and could neither go backward nor forward. The captain was terrified, and he told his passengers that there was someone on board who had not kept his word, which was why they could not sail on. At this the Bey came forward, and said that it was he who had not kept his word. They put him ashore so that he might keep his promise and then return to the ship.

The Bey walked along the seashore until he came to a great valley, and then he wandered on till he stood beside a large spring. He had scarcely trodden on the stones around it when suddenly a huge genie stood before him and asked him what he wanted.

"The stone-of-patience is of a yellow color and the knife-of-patience has a brown handle. Bring them both to me," said the Bey to the genie.

The next moment both the stone and the knife were in his hand, and he came back to the ship, went on board, and returned home. He gave the garment to his wife, but the stone and the knife he put in the kitchen.

The Bey was curious to know what the damsel would do with them, so one evening he crept down into the kitchen and watched her. When night approached she took the knife in her hand and placed the stone in front of her and began telling them her story. She told them what the little bird had thrice told her, and how it had terrified both her mother and herself.

And while she was looking at the stone, it suddenly began to swell, and its yellow color hissed and bubbled as if there were life in it.

Then the damsel went on to tell how she had wandered into the Bey's palace, how she had prayed beside him for forty days, and how she had left the slave girl to pray while she went to bathe and dress herself to look her best for the Bey. And the yellow stone swelled again, and hissed and foamed as if it were about to burst.

Then the damsel told how the slave girl had deceived her, and how the Bey had taken the slave as a wife; and all this time the yellow stone went on swelling and hissing and foaming as if there were a real living heart inside it—until suddenly it burst and turned to ashes.

Then the damsel took the little knife by the handle and said, "Oh, yellow patience-stone, you were only a stone, and yet you could not endure that I should thus be deceived and thrust out." And with that she would have buried the knife in her breast, but the Bey rushed forward and snatched it away.

"You are my true fate," cried the youth, and he took her into the upper chamber.

The treacherous slave they banished, and then they sent for the damsel's mother, and all lived together with great joy and happiness.

As for the little bird, it came sometimes and perched in the window of the palace to sing its joyful song. And this is what it sang: "Oh, little damsel, happy little damsel, at last you have found your fate!"

S•I•S•T•E•R•S
Resourceful and Steadfast

CLEVER MARIA
(Portugal)

Once upon a time there was a merchant whose wife had died leaving him with three lovely daughters. The youngest, Maria, was not only pretty but also wise. One day the king, who lived alongside the merchant, asked him to go on a journey for him. Though reluctant to leave his three daughters, the merchant agreed to go.

Before leaving he gave each daughter a pot of basil, saying, "While I am gone you must not let anyone into the house. The basil plants will tell me what has occurred during my absence."

"We will abide by your wishes," said the girls.

After the merchant had left, the king and two of his friends came to call on the girls. When they arrived, Maria suggested that the three girls fetch the king some wine.

"Do not trouble yourselves," the king replied. "We do not need anything to drink."

But Maria insisted, but instead of returning with the wine she slipped out to a neighbor woman's house, telling her that she had had a fight with her sisters and needed a place to sleep. The neighbor let her in and she spent the night safely. The next morning she returned home and found that her sisters' plants had withered away because of their disobedience.

That afternoon, Maria's sister spied some lemons in the king's garden just below their window. She begged Maria to get some for them. Maria knew she had to fetch them or she would never hear the end of it, and she swung down on a rope to the garden and gathered some lemons in her pockets.

"What have we here?" exclaimed the gardener. "A thief!"

"Don't call me a thief!" she cried, shoving the gardener into the bushes. She grabbed the rope and scrambled back up to the window.

The next day the other sister noticed some ripe bananas in the royal garden, and she insisted that Maria return for bananas. Reluctantly, Maria slipped down the rope, only to be met by the king himself.

The king began to question her and she wisely told him the truth about what she had done. He commanded her to follow him for her punishment, but as he started toward the palace she disappeared from sight. He searched everywhere, but she was never found. His anger at her disappearance made him so ill that his people began to fear for his life.

Many months passed. The two sisters married the king's friends and soon gave birth to daughters. One day Maria dressed as a boy, slipped into her sisters' houses, and quietly placed the babies into a basket covered with flowers. She strolled past the palace calling, "Who will carry this basket of flowers to the king?"

The king's bedroom window was open and when he heard her call, he sent someone to get the basket. When he opened the basket and saw the babies, he knew it was Maria tricking him. He was puzzling over how to get even with her when word came that the merchant had returned from his journey. He realized that now he could get his revenge. The king sent a message that the merchant was to bring him a coat made of stone the very next day or he would be punished.

The merchant had come home eager to see his daughters, but was immediately devastated that they had betrayed his trust. Then he received the message about making a coat of stone, and he became even more dismayed.

"Don't fret, father," Maria said, startling him with her appearance. "Take this chalk and go tell the king you have come to measure him."

Trusting her wisdom, he went to the palace as she suggested. When he told the king why he was there the king scoffed, "That will not work."

"Then I cannot make you the coat."

"In that case, if you want to live you must give me your daughter Maria."

The merchant returned to Maria, telling her of this new demand.

"Do not worry yourself, father. Now get a doll made to look just like me. Attach a string so that the doll can nod 'yes' or 'no.'"

The king felt confident that the merchant would soon be back with Maria and instructed his pages to put Maria in his room. Soon the merchant and Maria arrived and she was led to the king's room. As soon as she was left alone, she removed the doll from under her coat and hid herself behind the couch, while holding the doll's string. Soon the king came into the room.

"Maria," said the king, "I hope you are well."

The doll nodded its head.

The king began to discuss Maria's mischief, and at each recounting, the doll's head nodded quietly. "You only came to mock me!" he raged. And he rose and taking his sword, he cut off the doll's head. He realized that his anger had led him to act in haste, and he dropped to his knees in remorse.

"My Maria, you were so hard on me in life. Had I only spared you, perhaps you could have known my love."

Maria stood up from behind the couch, and as the king saw her there he rejoiced that she was as clever as she was wise. In time they were wed and had a happy life.

PATIENCE
(India, Punjab)

There was a king who dearly loved his two daughters, Kupti and Imani. One day he asked Kupti, "Are you content to have me manage your life and your wealth?"

"Of course, dear father. I would trust no other," Kupti replied.

Imani had a different response to his question. "Father, though I love you dearly, I would rather be in charge of my own life and fortune."

"You are young and perhaps foolish. But I shall grant you your wish and you shall learn the meaning of independence."

So the king presented his daughter Imani to an old, lame fakir (religious man) and told him that she would be staying with him and earning her own living. The fakir was quite amazed at this turn of events, but he hardly had a choice in the matter. He puzzled over how he could make her comfortable in his humble surroundings, but the princess interrupted his musings.

"Do you have any money?"

"I have only a penny," answered the fakir.

"That will do. Give me the penny and then borrow a spinning wheel and loom for me."

While the fakir went to borrow the wheel and loom, the princess took the penny and bought flax and oil. When she returned home she used the oil to soothe the fakir's withered leg and then set to work at the spinning wheel. By morning she had spun thread that was breathtaking. She used the thread at the loom, working until she had woven a cloth of unparalleled beauty.

She sent the fakir to the market to sell the cloth for two gold pieces while she took a rest. As the old man tried to sell the cloth, Kupti came by and upon seeing the cloth she asked the price. She was delighted at the price as the cloth was more beautiful than any she had seen.

Each day Imani used a penny to buy oil and flax. Each day she soothed the old man's crippled leg and wove lovely cloth. The fakir's leg improved from her massage, and people sought out her beautiful cloth, paying handsome prices for it.

As their wealth increased, the princess had a grand house built. When the king learned of her achievement, he was pleased by her success.

Shortly thereafter the king had to travel to another country and he asked Kupti what she would like as a gift.

"I would dearly love a necklace of rubies," she answered.

The king decided to ask Imani if she would also like a gift, but when the messenger arrived Imani was busy trying to untangle a knot in her loom.

The messenger bowed and said, "Your father must take a journey, and he asks what you would like as a gift."

Imani, absorbed with her task, mumbled, "Patience," intending the messenger to wait until she was free. But the messenger took her word as her answer and returned to the king stating that Imani had requested patience.

The king was perplexed, curious as to how one acquired patience, but he departed, hoping that he would be able to fulfill her request. When his journey was nearly over and he had found a ruby necklace for Kupti, he sent his servant into the marketplace to inquire if anyone had any patience for sale.

Feeling foolish, the servant nevertheless walked the marketplace, calling, "Has anyone any patience to sell?" Though he was taunted by many, he continued his calling until the resident king heard of the servant's request and sent for him.

"Why are you asking for patience?" the king inquired.

"My master wants it as a present for his daughter Imani," answered the servant.

"Well, the only patience this lady may have cannot be bought."

The servant did not realize that the king was having his fun with him, as the king's name, Subbar, means patience.

The servant answered, "I do not know why the princess wants patience, for she is not only beautiful and clever, but she is also very hard-working and loving."

The king left for a moment, returning with a fan that he put into a small box. "Here is a box. It will open only for the person who needs its contents. The person who opens it will receive patience of one sort or another."

The servant took it to his master and they returned home. When the box was delivered to Imani she was surprised as she had expected no gift. She took it to the fakir, but without a key or hinge he could not open it. But when Imani took it back and held it the box opened quite easily and Imani took out and began to use the fan. With the third stroke of the fan the king suddenly stood before her.

"I am King Subbar Khan," he stated, and he told them of the story of the servant who was searching for patience. Then he said, "This box and fan are magic. The box will not open to all, but with three strokes of the fan I will be here and with three taps of the fan I will be home again."

The fakir was delighted with his company and bade him stay the evening. That began many pleasurable evenings of chess and conversation for the men. Indeed they all became great friends, enjoying many hours together. As they often stayed up late visiting, a room was set aside for the king so that he could return home in the morning.

It became known throughout the town that a handsome king was visiting frequently, and Princess Kupti became quite jealous. She visited Imani, feigning interest in her home, asking for a tour of the rooms. Once Kupti had learned which was the visitor's room she sneaked back to it and spread finely ground, poisoned glass on the bed.

After that night's chess game Subbar Khan retired to his room, and as he lay down, the glass began to prick his skin. Trying to become comfortable, he turned and turned, fearing that he had been poisoned. In the morning he disguised his distress, returning to his home as usual.

None of his physicians could help him and he lay near death at his home. Meanwhile Princess Imani and the old fakir became more and more distraught because they could not summon their friend to visit them. Finally, Imani became so worried that she donned the dress of a young fakir and set out to the king's country.

One night she lay down under a tree to sleep, but her thoughts of the king kept her awake. Soon she heard two monkeys above her chattering to each other about the king and how he was dying of poisoned glass that had been spread on his bed.

"It's too bad," said one monkey, "that they don't know that this very tree's berries when soaked in hot water will stop the poison."

When Imani heard this she waited impatiently for daylight and then she gathered all the berries she could carry. Soon she had reached the king's city and she went to the palace stating that she had a medicine that might help the king.

Soon she was brought to the king's room, but he was so wasted by the poison that she could hardly recognize him. She asked for some boiling water and steeped the berries in it, asking the king's attendants to wash him with it. For the first night in many weeks, the king slept easily. The second day she directed the attendants to wash him again with the mixture. After this washing the king asked for some broth. After the third washing, he sat up, weak but alert. After the fourth washing he went to his throne and asked to see the physician who had cured him.

When Imani appeared before the king, he did not recognize her. She refused his offers of riches, asking instead that the king give her his ring and handkerchief. She made her goodbyes and returned to her country.

After her return, she and the fakir sent for the king with the magic fan. When he arrived they asked about his absence and he told them about his illness and recovery. The princess showed him the ring and handkerchief and asked if these had been his rewards to the physician.

The king realized that she had been the physician and he suddenly grabbed the magic fan.

"I will never be sent back to my country unless you accompany me as my wife!" the king declared.

And so it was that the fakir returned with Princess Imani and King Subbar Khan to the king's country, where the princess and the king were wed and lived happily ever after.

THE TWELVE BROTHERS
(Germany*)

A king and a queen lived together in peace with their twelve sons. But one day the king said to the queen, "If your thirteenth child is a girl, the twelve boys must die so that her riches may be greater and the kingdom hers alone." He had twelve coffins made and filled them with shavings and pillows. The coffins were put in a locked room and the king gave the key to the queen, telling her not to tell anyone about them.

But the queen sat grieving, and her youngest son, Benjamin, said to her, "Mother, dear, why are you so sad?"

"Dearest child, I cannot tell you."

But he persisted until she unlocked the room and showed him the coffins with the shavings and the pillows. "My dear Benjamin, your father had these coffins made for you and your eleven brothers, and if I give birth to a girl you are all to be put to death and buried in them."

As she wept, Benjamin comforted her, saying, "Don't cry, mother. We can take care of ourselves."

The queen said, "Son, go into the woods with your brothers, and take turns sitting on the top of the highest tree that can be found. Watch the castle each day, and if a boy is born I will put out a white flag and you can all return home. If it is a daughter, I will put out a red flag, and you must flee and dear God watch over you. Each night I will pray that you are keeping warm in the winter and finding respite from the heat in the summer."

After she had given her sons her blessing, they went away into the forest. Each took his turn on the tallest oak, looking toward the castle. When eleven days had passed and Benjamin's turn came, he saw a flag put out. It was not white, but was red, proclaiming they should die.

When the brothers heard of the red flag they became angry, saying, "Are we to die because of a girl? We will avenge ourselves! Whenever we find a girl we will spill her blood."

They went deeper into the wood and where it was darkest they found an empty, enchanted house. "We will dwell here; and you, Benjamin, will stay home and cook. The rest of us will hunt for food."

---

*Adapted from the Brothers Grimm.

So they hunted rabbits, deer, and birds, and brought them back for Benjamin to cook. In this way they lived for ten years with the time passing quickly.

By this time the queen's daughter was growing up with a beautiful face, a kind heart, and a golden star on her forehead. Once when there was a large wash she saw the twelve shirts and asked her mother, "Whose are these twelve shirts? They are too small to be my father's."

The mother answered sadly, "Dear child, they belong to your twelve brothers."

"Where are my brothers? I have never heard of them."

"God only knows where on this earth they are wandering." She led her daughter to the secret room, unlocked it and showed her the twelve coffins with the shavings and pillows. "These coffins were intended for your twelve brothers, but they went away when you were born." And she told her how this had happened.

"Dear mother, don't cry. I will find my brothers," she promised. And she took the shirts and began to search in the forest. In the evening she came upon the enchanted house and went in, finding a youth.

He was amazed at her beautiful clothes and the star on her forehead and asked, "Where are you from and what do you want?"

"I am a king's daughter, and I am searching for my twelve brothers. I will search everywhere under the blue sky until I find them." And she showed him the twelve shirts that belonged to them.

Benjamin saw that she was his sister and said, "I am Benjamin, your youngest brother."

She wept for joy. Benjamin joined her, and they embraced and kissed each other. But Benjamin soon said, "Sister, there is a problem. We brothers have sworn that any maiden we meet must die because we lost our kingdom to a girl."

"I will gladly die to save my brothers," she stated.

"No," he answered, "sit under this tub until my brothers return and I can change their minds."

She hid, and as night came the brothers returned from hunting. As they sat eating, they asked of Benjamin, "What is new?"

"Well, you have been in the forest, and I have stayed at home. Yet I know more than you," Benjamin stated.

"Tell us!" they cried.

"First promise me that the first maiden we see shall not be put to death."

"Yes, we promise," they all insisted. "Tell us now."

"Our sister is here," he said. And he lifted up the tub and she came out in her royal gown. With the golden star on her forehead, she seemed so beautiful and sweet that they all rejoiced and immediately loved her.

After this she stayed with them, helping Benjamin in the house with the work. The others continued to hunt wild animals for food for all of them. She fetched wood for cooking, gathered vegetables for cooking, and watched the pots on the fire. Supper was always ready for the brothers. She also made the house very tidy, with clean white beds. The brothers were content and harmonious.

One day the two of them had prepared a fine feast, and when the brothers came home they all sat down to eat and drink. They were full of happiness. There was a little garden behind the house and in it were twelve lilies. The maiden wanted to please them, and she went out to gather the flowers so as to give one to each brother as he ate. But as she broke off the flowers the brothers were changed into twelve ravens and they flew over the forest far away. The house with the garden also disappeared. The maiden stood alone in the wood and when she looked around she saw an old woman standing by her.

"My child," the old woman said, "what have you done? Why didn't you leave those twelve flowers alone? They were your twelve brothers, and they are now changed to ravens forever."

The maiden wept and begged, "Is there no way to set them free?"

"Only one possible way and that is difficult," said the old woman. "You can only release them by being silent for seven years. You can neither speak nor laugh one word, and if you do, even during the last hour of the seven years, all will be lost and your brothers will die."

The girl thought in her heart, "I know that I can set my brothers free." She went and found a tall tree, climbed up, and sat there spinning in silence. A king who was hunting in the wood had a large greyhound who ran to the tree, jumping up and barking. The king saw the beautiful girl with the golden star on her forehead and he was so taken with her that he asked her to be his wife. She said not a word, only nodding her head. The king climbed the tree, brought her down, set her on his horse, and took her home. The wedding was celebrated with great splendor and rejoicing, but the bride neither laughed nor spoke. They lived happily for a few years.

Then the king's mother, a wicked woman, said to the king, "She is only a lowly beggar whom you have taken. Who knows what mean tricks she is playing. Even if she truly cannot speak, at least she might laugh. One who doesn't laugh has a guilty conscience."

At first the king refused to believe her, but she kept after him so that he finally believed his mother and condemned his wife to death. A great fire was readied in the courtyard and she was to be burned to death. The king stood above at the window, watching with tears in his eyes, for he truly loved her. When she was tied to the stake and the red tongues of the flames were licking at her garments, the last moment of the seven years arrived.

There was a rushing sound in the air, and the twelve ravens came flying down. As they touched the earth and became her twelve brothers, they scattered the fire and put out the flames. They set their sister free, kissing and hugging her. Now that she could speak, she told the king why she had never laughed or spoken. The king was delighted to learn of her innocence and they all lived together in happiness. As for the king's wicked mother, she soon died a miserable death.

THE PRINCESS AND THE GIANT
(Scotland)

Once there were a king and a queen of Scotland. When the king died, a distant cousin inherited the throne. The cousin was a jealous sort and he sent the widowed queen and her three daughters to a remote country cottage to eke out an existence with a small field for their cow and garden.

The queen was industrious and did not let their sudden change in fortune unduly dismay her. She gathered her daughters around her and said, "Our first job is to gather stones from the moor. We must build a wall to keep the cow out of our field. Come, daughters. Let's begin."

Whenever the older daughter would complain about their new lowly existence and the unfairness of it all, her mother would admonish her to make the best of it. They continued to work hard at living comfortably in their new humble surroundings.

One morning the second daughter was going to the garden to get a cabbage. Suddenly she ran back to the cottage wailing for her mother. "Oh, dear mother, you must see this! Someone has taken a whole row of cabbages from our garden!"

They all rushed out to the garden and the three girls cried with frustration at seeing their garden ravished. But their mother reminded them that in no time even more new cabbages would grow on the remaining stalks. The two older girls continued to mourn their loss, but the youngest wandered off quietly. In a moment she came back.

"Mother, just look. There are huge prints of boots in the mud by our wall."

They all ran and looked, and the queen decided that only a giant could make such huge prints. Having been raised as royalty the girls were not afraid of much, and having not experienced giants they were not particulary threatened by the thought of a giant in their midst. They were mostly outraged that anyone had ravished their garden.

"I will stay out tonight and watch for that giant!" declared the oldest daughter. And that night she took a shawl and milking stool and hid herself by the garden. As the moon rose she watched quietly. Suddenly she heard a tramping and soon a huge giant stepped over the wall and into the garden. He bent his large body toward the ground and began to cut off some cabbages.

"Why are you stealing our cabbages?" she cried out.

"What concern is it to you?" asked the giant, surprised at being challenged.

The oldest daughter was even more surprised at his effrontery and said, "Those are our cabbages! Leave them and leave this garden!"

Instead of leaving the garden, the giant reached over and plucked her like a cabbage and popped her into his sack of cabbages. Putting the sack over his shoulder he quickly passed over hill and dale until he came to his house.

The oldest daughter climbed painfully out of the sack, only to be told that she was to begin her chores by driving the cow to pasture. After she had finished with the cow, she returned to the house to make a bit of porridge. She had just sat down to eat it when she heard a knock at the door.

"Who is there?" she asked.

"It is a weary traveler in need of a bite to eat."

The oldest daughter told him to leave or be faced with the wrath of the giant. Then she set the pot of porridge over the fire and began to comb the wool. The wool became more and more tangled and she became more and more impatient with her task. When the giant returned the porridge was burning and the wool was ruined. He threw her into the loft, telling her she was of no use to him.

Meanwhile, the second daughter had decided to sit up and watch for the giant the next night. She fully intended to make the giant give back her older sister, but the giant was watchful and when he saw her he tossed her into his sack before gathering more cabbages. She arrived at his house bruised and nearly smothered.

He set her to work, and like her older sister she made an awful mess of it. The poor traveler arrived as the night before, and she also turned him away. When the giant found his house just as unkempt as the night before he threw her into the loft where she found her sister. They hugged each other with relief, and slept the night in each other's arms.

That night when the giant approached the garden, the third daughter was sitting on the stone wall.

"Good evening, giant," she said politely.

"You will come with me," said the giant.

"Thank you," she said, "I am ready."

The giant was quite impressed with her manners and he picked his cabbages before placing her gently on top of them in his sack. The youngest daughter had a small pair of scissors with her, and she cut a hole through which to watch the way to the giant's house. When they arrived, she cheerfully stepped out of the sack.

The giant bade her to drive the cow to the pasture, make the porridge, and comb, card, and spin the wool. She nodded at each directive and said she would try her best, even though she had never worked with wool. The giant went off to sleep while she took the cow to pasture and made the porridge.

Just as she was about to eat she heard a knock at the door. She opened the door and greeted the traveler, a strange little fellow with red hair and blue eyes set in a thin white face. His tartan kilt was handsome, but it was clear that he was terribly hungry. He told her that he was lost and starving.

The youngest daughter gave him her own dinner, and afterward he saw the pile of wool and asked if he could repay her kindness by carding it for her. She was delighted at his offer, and in no time he had combed it, carded it, and spun it into beautiful white wool. When he was done he turned and disappeared just as quickly as he had arrived.

When the giant came in, he found a pot full of porridge, a lovely length of wool, and a cheerful girl ready to wait on him.

"Your work is good. If you can teach your sisters how to do as well, I will let them down from the loft. Take the ladder and you can visit with them."

Their reunion was joyful, and the next morning the youngest daughter came down the ladder ready to be of service again.

As she gave the giant his breakfast, she said, "Please, sir, as there is no one left to help my mother, would you mind taking her a basket of heather for the cow's bed?"

She inquired so daintily that the giant was quite charmed by her and couldn't turn her down. Soon he was on his way with the basket while she kept herself busy at his house. That evening he was so pleased with her work that he told her she might be allowed to teach her sisters how to be such good workers some morning.

The next morning there was a pile of grass in the yard. She asked the giant if he would be so kind as to carry it to her mother for fodder for the cow. The giant cheerfully filled up the basket and later carried it to her mother.

That evening he told the youngest daughter that he was so pleased with her that she could have them come down and help her the next day. He was going on a journey and wanted the house sparkling when he returned.

"Would you mind terribly delivering this basket of myrtle to my mother on your way tomorrow? My mother could use it and would be ever so grateful."

The errand was not out of his way, and he agreed. The next morning he left early and did not notice that the girl was not down from the loft as yet. He left the basket in the field and departed, not realizing that he had carried the youngest daughter home, just as he had unwittingly carried her sisters.

She crept out of the basket and ran to the cottage where her mother and sisters were preparing breakfast. After many hugs and kisses they began to eat, but were interrupted by a messenger from the king. He had decided to invite the queen and her daughters to join him at the palace and had sent his coach for their journey.

When the giant returned that night, expecting to find the three sisters hard at work, he instead found a cold fire in an empty house. He rushed to the queen's cottage, but could not find even a cabbage, for the queen had carried them all away with them.

THE SNOW QUEEN
(Denmark*)

here was once a dreadfully wicked hobgoblin. One day he was in capital spirits because he had made a looking-glass which reflected everything that was good and beautiful in such a way that it dwindled almost to nothing, but anything that was bad and ugly stood out very clearly and looked much worse. The most beautiful landscapes looked like boiled spinach, and the best people looked repulsive or seemed to stand on their heads with no bodies; their faces were so changed that they could not be recognized, and if anyone had a freckle you might be sure it would be spread over the nose and mouth.

That was the best part of it, said the hobgoblin.

But one day the looking-glass was dropped, and it broke into a million-billion and more pieces.

And now came the greatest misfortune of all, for each of the pieces was hardly as large as a grain of sand, and they flew about all over the world, and if anyone had a bit in his eye there it stayed, and then he would see everything awry, or else could only see the bad sides of a case. For every tiny splinter of the glass possessed the same power that the whole glass had.

Some people got a splinter in their hearts, and that was dreadful, for then it began to turn into a lump of ice.

The hobgoblin laughed till his sides ached, but still the tiny bits of glass flew about.

And now we will hear all about it.

In a large town, where there were so many people and houses that there was not room enough for everybody to have gardens, lived two poor children. They were not brother and sister, but they loved each other just as much as if they were. Their parents lived opposite one another in two attics, and out on the leads they had put two boxes filled with flowers. There were sweet peas in it, and two rose trees, which grew beautifully, and in summer the two children were allowed to take their little chairs and sit out under the roses. Then they had splendid games.

*Translated from the German of Hans Christian Andersen by Alma Alleyne.

In the winter they could not do this, but then they put hot pennies against the frozen windowpanes, and made round holes to look at each other through.

His name was Kay, and hers was Gerda.

Outside it was snowing fast.

"Those are the white bees swarming," said the old grandmother.

"Have they also a queen bee?" asked the little boy, for he knew that the real bees have one.

"To be sure," said the grandmother. "She flies wherever they swarm the thickest. She is larger than any of them, and never stays upon the earth, but flies again up into the black clouds. Often at midnight she flies through the streets, and peeps in at all the windows, and then they freeze in such pretty patterns and look like flowers."

"Yes, we have seen that," said both children; they knew that it was true.

"Can the Snow Queen come in here?" asked the little girl.

"Just let her!" cried the boy, "I would put her on the stove, and melt her!"

But the grandmother stroked his hair, and told some more stories.

In the evening, when little Kay was going to bed, he jumped on the chair by the window, and looked through the little hole. A few snowflakes were falling outside, and one of them, the largest, lay on the edge of one of the window boxes. The snowflake grew larger and larger till it took the form of a maiden, dressed in finest white gauze.

She was so beautiful and dainty, but all of ice, hard bright ice.

Still she was alive; her eyes glittered like two clear stars, but there was no rest or peace in them. She nodded at the window, and beckoned with her hand. The little boy was frightened, and sprang down from the chair. It seemed as if a great white bird had flown past the window.

The next day there was a harder frost than before.

Then came the spring, and then the summer, when the roses grew and smelt more beautifully than ever.

Kay and Gerda were looking at one of their picture books—the clock in the great church-tower had just struck five, when Kay exclaimed, "Oh! something has stung my heart, and I've got something in my eye!"

The little girl threw her arms round his neck; he winked hard with both his eyes; no, she could see nothing in them.

"I think it is gone now," said he; but it had not gone. It was one of the tiny splinters of the glass of the magic mirror which we have heard about, that turned everything great and good reflected in it small and ugly. And poor Kay had also a splinter in his heart, and it began to change into a lump of ice. It did not hurt him at all, but the splinter was there all the same.

"Why are you crying?" he asked; "it makes you look so ugly! There's nothing the matter with me. Just look! that rose is all slug-eaten, and this one is stunted! What ugly roses they are!"

And he began to pull them to pieces.

"Kay, what *are* you doing?" cried the little girl.

And when he saw how frightened she was, he pulled off another rose, and ran in at his window away from dear little Gerda.

When she came later on with the picture book, he said that it was only fit for babies, and when his grandmother told them stories, he was always interrupting with, "But—" and then he would get behind her and put on her spectacles, and speak just as she did. This he did very well, and everybody laughed. Very soon he could imitate the way all the people in the street walked and talked.

His games were now quite different. On a winter's day he would take a burning glass and hold it out on his blue coat and let the snowflakes fall on it.

"Look in the glass, Gerda! Just see how regular they are! They are much more interesting than real flowers. Each is perfect; they are all made according to rule. If only they did not melt!"

One morning Kay came out with his warm gloves on, and his little sledge hung over his shoulder. He shouted to Gerda, "I am going to the marketplace to play with the other boys," and away he went.

In the marketplace the boldest boys used often to fasten their sledges to the carts of the farmers, and then they got a good ride.

When they were in the middle of their games there drove into the square a large sledge, all white, and in it sat a figure dressed in a rough white fur pelisse with a white fur cap on.

The sledge drove twice round the square, and Kay fastened his little sledge behind it and drove off. It went quicker and quicker into the next street. The driver turned round, and nodded to Kay in a friendly way as if they had known each other before. Every time that Kay tried to unfasten his sledge the driver nodded again, and Kay sat still once more. Then they drove out of the town, and the snow began to fall so thickly that the little boy could not see his hand before him, and on and on they went. He quickly unfastened the cord to get loose from the big sledge, but it was of no use; his little sledge hung on fast, and it went on like the wind.

Then he cried out, but nobody heard him. He was dreadfully frightened.

The snowflakes grew larger and larger till they looked like great white birds. All at once they flew aside, the large sledge stood still, and the figure who was driving stood up. The fur cloak and cap were all of snow. It was a lady, tall and slim, and glittering. It was the Snow Queen.

"We have come at a good rate," she said; "but you are almost frozen. Creep in under my cloak."

And she set him close to her in the sledge and drew the cloak over him. He felt as though he were sinking into a snowdrift.

"Are you cold now?" she asked, and kissed his forehead. The kiss was cold as ice and reached down to his heart, which was already half a lump of ice.

"My sledge! Don't forget my sledge!" He thought of that first, and it was fastened to one of the white birds who flew behind with the sledge on its back.

The Snow Queen kissed Kay again, and then he forgot all about little Gerda, his grandmother, and everybody at home.

"Now I must not kiss you any more," she said, "or else I should kiss you to death."

Then away they flew over forests and lakes, over sea and land. Round them whistled the cold wind, the wolves howled, and the snow hissed; over them flew the black shrieking crows. But high up the moon shone large and bright, and thus Kay passed the long winter night. In the day he slept at the Snow Queen's feet.

But what happened to little Gerda when Kay did not come back?

What had become of him? Nobody knew. The other boys told how they had seen him fasten his sledge onto a large one which had driven out of the town gate.

Gerda cried a great deal. The winter was long and dark to her.

Then the spring came with warm sunshine. "I will go and look for Kay," said Gerda.

So she went down to the river and got into a little boat that was there. Presently the stream began to carry it away.

"Perhaps the river will take me to Kay," thought Gerda. She glided down, past trees and fields, till she came to a large cherry garden, in which stood a little house with strange red and blue windows and a straw roof. Before the door stood two wooden soldiers, who were shouldering arms.

Gerda called to them, but they naturally did not answer. The river carried the boat onto the land.

Gerda called out still louder, and there came out of the house a very old woman. She leant upon a crutch, and she wore a large sun-hat which was painted with the most beautiful flowers.

"You poor little girl!" said the old woman.

And then she stepped into the water, brought the boat in close with her crutch, and lifted little Gerda out.

"And now come and tell me who you are, and how you came here," she said.

Then Gerda told her everything, and asked her if she had seen Kay. But she said he had not passed that way yet, but he would soon come.

She told Gerda not to be sad, and that she should stay with her and take of the cherry trees and flowers, which were better than any picture book, as they could each tell a story.

She then took Gerda's hand and led her into the little house and shut the door.

The windows were very high, and the panes were red, blue, and yellow, so that the light came through in curious colors. On the table were the most delicious cherries, and the old woman let Gerda eat as many as she liked, while she combed her hair with a gold comb.

The beautiful sunny hair rippled and shone round the dear little face, which was so soft and sweet. "I have always longed to have a dear little girl just like you, and you shall see how happy we will be together."

And as she combed Gerda's hair, Gerda thought less and less about Kay, for the old woman was a witch, but not a wicked witch, for she only enchanted now and then to amuse herself, and she did want to keep little Gerda very much.

So she went into the garden and waved her stick over all the rose bushes and blossoms and all; they sank down into the black earth, and no one could see where they had been.

The old woman was afraid that if Gerda saw the roses she would begin to think about her own, and then would remember Kay and run away.

Then she led Gerda out into the garden. How glorious it was, and what lovely scents filled the air! All the flowers you can think of blossomed there all the year round.

Gerda jumped for joy and played there till the sun set behind the tall cherry trees, and then she slept in a beautiful bed with red silk pillows filled with violets; and she slept soundly and dreamed as a queen does on her wedding day.

The next day she played again with the flowers in the warm sunshine and so many days passed by. Gerda knew every flower, but although there were so many, it seemed to her as if *one* were not there, though she could not remember which.

She was looking one day at the old woman's sun-hat which had the painted flowers on it, and there she saw a rose.

The witch had forgotten to make that vanish when she had made the other roses disappear under the earth. It is so difficult to think of everything.

"Why, there are no roses here!" cried Gerda, and she hunted among all the flowers, but not one was to be found. Then she sat down and cried, but her tears fell just on the spot where a rose bush had sunk, and when her warm tears watered the earth, the bush came up in full bloom just as it had been before. Gerda kissed the roses and thought of the lovely roses at home, and with them came the thought of little Kay.

"Oh, what have I been doing!" said the little girl. "I wanted to look for Kay."

She ran to the end of the garden. The gate was shut, but she pushed against the rusty lock so that it came open.

She ran out with her little bare feet. No one came after her. At last she could not run any longer, and she sat down on a large stone. When she looked round she saw that the summer was over; it was late autumn. It had not changed in the beautiful garden, where there were sunshine and flowers all the year round.

"Oh, dear, how late I have made myself!" said Gerda. "It's autumn already! I cannot rest!" And she sprang up to run on.

Oh, how tired and sore her little feet grew, and it became colder and colder.

She had to rest again, and there on the snow in front of her was a large crow.

It had been looking at her for some time, and it nodded its head and said, "Caw! caw! good day." Then it asked the little girl why she was alone in the world. She told the crow her story, and asked if he had seen Kay.

The crow nodded very thoughtfully and said, "It might be! It *might* be!"

"What! Do you think you have?" cried the little girl, and she almost squeezed the crow to death as she kissed him.

"Gently, gently!" said the crow. "I think—I know—I think—it might be little Kay, but now he has forgotten you for the princess!"

"Does he live with a princess?" asked Gerda.

"Yes, listen," said the crow.

Then he told all he knew.

"In the kingdom in which we are now sitting lives a princess who is dreadfully clever. She has read all the newspapers in the world and has forgotten them again. She is as clever as that. The other day she came to the throne, and that is not so pleasant as people think. Then she began to say, 'Why should I not marry?' But she wanted a husband who could answer when he was spoken to, not one who would stand up stiffly and look respectable—that would be too dull.

"When she told all the Court ladies, they were delighted. You can believe every word I say," said the crow. "I have a tame sweetheart in the palace, and she tells me everything."

Of course his sweetheart was a crow.

"The newspapers came out next morning with a border of hearts round it, and the princess's monogram on it, and inside you could read that every good-looking young man might come into the palace and speak to the princess, and whoever should speak loud enough to be heard would be well fed and looked after, and the one who spoke best should become the princess's husband. Indeed," said the crow, "you can quite believe me. It is as true as that I am sitting here.

"Young men came in streams, and there was such a crowding and a mixing together! But nothing came of it on the first nor on the second day. They could all speak quite well when they were in the street, but as soon as they came inside the palace door, and saw the guards in silver, and upstairs the footmen in gold, and the great hall all lighted up, then their wits left them! And when they stood in front of the throne where the princess was sitting, then they could not think of anything to say except to repeat the last word she had spoken, and she did not much care to hear that again. It seemed as if they were walking in their sleep until they came out into the street again, when they could speak once more. There was a row stretching from the gate of the town up to the castle.

"They were hungry and thirsty, but in the palace they did not even get a glass of water.

"A few of the cleverest had brought some slices of bread and butter with them, but they did not share them with their neighbor, for they thought, 'If he looks hungry, the princess will not take him!' "

"But what about Kay?" asked Gerda. "When did he come? Was he in the crowd?"

"Wait a bit; we are coming to him! On the third day a little figure came without horse or carriage and walked jauntily up to the palace. His eyes shone as yours do; he had lovely curling hair, but quite poor clothes."

"That was Kay!" cried Gerda with delight. "Oh, then I have found him!" and she clapped her hands.

"He had a little bundle on his back," said the crow.

"No, it must have been his skates, for he went away with his skates!"

"Very likely," said the crow, "I did not see for certain. But I know this from my sweetheart, that when he came to the palace door and saw the royal guards in silver, and on the stairs the footmen in gold, he was not the least put out. He nodded to them, saying, 'It must be rather dull standing on the stairs; I would rather go inside!'

"The halls blazed with lights; councillors and ambassadors were walking about in noiseless shoes carrying gold dishes. It was enough to make one nervous! His boots creaked dreadfully loud, but he was not frightened."

"That *must* be Kay!" said Gerda. "I know he had new boots on; I have heard them creaking in his grandmother's room!"

"They *did* creak, certainly!" said the crow. "And, not one bit afraid, up he went to the princess, who was sitting on a large pearl as round as a spinning wheel. All the ladies-in-waiting were standing round, each with their attendants, and the lords-in-waiting with *their* attendants. The nearer they stood to the door the prouder they were."

"It must have been dreadful!" said little Gerda. "And Kay did win the princess?"

"I heard from my tame sweetheart that he was merry and quick-witted; he had not come to woo, he said, but to listen to the princess's wisdom. And the end of it was that they fell in love with each other."

"Oh, yes; that was Kay!" said Gerda. "He was so clever; he could do sums with fractions. Oh, do lead me to the palace!"

"That's easily said!" answered the crow, "but how are we to manage that? I must talk it over with my tame sweetheart. She may be able to advise us, for I must tell you that a little girl like you could never get permission to enter it."

"Yes, I will get it!" said Gerda. "When Kay hears that I am there he will come out at once and fetch me!"

"Wait for me by the railings," said the crow, and he nodded his head and flew away.

It was late in the evening when he came back.

"Caw, caw!" he said, "I am to give you her love, and here is a little roll for you. She took it out of the kitchen; there's plenty there, and you must be hungry. You cannot come into the palace. The guards in silver and the footmen in gold would not allow it. But don't cry! You shall get in all right. My sweetheart knows a little back-stairs which leads to the sleeping-room, and she knows where to find the key."

They went into the garden, and when the lights in the palace were put out one after the other, the crow led Gerda to a back-door.

Oh, how Gerda's heart beat with anxiety and longing! It seemed as if she were going to do something wrong, but she only wanted to know if it were little Kay. Yes, it must be he! She remembered so well his clever eyes, his curly hair. She could see him smiling as he did when they were at home under the rose trees! He would be so pleased to see her, and to hear how they all were at home.

Now they were on the stairs; a little lamp was burning, and on the landing stood the tame crow. She put her head on one side and looked at Gerda, who bowed as her grandmother had taught her.

"My betrothed has told me many nice things about you, my dear young lady," she said. "Will you take the lamp while I go in front? We go this way so as to meet no one."

Through beautiful rooms they came to the sleeping-room. In the middle of it, hung on a thick rod of gold, were two beds, shaped like lilies, one all white, in which lay the princess, and the other red, in which Gerda hoped to find Kay. She pushed aside the curtain, and saw a brown neck. Oh, it *was* Kay! She called his name out loud, holding the lamp toward him.

He woke up, turned his head and—it was *not* Kay!

It was only his neck that was like Kay's, but he was young and handsome. The princess sat up in her lily-bed and asked who was there.

Then Gerda cried, and told her story and all that the crows had done.

"You poor child!" said the prince and princess, and they praised the crows, and said that they were not angry with them, but that they must not do it again. Now they should have a reward.

"Would you like to fly away free?" said the princess, "or will you have a permanent place as court crows with what you can get in the kitchen?"

And both crows bowed and asked for a permanent appointment, for they thought of their old age.

And they put Gerda to bed, and she folded her hands, thinking, as she fell asleep, "How good people and animals are to me!"

The next day she was dressed from head to foot in silk and satin. They wanted her to stay on in the palace, but she begged for a little carriage and a horse, and a pair of shoes so that she might go out again into the world to look for Kay.

They gave her a muff as well as some shoes; she was warmly dressed, and when she was ready, there in front of the door stood a coach of pure gold, with a coachman, footmen, and postilions with gold crowns on.

The prince and princess helped her into the carriage and wished her good luck.

The wild crow who was now married drove with her for the first three miles; the other crow could not come because she had a bad headache.

"Good-bye, good-bye!" called the prince and princess; and little Gerda cried, and the crow cried.

When he said good-bye, he flew on to a tree and waved with his black wings as long as the carriage, which shone like the sun, was in sight.

They came at last to a dark wood, but the coach lit it up like a torch. When the robbers saw it, they rushed out, exclaiming, "Gold! Gold!"

They seized the horses, killed the coachman, footmen, and postilions, and dragged Gerda out of the carriage.

"She is plump and tender! I will eat her!" said the old robber-queen, and she drew her long knife, which glittered horribly.

"You shall not kill her!" cried her little daughter. "She shall play with me. She shall give me her muff and her beautiful dress, and she shall sleep in my bed."

The little robber-girl was as big as Gerda, but was stronger, broader, with dark hair and black eyes. She threw her arms round Gerda and said, "They shall not kill you, so long as you are not naughty. Aren't you a princess?"

"No," said Gerda, and she told all that had happened to her, and how dearly she loved little Kay.

The robber-girl looked at her very seriously, and nodded her head, saying, "They shall not kill you, even if you are naughty, for then I will kill you myself!"

And she dried Gerda's eyes, and stuck both her hands in the beautiful warm muff.

The little robber-girl took Gerda to a corner of the robbers' camp where she slept.

All round were more than a hundred wood-pigeons which seemed to be asleep, but they moved a little when the two girls came up.

There was also, nearby, a reindeer which the robber-girl teased by tickling it with her long sharp knife.

Gerda lay awake for some time.

"Coo, coo!" said the wood-pigeons. "We have seen little Kay. A white bird carried his sledge; he was sitting in the Snow Queen's carriage which drove over the forest when our little ones were in the nest. She breathed on them, and all except we two died. Coo, coo!"

"What are you saying over there?" cried Gerda. "Where was the Snow Queen going to? Do you know at all?"

"She was probably traveling to Lapland, where there is always ice and snow. Ask the reindeer."

"There is capital ice and snow there!" said the reindeer. "One can jump about there in the great sparkling valleys. There the Snow Queen has her summer palace, but her best palace is up by the North Pole, on the island called Spitzbergen."

"O Kay, my little Kay!" sobbed Gerda.

"You must lie still!" said the little robber-girl, "or else I shall stick my knife into you!"

In the morning Gerda told her all that the wood-pigeons had said. She nodded. "Do you know where Lapland is?" she asked the reindeer.

"Who should know better than I?" said the beast, and his eyes sparkled. "I was born and bred there on the snowfields."

"Listen!" said the robber-girl to Gerda; "you see that all the robbers have gone; only my mother is left, and she will fall asleep in the afternoon—then I will do something for you!"

When her mother had fallen asleep, the robber-girl went up to the reindeer and said, "I am going to set you free so that you can run to Lapland. But you must go quickly and carry this little girl to the Snow Queen's palace, where her playfellow is. You must have heard all that she told about it, for she spoke loud enough!"

The reindeer sprang high for joy. The robber-girl lifted little Gerda up, and had the foresight to tie her on firmly, and even gave her a little pillow for a saddle. "You must have your fur boots," she said, "for it will be cold; but I shall keep your muff, for it is so cosy! But, so that you may not freeze, here are my mother's great fur gloves; they will come up to your elbows. Creep into them!"

And Gerda cried for joy.

"Don't make such faces!" said the little robber-girl. "You must look very happy. And here are two loaves and a sausage; now you won't be hungry!"

They were tied to the reindeer, the little robber-girl opened the door, made all the big dogs come away, cut through the halter with her sharp knife, and said to the reindeer, "Run now! But take care of the little girl."

And Gerda stretched out her hands with the large fur gloves toward the little robber-girl and said, "Good-bye!"

Then the reindeer flew over the ground, through the great forest, as fast as he could.

The wolves howled, the ravens screamed, the sky seemed on fire.

"Those are my dear old northern lights," said the reindeer; "see how they shine!"

And then he ran faster still, day and night.

The loaves were eaten, and the sausage also, and then they came to Lapland.

They stopped by a wretched little house; the roof almost touched the ground, and the door was so low that you had to creep in and out.

There was no one in the house except an old Lapland woman who was cooking fish over an oil-lamp. The reindeer told Gerda's whole history, but first he told his own, for that seemed to him much more important, and Gerda was so cold that she could not speak.

"Ah, you poor creatures!" said the Lapland woman; "you have still further to go! You must go over a hundred miles into Finland, for there the Snow Queen lives, and every night she burns Bengal lights. I will write some words on a dried stock-fish, for I have no paper, and you must give it to the Finland woman, for she can give you better advice than I can."

And when Gerda was warmed and had had something to eat and drink, the Lapland woman wrote on a dried stock-fish, and begged Gerda to take care of it, tied Gerda securely on the reindeer's back, and away they went again.

The whole night was ablaze with northern lights, and then they came to Finland and knocked at the Finland woman's chimney, for door she had none.

Inside it was so hot that the Finland woman wore very few clothes; she loosened Gerda's clothes and drew off her fur gloves and boots. She laid a piece of ice on the reindeer's head, and then read what was written on the stock-fish. She read it over three times till she knew it by heart, and then put the fish in the saucepan, for she never wasted anything.

Then the reindeer told his story, and afterward little Gerda's, and the Finland woman blinked her eyes but said nothing.

"You are very clever," said the reindeer, "I know. Cannot you give the little girl a drink so that she may have the strength of twelve men and overcome the Snow Queen?"

"The strength of twelve men!" said the Finland woman; "*that* would not help much. Little Kay is with the Snow Queen, and he likes everything there very much and thinks it the best place in the world. But that is because he has a splinter of glass in his heart and a bit in his eye. If these do not come out, he will never be free, and the Snow Queen will keep her power over him."

"But cannot you give little Gerda something so that she can have power over her?"

"I can give her no greater power than she has already; don't you see how great it is? Don't you see how men and beasts must help her when she wanders into the wide world with her bare feet? She is powerful already, because she is a dear little innocent child. If she cannot by herself conquer the Snow Queen and take away the glass splinters from little Kay, *we* cannot help her! The Snow Queen's garden begins two miles from here. You can carry the little maiden so far; put her down by the large bush with red berries growing in the snow. Then you must come back here as fast as you can."

Then the Finland woman lifted little Gerda on the reindeer and away he sped.

"Oh, I have left my gloves and boots behind!" cried Gerda. She missed them in the piercing cold, but the reindeer did not dare to stop. On he ran till he came to the bush with red berries. Then he set Gerda down and kissed her mouth, and great big tears ran down his cheeks, and then he ran back. There stood poor Gerda without shoes or gloves in the middle of the bitter cold of Finland.

She ran on as fast as she could. A regiment of gigantic snowflakes came against her, but they melted when they touched her, and she went on with fresh courage.

And now we must see what Kay was doing. He was not thinking of Gerda, and never dreamt that she was standing outside the palace.

The walls of the palace were built of driven snow, and the doors and windows of piercing winds.

There were more than a hundred halls in it all of frozen snow. The largest was several miles long; the bright northern lights lit them up, and very large and empty and cold and glittering they were! In the middle of the great hall was a frozen lake which had cracked in a thousand pieces; each piece was exactly like the other. Here the Snow Queen used to sit when she was at home.

Little Kay was almost blue and black with cold, but he did not feel it, for she had kissed away his feelings and his heart was a lump of ice.

He was pulling about some sharp, flat pieces of ice, and trying to fit one into the other. He thought each was most beautiful, but that was because of the splinter of glass in his eye. He fitted them into a great many shapes, but he wanted to make them spell the word "Love." The Snow Queen had said, "If you can spell out that word you shall be your own master. I will give you the whole world and a new pair of skates."

But he could not do it.

"Now I must fly to warmer countries," said the Snow Queen. "I must go and powder my black kettles!" (This was what she called Mount Etna and Mount Vesuvius.) "It does the lemons and grapes good."

And off she flew, and Kay sat alone in the great hall trying to do his puzzle.

He sat so still that you would have thought he was frozen.

Then it happened that little Gerda stepped into the hall. The biting cold winds became quiet as if they had fallen asleep when she appeared in the great, empty, freezing hall.

She caught sight of Kay; she recognized him, ran and put her arms round his neck, crying, "Kay! dear little Kay! I have found you at last!"

But he sat quite still and cold. Then Gerda wept hot tears which fell on his neck and thawed his heart and swept away the bit of the looking-glass. He looked at her and then he burst into tears. He cried so much that the glass splinter swam out of his eye; then he knew her, and cried out, "Gerda! dear little Gerda! Where have you been so long? and where have I been?"

And he looked round him.

"How cold it is here! How wide and empty!" and he threw himself on Gerda, and she laughed and wept for joy. It was such a happy time that the pieces of ice even danced round them for joy, and when they were tired and lay down again they formed themselves into the letters that the Snow Queen had said he must spell in order to become his own master and have the whole world and a new pair of skates.

And Gerda kissed his cheeks and they grew rosy; she kissed his eyes and they sparkled like hers; she kissed his hands and feet and he became warm and glowing. The Snow Queen might come home now; his release—the word "Love"—stood written in sparkling ice.

They took each other's hands and wandered out of the great palace; they talked about the grandmother and the roses on the leads, and wherever they came the winds hushed and the sun came out. When they reached the bush with red berries there stood the reindeer waiting for them.

He carried Kay and Gerda first to the Finland woman, who warmed them in her hot room and gave them advice for their journey home.

Then they went to the Lapland woman, who gave them new clothes and mended their sleigh. The reindeer ran with them till they came to the green fields fresh with the spring green. Here he said good-bye.

They came to the forest, which was bursting into bud, and out of it came a splendid horse which Gerda knew; it was one which had drawn the gold coach ridden by a young girl with a red cap on and pistols in her belt. It was the little robber-girl who was tired of being at home and wanted to go out into the world. She and Gerda knew each other at once.

"You are a nice fellow!" she said to Kay. "I should like to know if you deserve to be run after all over the world!"

But Gerda patted her cheeks and asked after the prince and princess.

"They are traveling about," said the robber-girl.

"And the crow?" asked Gerda.

"Oh, the crow is dead!" answered the robber-girl. "His tame sweetheart is a widow and hops about with a bit of black crape round her leg. She makes a great fuss, but it's all nonsense. But tell me what happened to you, and how you caught him."

And Kay and Gerda told her all.

"Dear, dear!" said the robber-girl, shook both their hands, and promised that if she came to their town she would come and see them. Then she rode on.

But Gerda and Kay went home hand in hand. There they found the grandmother and everything just as it had been, but when they went through the doorway they found they were grown-up.

There were the roses on the leads; it was summer, warm, glorious summer.

FOWLER'S FOWL

(Germany*)

There once was a wizard who would dress up as a poor man and go begging at houses and capture pretty girls. No one knew what happened to the girls because they were never seen again.

One day he came to the door of a man who had three lovely daughters. The wizard looked pathetic and feeble, carrying a basket on his back for handouts. He pleaded for something to eat, and when the eldest daughter brought him some bread he only had to touch her and she felt herself leap into the basket. He strode off, making for his house in the middle of a dark forest. The house was quite grand and he gave her anything she wished for.

"My darling," he said to her, "I am sure you'll be happy here, for you may have whatever your heart desires."

After a few days had passed he said, "I am going away and must leave you alone. Here are the keys to the house. You may go into any room except the one that this little key opens. If you defy me, you will die." He also gave her an egg and said, "You must also take care of this egg. Keep it safe with you, because if it is lost something terrible will happen."

She took the keys and the egg and promised to take good care of both. After he left, she looked through the house from cellar to attic. The rooms sparkled with silver and gold. She had never seen such richness. At last she came to the forbidden door. She tried to pass by it, but her curiosity stopped her. She looked at the key and it seemed to be like all the others. She put it into the lock and turned it just a little. The door sprang open. Inside this room was no silver or gold. Instead there was a huge tub of bloody dead bodies that had been chopped into pieces. Next to the tub was a block of wood with an ax on it. She was so terrified that she dropped the egg into the tub. She took it out and wiped the blood off, but the blood reappeared an instant later. She wiped and wiped, but the blood remained.

---

*Adapted from the Brothers Grimm.

Soon the wizard returned from his trip and he immediately asked her for the keys and the egg. Shakily she gave them to him, and he knew by the red stain on the egg that she had been in the forbidden room.

"You went into the room against my wishes and now you'll go in against yours. You must die." And the wizard dragged her in, chopped her up, and threw her into the tub. "Now I'll have the second daughter," said the wizard.

And he again dressed like a poor beggar, went to the house, and asked for some bread. The second daughter brought him some bread and was caught just like the first. Her fate was the same as her sister's, as she also fell victim to her curiosity.

The wizard then fetched the third daughter, but she was quite clever. When he left her with the egg and keys, she put the egg away in a safe place. When she entered the forbidden room she found her murdered sisters in the tub. She immediately began to put their body parts into their proper places. When the pieces were joined, they began to move and soon the sisters were whole again. They hugged and kissed and were full of joy.

When the wizard returned and asked for the key and egg he found no trace of blood on the egg. He said, "You have stood the test. You shall be my wife." But in so doing, he had lost his power over her and had to grant her wishes.

The youngest daughter said, "Very well, but first you must carry a basket of gold on your back to my father and mother. I will meanwhile prepare for the wedding." And she ran to her hiding sisters and said, "I can save you now. The wizard will carry you back. But when you get home you must send me help." She put them in the basket and covered them with gold. Then she called the wizard in and told him he could leave, but that she would be watching from the window and he was not to tarry or rest.

The wizard put the basket on his back and started on his way, but the basket was so heavy that he had to stop. One of the sisters called out, "I am watching from my window and can see you resting. Keep moving!" He thought it was his bride and moved on, and each time he rested he heard the same voice. Finally he made it to his bride's home, delivering the heavy basket.

In the meantime, the bride was preparing the wedding feast, inviting all the wizard's friends. She took a grinning skull, decorated it with jewels and flowers and set it in the attic window looking out. Next she covered herself with honey, slit open a feather bed, and rolled in the feathers. Looking like a strange bird, she left the house. On her way, she met some of the wedding guests who asked, "Oh Fowler's fowl, where are you from?"

"From Fitz the Fowler's house I've come."

"Tell us what the bride is doing."

"She has swept the whole house and looks out the attic window."

Soon she met the wizard who was walking home slowly. He also asked, "Oh Fowler's fowl, where are you from?"

"From Fitz the Fowler's house I've come."

"Tell me what the bride is doing."

"She has swept the whole house and looks out the attic window."

He looked up and thought the decorated skull was his bride. He nodded and waved. When he and his guests were inside, the girl's brothers and cousins arrived to rescue her. They locked all the doors and set fire to the house. The wizard and all his friends were burned to death.

THE WATER OF LIFE
(Spain)

Three brothers and one sister lived together in a small cottage, and they loved one another dearly. One day the eldest brother, who had never done anything but amuse himself from sunrise to sunset, said to the rest, "Let us all work hard, and perhaps we shall grow rich, and be able to build ourselves a palace."

And his brothers and sister answered joyfully, "Yes, we will all work!"

So they fell to working with all their might, till at last they became rich, and were able to build themselves a beautiful palace; and everyone came from miles round to see its wonders, and to say how splendid it was. No one thought of finding any faults, till at length an old woman, who had been walking through the rooms with a crowd of people, suddenly exclaimed, "Yes, it is a splendid palace, but there is still something it needs!"

"And what may that be?"

"A church."

When they heard this the brothers set to work again to earn some more money, and when they had got enough they set about building a church, which should be as large and beautiful as the palace itself.

And after the church was finished greater numbers of people than ever flocked to see the palace and the church and vast gardens and magnificent halls.

But one day, as the brothers were as usual doing the honors to their guests, an old man turned to them and said, "Yes, it is all most beautiful, but there is still something it needs!"

"And what may that be?"

"A pitcher of the water of life, a branch of the tree the smell of whose flowers gives eternal beauty, and the talking bird."

"And where am I to find all those?"

"Go to the mountain that is far off yonder, and you will find what you seek."

After the old man had bowed politely and taken farewell of them the eldest brother said to the rest, "I will go in search of the water of life, and the talking bird, and the tree of beauty."

"But suppose some evil thing befalls you?" asked his sister. "How shall we know?"

"You are right," he replied; "I had not thought of that!"

Then they followed the old man, and said to him, "My eldest brother wishes to seek for the water of life, and the tree of beauty, and the talking bird, that you tell him are needful to make our palace perfect. But how shall we know if any evil thing befalls him?"

So the old man took them a knife, and gave it to them, saying, "Keep this carefully, and as long as the blade is bright all is well; but if the blade is bloody, then know that evil has befallen him."

The brothers thanked him, and departed, and went straight to the palace, where they found the young man making ready to set out for the mountain where the treasures he longed for lay hid.

And he walked, and he walked, and he walked, till he had gone a great way, and there he met a giant.

"Can you tell me how much further I have still to go before I reach that mountain yonder?"

"And why do you wish to go there?"

"I am seeking the water of life, the talking bird, and a branch of the tree of beauty."

"Many have passed by seeking those treasures, but none have ever come back; and you will never come back either, unless you mark my words. Follow this path, and when you reach the mountain you will find it covered with stones. Do not stop to look at them, but keep on your way. As you go you will hear scoffs and laughs behind you; it will be the stones that mock. Do not heed them; above all, do not turn round. If you do you will become as one of them. Walk straight on till you get to the top, and then take all you wish for."

The young man thanked him for his counsel, and walked, and walked, and walked, till he reached the mountain. And as he climbed he heard behind him scoffs and jeers, but he kept his ears steadily closed to them. At last the noise grew so loud that he lost patience, and he stooped to pick up a stone to hurl into the midst of the clamor, when suddenly his arm seemed to stiffen, and the next moment he was a stone himself!

That day his sister, who thought her brother's steps were long in returning, took out the knife and found the blade was red as blood. Then she cried out to her brothers that something terrible had come to pass.

"I will go and find him," said the second. And he went.

And he walked, and he walked, and he walked, till he met the giant, and asked him if he had seen a young man traveling toward the mountain.

And the giant answered, "Yes, I have seen him pass, but I have not seen him come back. The spell must have worked upon him."

"Then what can I do to disenchant him, and find the water of life, the talking bird, and a branch of the tree of beauty?"

"Follow this path, and when you reach the mountain you will find it covered with stones. Do not stop to look at them, but climb steadily on. Above all, heed not the laughs and scoffs that will arise on all sides, and never turn round. And when you reach the top you can then take all you desire."

The young man thanked him for his counsel, and set out for the mountain. But no sooner did he reach it than loud jests and gibes broke out on every side, and almost deafened him. For some time he let them rail, and pushed boldly on, till he had passed the place which his brother had gained; then suddenly he thought that among the scoffing sounds he heard his brother's voice. He stopped and looked back; and another stone was added to the number.

Meanwhile the sister left at home was counting the days when her two brothers should return to her. The time seemed long, and it would be hard to say how often she took out the knife and looked at its polished blade to make sure that this one at least was still safe. The blade was always bright and clear; each time she looked she had the happiness of knowing that all was well, till one evening, tired and anxious, as she frequently was at the end of the day, she took it from its drawer, and behold! the blade was red with blood. Her cry of horror brought her youngest brother to her, and, unable to speak, she held out the knife!

"I will go," he said.

So he walked, and he walked, and he walked, until he met the giant, and he asked, "Have two young men, making for yonder mountain, passed this way?"

And the giant answered, "Yes, they have passed by, but they never came back, and by this I know that the spell has fallen upon them."

"Then what must I do to free them, and to get the water of life, and the talking bird, and the branch of the tree of beauty?"

"Go to the mountain, which you will find so thickly covered with stones that you will hardly be able to place your feet, and walk straight forward, turning neither to the right hand nor to the left, and paying no heed to the laughs and scoffs which will follow you, till you reach the top, and then you may take all that you desire."

The young man thanked the giant for his counsel, and set forth to the mountain. And when he began to climb there burst forth all around him a storm of scoffs and jeers; but he thought of the giant's words, and looked neither to the right hand nor to the left, till the mountaintop lay straight before him. A moment now and he would have gained it, when, through the groans and yells, he heard his brothers' voices. He turned, and there was one stone the more.

And all this while his sister was pacing up and down the palace, hardly letting the knife out of her hand, and dreading what she knew she would see, and what she *did* see. The blade grew red before her eyes, and she said, "Now it is my turn."

So she walked, and she walked, and she walked till she came to the giant, and prayed him to tell her if he had seen three young men pass that way seeking the distant mountain.

"I have seen them pass, but they have never returned, and by this I know that the spell has fallen upon them."

"And what must I do to set them free, and to find the water of life, and the talking bird, and a branch of the tree of beauty?"

"You must go to that mountain, which is so full of stones that your feet will hardly find a place to tread, and as you climb you will hear a noise as if all the stones in the world were mocking you; but pay no heed to anything you may hear, and, once you gain the top, you have gained everything."

The girl thanked him for his counsel, and set out for the mountain; and scarcely had she gone a few steps upward when cries and screams broke forth around her, and she felt as if each stone she trod on was a living thing. But she remembered the words of the giant, and knew not what had befallen her brothers, and kept her face steadily toward the mountaintop, which grew nearer and nearer every moment. But as she mounted the clamor increased sevenfold: high above them all rang the voices of her three brothers. But the girl took no heed, and at last her feet stood upon the top.

Then she looked round, and saw, lying in a hollow, the pool of the water of life. And she took the brazen pitcher that she had brought with her, and filled it to the brim. By the side of the pool stood the tree of beauty, with the talking bird on one of its boughs; and she caught the bird, and placed it in a cage, and broke off one of the branches.

After that she turned, and went joyfully down the hill again, carrying her treasures, but her long climb had tired her out, and the brazen pitcher was very heavy, and as she walked a few drops of the water spilt on the stones, and as it touched them they changed into young men and maidens, crowding about her to give thanks for their deliverance.

So she learnt by this how the evil spell might be broken, and she carefully sprinkled every stone till there was not one left—only a great company of youths and girls who followed her down the mountain.

When they arrived at the palace she did not lose a moment in planting the branch of the tree of beauty and watering it with the water of life. And the branch shot up into a tree, and was heavy with flowers, and the talking bird nestled in its branches.

Now the fame of these wonders was noised abroad, and the people flocked in great numbers to see the three marvels, and the maiden who had won them; and among the sightseers came the king's son, who would not go till everything was shown him, and till he had heard how it had all happened. And the prince admired the strangeness and beauty of the treasures in the palace, but more than all he admired the beauty and courage of the maiden who had brought them there. So he went home and told his parents, and gained their consent to wed her for his wife.

Then the marriage was celebrated in the church adjoining the palace. Then the bridegroom took her to his own home, where they lived happily ever after.

HANSEL AND GRETEL
(Germany*)

ear a great forest lived a poor woodcutter, his wife, and his two children, Hansel and Gretel. They had little to eat or drink, and when famine swept the land there was not even bread to eat.

The woodcutter tossed and turned in his bed one night. "What will become of us? We cannot feed our children or ourselves."

His wife replied, "I will tell you what to do. We will take the children into the forest tomorrow morning, make them a fire, give them some bread, and go to our work without them. They will never find their way home again, and we shall be rid of them."

The woodcutter protested, "No wife, I can't leave my children in the forest. The wild animals would soon devour them."

"You are a fool," she said. "We will all starve instead. You might as well build the coffins." And she badgered him until he consented to her plan.

The two children had not been sleeping because of hunger pangs, and they heard what their stepmother had said to their father.

Gretel wept and said to Hansel, "It is over for us."

"Be quiet and don't worry," said Hansel. "I will think of something." When the parents had gone to sleep he put on his coat and slipped out the back door. The moon shone brightly, and white stones glistened like silver. Hansel filled the pockets of his coat with the stones and went back to Gretel.

"Go to sleep, dear sister. God will help us," Hansel said, and he lay down in the bed.

Early the next morning the stepmother woke the children, saying, "Get up, you lazybones. We are going into the forest to cut wood. Here is your bread for dinner, and see that you save it till then, as you will get no more."

---

*Adapted from the Brothers Grimm.

75

Gretel carried the bread under her apron, for Hansel's pockets were filled with the stones. When they had gone a little way into the forest, Hansel stood still and looked back toward the house. He did this again and again, until his father asked what he was doing.

"Oh father," said Hansel, "I am looking at my little white kitten, who is sitting up on the roof to bid me good-bye."

"You fool," said the stepmother. "That is not your kitten, but the sunshine on the chimney."

But Hansel had not been looking at his kitten, but had been dropping white stones onto the path every now and then. When they reached the middle of the forest, the father told the children to collect wood to make a warm fire.

When the fire was burning, the stepmother said, "Lie down and rest. We will go and cut wood, and when we are finished we will come for you."

Hansel and Gretel sat by the fire and at noon they ate their pieces of bread. They seemed to hear the strokes of an ax and thought their father was nearby, but it was only a branch moving in the wind. They became weary and fell asleep. When they woke up it was night.

"How can we get out of this forest?" Gretel asked.

Hansel comforted her, saying, "Wait a while longer and when the moon rises we will be able to find our way home."

And when the moon rose, Hansel and Gretel followed the white stones that shone like silver. They walked through the night and at daybreak came to their father's house. They knocked at the door, and the stepmother opened it.

"Oh, you naughty children! Why did you sleep so long in the forest? We thought you would never come home again!"

But the father was secretly glad, for he had never wanted to leave them in the woods.

However, it was not long before food was even more scarce, and the children heard their stepmother say to their father, "All the food is gone except a half a loaf of bread. The children must go. We will take them deeper into the forest this time so that they can't find their way back. This is the only way."

The father's heart ached and he thought that it would be better to share one's last food with one's children. But his wife wouldn't listen to him, and since he had given in to her once before, he found he could not resist her demands.

Again the children had heard their discussion, and when the parents had gone to sleep, Hansel got up to get more white stones. But the wife had locked the door and he could not go out.

He comforted his sister, saying, "Don't cry, Gretel. Go to sleep, and God will help us."

Early the next morning the wife came and pulled the children out of bed. She gave them each a small piece of bread, even smaller than before. On the way to the forest Hansel crumbled the bread in his pocket, stopping along the way to throw a crumb on the ground.

"Hansel, what are you stopping and staring at?" asked his father.

"I am looking at my little pigeon sitting on the roof," said Hansel.

"You fool," said the wife. "That is no pigeon, but the morning sun shining on the chimney."

Hansel continued to strew the bread crumbs along the road. The woman led the children deeper into the woods, where they had never been before. They made another large fire.

The stepmother said, "Stay there, children, and when you are tired you can go to sleep. We are going to cut wood, and when we are ready to go home we will come and get you."

When noon came, Gretel shared her bread with Hansel who had strewn his along the road. Then they slept until nighttime. Again they planned to wait till the moon rose so they could see the way home by the crumbs of bread.

But when the moon rose they couldn't find any bread, for the birds had eaten them. Hansel thought they might still find their way, but they could not. They walked through that night and into the next day and evening, but they could not find their way. They ate a few berries, but had nothing else to eat and were very hungry. At last they lay down under a tree to sleep.

Three mornings had passed since they had left their father's house. They kept trying to return to it, but instead they found themselves deeper in the forest. They were quite faint from hunger. At noon they saw a pretty white bird sitting on a branch, singing so sweetly that they stopped to listen. When it flew away they followed it till they came to a little house where the bird was perched on the roof. As they came close they realized the house was made of bread, roofed with cakes, with windows of sparkling sugar.

"Let's eat," said Hansel. "It will make a fine meal. I will eat a piece of the roof, Gretel, and you can have some of that sweet window."

Hansel reached up and broke off a bit of the roof and Gretel chewed on the window. Then they heard a thin voice call out from inside,

> Nibble, nibble, like a mouse,
> Who is nibbling at my house?

And the children answered,

> Never mind.
> It is the wind.

And they went on eating as before. Hansel took down a large piece of the roof and Gretel pulled out a large round windowpane. Then the door opened, and an old woman came out leaning upon a cane. Hansel and Gretel dropped their food in fear.

The old woman nodded her head and said, "Ah, my dear children, why are you out here? Don't be afraid. Come inside with me."

She led them into the house and gave them a fine meal of milk and pancakes, with sugar, apples, and nuts. Then she showed them two little beds, and they lay down on them and thought they were in heaven.

The old woman was not really so kind, but was a wicked witch who waited for children who would be attracted to her little house. Once they were inside she would kill them, cook them, and eat them, having a feast day. Her eyes were red, and she couldn't see very far, but she had a strong sense of smell and knew when humans were near. When she had realized Hansel and Gretel were nearby, she had cackled and said, "They are mine, and they will never get away!"

Early the next morning, before the children were awake, she got up to look at them, and as they lay sleeping so sweetly, she said to herself, "What a fine feast I shall have!"

And she grabbed Hansel with her withered hand and took him into a shed and shut him up in a cage. He screamed as loud as he could, but it was no use.

She went back to Gretel and shook her awake, saying, "Get up, you lazybones. Fetch some water and cook something nice for your brother. He is in the shed and must be fattened up so I can eat him!"

Gretel wept bitterly, but she had no choice but to do as the witch told her. Hansel had the best kind of food while Gretel was given very little.

Each morning the old woman visited the shed and said, "Hansel, hold out your finger so I can tell if you are fat enough."

But Hansel held out a bone, and the witch, with her weak eyes, thought it was his finger. She wondered why he was not getting fatter. After four weeks Hansel was still thin, but she had lost patience and would wait no longer.

"Now, Gretel," she cried, "go and fetch some water. Skinny or fat, tomorrow I must kill and cook Hansel."

"Oh, dear God, please help us!" Gretel wept. "If we had been devoured by beasts, at least we would have died together."

"Stop that wailing," cried the witch. "It won't help either of you."

Early the next morning Gretel rose to make the fire and fill the kettle.

"First we will do the baking," said the old woman. "I have heated the oven and kneaded the dough." She pushed Gretel toward the oven door. "Climb in and see if it is hot enough for the bread." Once Gretel was inside the witch planned to close the door and roast her.

But Gretel knew what she intended and said, "I don't know how to get in. Please show me."

"Stupid girl, the opening is big enough for me!" And she bent down and put her head in the opening.

Gretel gave her a big push all the way into the oven, shut the door and fastened the bolt. How the witch howled! But Gretel ran out, leaving her to burn to her death.

Gretel ran to the shed, releasing Hansel, crying, "We are free! Hansel, the old witch is dead!"

Hansel flew out of the cage like a bird and they danced and hugged and kissed. They searched all through the witch's house and found chests of pearls and precious stones.

"This is better than stones," said Hansel, as he filled his pockets with the jewels. Gretel filled her apron as well.

"Now we'd better leave," said Hansel. "I hope we can find our way out of the witch's wood."

When they had walked for a few hours they came to a large body of water.

"We can never get across," said Hansel. "There are no stepping stones or bridge."

"There is no boat either," said Gretel. "But there is a white duck. I'll ask her to help us." And she cried out,

> Duck, duck, here we stand.
> Hansel and Gretel, hand in hand.
> No bridge or stones far and wide,
> Duck, duck, give us a ride.

And the duck came and Hansel climbed on, telling his sister to join him.

"No," said Gretel, "that would be too much. You go and then it can return for me."

And that is what the kind duck did. When they had walked a bit further the forest began to look more familiar. At last they saw their father's house. They ran to the house, and flew into his arms. The man had been heavy of heart since they had left the children in the forest and since then his wife had died. When Gretel opened her apron the jewels bounced across the room and Hansel threw handfuls after them. All their troubles were over and they lived together in great joy.

FORTUNÉE

(France)

Once upon a time there were two orphans whose father was very poor when he died. The father had left his daughter Fortunée a silver ring and a pot of pinks that he had been given years before. It had been the father's habit to keep them with great care, and Fortunée also tended them lovingly. He left his son Bedou the remainder of his possessions.

Some time after his death, Fortunée was called by her brother and he said, "You have your ring and your flowers. Take care of them, but leave my house and belongings alone. They are mine alone!"

Her eyes filled with tears, but she said nothing. At supper Bedou threw her the scraps of his meal and told her that she could find her own food if that was not enough. Fortunée went to her room where she kept her pot of pinks.

"Dear flowers, I do enjoy your lovely color and smell. You are all I have and I will always keep you safe."

And though it was growing dark, she took a jug to the stream to get the flowers some water. As she approached the stream she saw a beautiful lady sitting at an ornate table laden with fine food. The lady, who was a queen, saw Fortunée and sent one of her several attendants to fetch her.

After Fortunée bowed to her, the queen asked, "Why are you out here? It is quite dangerous to be here alone."

"You are kind to worry about me, your majesty, but I have nothing worthy of stealing. My father died and all I have is a silver ring and a pot of pinks."

"But you do have a heart. Would you let your heart be stolen?" asked the queen.

"Your majesty, without a heart I would die, and though I am poor I do want to live."

"You are wise to defend your heart. Tell me, have you eaten tonight?"

"No, my brother ate all our food."

The queen invited Fortunée to join her, but though the girl was hungry, she was unable to eat much of anything.

"Why had you come to the stream?" the queen asked.

"I came to get water for my pinks," said Fortunée. As she picked up her jug to show it to the queen, she was stunned to see that it was no longer a common jug, but was now gold, encrusted with diamonds. It was filled with fragrant water.

"It is for you, Fortunée," said the queen. "Take care of your flowers and remember that the queen of the woods is now your friend."

"You are so kind, your majesty. I thank you for this honor. If you will wait here I would bring to you half of my flowers so that you could enjoy them as well."

Fortunée ran home, carefully cradling the jug. At home she found that Bedou had taken her flowers and left a cabbage in their place. She took her ring from its hiding place and returned to the queen.

"Your majesty, my flowers were taken by my brother. All I have left is my ring. Please accept it instead of the flowers."

"But it is all that you have," replied the queen.

Fortunée said, "No, your majesty, for I have your favor. It is all I need."

The queen put on the ring and climbed into her jeweled carriage drawn by six magnificent horses. Fortunée watched as the queen drove away.

When Fortunée returned home, she went to her room and threw the cabbage out of the window.

"You have killed me!" she heard. In amazement she went to her window, but she could see nothing. She was puzzled, but she went to bed for the night.

The next morning she went into the garden and seeing the cabbage she said, "What are you worth to me? I wish I had my lovely flowers."

"I never wished to be there. If you would be so kind as to put me back in the garden, you will find your pinks in Bedou's bed."

Fortunée was astonished, but she picked up the talking cabbage and carried it to the vegetable garden. As she put it down she noticed Bedou's hen. She picked it up and said, "I should make you my dinner to pay for Bedou's unkindness."

"Please spare me and I will tell you things you do not know," begged the hen.

Fortunée, who really had a kind heart, put down the hen.

"Thank you, kind child. You must know some things. Just as I am not a hen, you are not the daughter of this man who raised you. Your mother was a queen who had six daughters. She was told she would be killed if her seventh child was also a girl. The queen's sister was a fairy and when the queen had another daughter and the fairy sister had a son, the fairy used her magic and sent the babe on the wind to the queen. But the queen had become too frightened to wait and she had run away with the baby girl. She came to this hut when I was still a poor, but good woman. She gave you to me and then died. I was raising you, but I couldn't resist talking about the queen who brought you, and when I told this to a beautiful lady she touched me with her wand and turned me into a hen. My husband assumed I had been killed by the beasts of the forest. But one day this lady returned and gave him the pot of pinks and the silver ring. While she was there, twenty-five of the king's soldiers came looking for you and your mother. But the lady turned them all into cabbages, one of which you threw out the window last night. I had never heard one speak before. Indeed I have not been able to speak until now."

Fortunée was amazed by all she had heard. "I am sorry that you have suffered so much. Do not worry, though; I am going to look for my pinks and I believe that things will soon be better."

Fortunée knew that Bedou was out of the house and she entered his room. In front of his bed was a group of huge rats with enormous mice behind them. The rats lunged at her, forcing her back so that she could not get at her flowers. She suddenly remembered the perfumed water in her jug and retrieved it. As soon as she sprinkled some of the water on the rats and mice they disappeared into their holes. She watered the pinks, enjoying their fragrance.

Suddenly she heard a voice from the leaves saying, "Today, dear Fortunée, I can tell of my love for you. You are so beautiful that even these flowers bow to you."

This was all too much for Fortunée. She had listened to a cabbage and a hen talk, fought off rats and mice, and now been talked to by a plant. As she felt faint with confusion, Bedou returned and threw her out of the house.

The queen of the woods stood before her. "Your brother is hateful. Do you wish to have your revenge on him?"

"Your majesty, I do not understand his wickedness. But I will not become like him and seek revenge."

"But, Fortunée, he is not your true brother. Haven't you been told you are a princess?" asked the queen.

"I have been told that, but until I have proof there is little I can do about it."

"My child, it is clear that your blood is noble. You are truly a princess and I am now able to help you."

Just then a handsome prince appeared, dressed in rich clothing with a crown of pinks on his head. He knelt before the queen.

The queen looked at him fondly and said, "Dear Pink, your enchantment has been ended with the help of Fortunée." She turned to Fortunée and continued, "I know the hen has told you much, but what she did not know was that when I sent my son to be exchanged for you, the wind carried him to a flowerbed and an evil fairy turned him into a pot of pinks. I arranged for you to care for the pot, knowing that my magic water would restore him. If you could find it in your heart to marry him the enchantment will be forever ended."

"Your majesty, I could never agree to marry a man without knowing more of him and if he cared for me."

The prince spoke, "I have loved you for years. You have shown your kindness in spite of the wickedness around you. If you will not have me for your husband, I would ask only to be your pot of pinks once again and have you tend to me as in the past."

The princess, Fortunée, was touched by his words and as she considered his plea the queen touched her with her wand, transforming her clothes into exquisite jeweled garments. Just then Bedou came along, stopping in shock as he saw Fortunée looking like a princess.

Fortunée turned to the queen, "Won't you spare him? I don't want revenge."

The queen admired her generous spirit and acted in kind. She turned Bedou's hut into a beautiful palace and changed his wickedness to benevolence. Then she changed the cabbages back into men and the hen into a woman.

Everyone was content, except for Prince Pink who waited for Fortunée to look upon him with favor. Finally she agreed that he could court her. At last they married and they lived happily ever after.

MOLLY WHUPPIE
(Scotland)

A husband and wife who had many children were so poor that they could not feed them all. So they took their three youngest daughters into the forest and left them there. The children set out and walked and walked until it was dark. At last they saw the lights of a house and knocked at the door.

"What do you want?" said a woman.

"We are lost and hungry. Could we come in and have something to eat?" the girls asked.

"No," said the woman. "My husband is a giant and he will kill you if he finds you here."

"We won't stay but a bit, ma'am, and we'll be gone before he comes home."

She took pity on them and let them come in for some bread and milk. But as they began to eat, there was a loud knock at the door and they heard a frightful voice crying,

Fee, fi, fo, fum
I smell the blood of an earthly one.
Who is there, my wife?

His wife answered, "It is just three poor children who needed some food and comfort. They'll soon be gone. Leave them alone."

The giant said nothing, ate a huge supper, and insisted they spend the night. This giant had three daughters of his own, and they were going to share their bed with the three visitors, the youngest of whom was Molly Whuppie. Molly was a resourceful child and she noticed that the giant had put straw ropes around her and her sisters' necks and gold chains around his daughters' necks. Molly stayed awake and when the rest were sleeping, she slid out of bed and switched their straw ropes for the giant's daughters' gold chains. Then she quietly slipped back into bed.

When the night was dark, the giant got up, picked up a club, came over to the bed, and felt for the necks with the straw ropes. When he found them, he unwittingly took his own three daughters out of bed and beat them to death. Then he went back to bed, dreaming of the feast he would soon have.

Molly woke her sisters, admonished them to be quiet, and they stole out of the house. They ran until morning, when they saw a palace before them. Molly went in and asked to tell her story to the king.

"Molly, you are indeed a clever girl. If you would now go back to the giant's house and bring me the magic sword that hangs on his bedpost, I would allow your oldest sister to marry my oldest son."

"I will do my best," answered Molly.

She ran back to the giant's house and sneaked under his bed. Soon he came home, enjoyed a huge supper, and went to sleep. When Molly heard his snores, she slipped out and reached over the sleeping giant and lifted down the sword. But suddenly he woke up and Molly had to flee, carrying his sword. She ran and ran, with the giant close behind, till they reached a tiny bridge. She could run over it, but he was too large.

He bellowed, "Woe to ye, Molly Whuppie! Never ye come again."

But she said, "Twice more, I'll come again."

Then Molly ran to the palace, gave the sword to the king, and her eldest sister was married to the king's first son.

The king called Molly to him. "Well, Molly, you have done well. But if you could only get the giant's magic purse of gold that is under his pillow, I would marry your second sister to my second son."

"I will do my best," answered Molly.

Again she sneaked into the giant's house and waited under his bed as he ate his supper and fell asleep. She waited till she heard his snores, then slipped out from under the bed, slid her hand under his pillow, and carefully pulled out the purse. Just then he woke up and chased Molly out the door. She ran with him after her until they reached the tiny bridge. Again she ran over it, but he could not.

He howled, "Woe to ye, Molly Whuppie! Never ye come again."

And she replied, "Once more I'll come again."

Then Molly took the purse to the king and her second sister was married to his second son.

"Molly," the king said. "You are indeed most clever. Now if you could bring me the giant's ring of invisibility that he wears on his finger, I would marry you to my youngest son."

That pleased Molly, so she replied, "I will do my best."

She went again to the giant's house and hid under his bed. She waited for his snores and then she slipped out, reached for his hand, and pulled and pulled till she got off the ring. But just then the giant woke and caught her by the hand.

"Now I have you, Molly Whuppie!" howled the giant. "You think you are so clever. Answer this: If I had served you as you've served me, what would you do with me?"

Molly thought quickly and said, "Sir, I would put you into a sack along with the cat and dog. Then I would hang the sack on the wall, go into the woods, find the biggest and thickest stick, and beat the sack till you were dead."

"So be it, Molly. I will do just that to you!"

He put Molly, the cat, and the dog into a sack and hung it up on the wall. He went into the wood to hunt for a stick. As soon as he had gone, Molly began to sing, "Oh, if you could only see what I see!"

"Oh what do you see, Molly?" asked the giant's wife.

But Molly just sang on, "Oh, if you could only see what I see!"

The giant's wife begged Molly to take her into the sack so she could see what Molly saw. Molly agreed, and the giant's wife cut a hole in the sack. Molly jumped down and helped the giant's wife into the sack and sewed up the hole.

The giant's wife could see nothing in the sack and asked Molly to let her down again, but Molly hid behind the door. Soon the giant returned with a huge stick in his hand, and he took down the sack and began to beat it.

The giant's wife screamed at him, "It's me, your wife!" But the dog barked and the cat screeched and he could not tell her voice. Molly took pity on the wife and came out from behind the door. The giant took one look at her and ran after her. They ran and ran till Molly crossed over the tiny bridge. He said again, "Woe to ye, Molly Whuppie! Never ye come again."

And Molly said, "Never more will I come."

Molly took the ring to the king and was married to his youngest son. She never saw the giant again.

THE WITCH
(Russia)

Once upon a time there was a peasant whose wife died, leaving him with twins, a boy and a girl. The peasant tried to raise them, but it was too hard without a wife and he decided to marry again. The stepmother was cruel to the children and gave them little to eat. She often thought of how she could rid herself of them, and finally she decided to send them into a gloomy wood where a wicked witch lived.

One morning she said to them, "You have been such good children that I am going to send you to visit my granny in the woods. You will have to help her out, but she will take good care of you, rewarding you hand-somely for your help."

So the children left, but the sister, who was quite wise, said, "Let us first go see our own dear grandmother and tell her where we are going."

When they told their grandmother, she cried, "Your stepmother isn't sending you to her granny! She is sending you to a wicked witch who lives in the darkest part of the forest. Now take heed, children. You must be polite to everyone. Never take anything that belongs to anyone else. I'll try to find some help."

She gave them some milk, a bit of meat, and some bread, and the children set out for the woods. After a long walk they found a strange little hut.

"Who's there?" snarled the witch.

Remembering their grandmother's advice to be polite, they said, "Good morning, granny. Our stepmother has sent us to wait upon you and serve you."

"See that you do, and if you are good, I will reward you. If not, I'll have you both for dinner."

She set the girl down to spin yarn, and she gave the boy a sieve in which to carry water from the well. She then went out into the wood. The girl was sitting, trying to puzzle out how to spin, when she heard the sound of hundreds of little feet. From every corner of the room came little mice, saying, "Little girl, give us some bread and we will help."

She gave them some of the bread her grandmother had given her. Then the mice told her that they would do her spinning, and if she gave the witch's cat some meat it would show them the way out of the wood. She went to look for the cat and the mice began to spin the yarn for her.

As she looked for the cat, she found her brother trying to carry water from the well with the sieve. The water would run out as fast as he put it into the sieve. "Brother, fill up the holes with clay," she said. So he did and carried the water into the house without spilling a drop.

They found the cat curled up by the hearth and fed her the meat, saying, "Kitty, please tell us how to get away from the witch."

The cat stretched and purred and gave them a handkerchief and a comb. It told them that when the witch chased them they should throw the handkerchief on the ground and run. A river would spring up, and if the witch got across they should throw the comb behind them and run for their lives. A forest would grow up behind them, and they would be able to get away.

As the cat finished speaking, the witch returned to see if the children had finished their work.

"Well, you have done well enough for today, but tomorrow will be harder, and if you don't do it well it'll be the oven for you," threatened the witch.

That night the children lay awake, hardly daring to breathe. The next morning the witch gave the girl two pieces of linen to weave before night and told the boy to cut a pile of wood into chips.

Once she had left, they took the comb and handkerchief and ran away from the witch's hut as fast as they could. First they met the watchdog who snarled and crouched as if to leap on them, but they threw the last of their bread to him and he stopped to eat. The branches of birch trees pushed and pulled at them, but the girl used her hair ribbon to tie the branches together. They ran on through the forest and came to an open field.

Back at the witch's hut the cat was busily weaving the linen, though tangling the threads as she worked. The witch came up to the window and whispered, "Are you weaving, my dear?"

"Yes, granny," answered the cat.

But the witch saw that the children had left. She hit the cat and said, "Why did you let the children leave? You should have scratched out their eyes!"

But the cat sat defiantly and said, "In all these years you have never even given me a bone, but the children gave me their only piece of meat!"

The witch went to the watchdog and asked why he let the children pass. He answered, "I have served you well and in all these years you did not give me so much as a bread crust. Those dear children gave me their last bit of bread."

The birch trees whispered, "We too have served you well and you never tied even a bit of yarn around my branches. But the children bound up my branches with their brightest ribbon."

The witch saw that she must pursue the children on her own and she mounted her broom and set off after them. The children heard the swish of her broom sweeping the ground behind them, so they threw the handkerchief down. In a moment a deep, broad river flowed behind them. When the witch came to the river she had to take time to find a shallow place to cross. After she crossed, she pursued them faster than before.

As the children ran they again heard the swishing of the broom behind them. The girl threw down the comb and instantly a thick forest sprang up. The roots and branches were so densely intertwined that it was impossible to pass through. The witch searched and searched for passage, but finally gave up and returned to her hut.

The twins ran on and on until they came to their home. They told their father all that had happened and he banished their stepmother from the house. He took care of the children himself and they lived happily together.

M·A·I·D·E·N·S

Clever and True

THE ROBBER BRIDEGROOM

(Germany*)

There once was a miller who had a beautiful daughter. When she was grown, he decided that she needed a fine husband who would take care of her. Soon a rich man showed interest in her, and since the miller found nothing wrong with him, he promised his daughter to him. But she did not share his confidence in the suitor. Indeed whenever she saw or thought about him she felt her heart grow cold.

One day the bridegroom said to her, "You are soon to be my bride, yet you never come to see me."

"I don't know where you live," she replied evasively.

"My house is but a way through the forest."

She tried to find an excuse, but he insisted she come.

"You must visit me next Sunday. Guests are already invited and I will strew ashes along the path to guide you."

When Sunday came and she set out on her way, she was very uneasy, although she didn't know why. She filled both pockets full of peas and lentils, and as she followed the ashes she cast a few peas and lentils to the ground. After a day of walking, she came to the middle of the forest and where it was the darkest stood a desolate, dreary house. She walked in, but quiet prevailed. Suddenly she heard a voice cry,

> Turn back, turn back thou pretty bride,
> Within this house thou must not bide,
> For here do evil things betide.

She looked around and saw a bird in a cage by the wall. Again it cried,

> Turn back, turn back thou pretty bride,
> Within this house thou must not bide,
> For here do evil things betide.

She went searching through the house, but found no one in it. At last she reached the cellar, and there sat a very old woman.

---

*Adapted from the Brothers Grimm.

"Can you tell me if my bridegroom lives here?" she asked.

The old woman answered, "Oh, dear child, do you know where you are? You are in a den of thieves. Your only marriage will be to death. See this kettle of water? They will cut you into pieces, cook, and eat you. They are merciless cannibals. Without my help you are lost."

With that she had the bride hide behind a barrel where she could not be seen. "Be still as a mouse. Do not move and tonight when the robbers are asleep we will flee. I have been waiting a long time for this chance to escape."

In moments the robbers came back. They had another young woman with them. They drunkenly ignored her pleas for mercy, and gave her three glasses of wine to drink, one white, one red, and one yellow. Soon she was dead and they threw her on the table, tore off her clothes, and cut her into pieces. One thief noticed a gold ring on a little finger and when he couldn't remove it, he chopped off the finger, causing it to fly into the bride's lap. He began to search for it, but could not find it.

"Have you looked behind the barrel?" one of the others asked.

But just then the old woman cried, "Come to supper. You can find it tomorrow. It is going nowhere."

The robbers gave up the search and began to eat. The old woman had slipped a sleeping potion into their wine, and soon they were sleeping, sprawled about on the floor. When the bride heard their snores she carefully stepped through them and made her way to the door.

The old woman joined her as they hastily set out into the woods. The ashes had been blown away, but the peas and lentils had spouted, shining in the moonlight. They traveled all night, reaching the mill in the morning. The girl told her father all that had happened.

When the planned wedding day came, the bridegroom arrived, along with all the friends and neighbors of the miller. As they sat down at the table, each guest was invited to tell a story.

At last the bridegroom asked his bride, "Sweetheart, surely you know a story. Tell us."

"Instead of a story, I will tell you a dream. I was walking through a forest alone and at last I came to a house. When I went in I couldn't find a living soul, but by the wall was a bird in a cage who cried,

> Turn back, turn back thou pretty bride,
> Within this house thou must not bide,
> For here do evil things betide.

"And then it said it again. I searched through all the rooms and they were all empty. At last I went down into a cellar, and there sat an old woman. I asked her if my bridegroom lived in that house and she answered, 'Oh, dear child, do you know where you are? You are in a den of thieves. Your only marriage will be to death. See this kettle of water? They will cut you into pieces, cook, and eat you.' Darling, it was only a dream, but next the old woman hid me behind a great barrel. In came the thieves, bringing with them a helpless young woman. They gave her three kinds of wine—white, red, and yellow—killed her, and cut her into pieces. Of course, my dear, it was only a dream. One of the robbers saw a gold ring on her finger, and when he couldn't get it off he chopped off her little finger. It flew behind the barrel onto my lap.

"And here is the finger with the ring!"

With those words, she drew it forth and showed it to the guests. The robber, who had grown deadly white, sprang up to escape. But the people held him until the authorities arrived. He and his gang were executed for their crimes.

THE LITTLE ORPHAN GIRL
(Chile)

There was once a married couple who worked faithfully their whole lives as coal gatherers for a very wealthy rancher who lived in the mountains. This couple had a single daughter and a dog. The wife died one day, and with the years, the husband followed her, charging his daughter to bury him behind the ranch beside his wife's body. He warned her not to tell anyone that she was left alone so that people would continue to respect her.

About a year had passed, and finally the nearest neighbors, who were a mother and two daughters, realized that the girl was all alone. Meanwhile, a voice surprised her in the house one afternoon.

"Leave a washbowl of water just inside your door, for I wish to keep you company." She looked all about and saw only a little bird perched on the branch of a tree in the dooryard. She agreed gladly and left a bowl of water. That evening when she lay down to sleep, the girl heard a little bird bathing himself in the bowl, and at the very same moment a young man sat down on the bed to talk to her. He offered to visit her the following night as well, and immediately disappeared. At the same hour the next evening, she placed the bowl of water by her door and went to bed to wait. The youth came again, and soon they were intimate friends. He filled her life with all she had lacked.

Meanwhile the neighbor women were discussing the idea of offering the girl some company and seeing, incidentally, what she did all by herself in that lonely little cottage. They had nicknamed her *La Guacha* (Little Orphan). One afternoon the older daughter from next door strolled over to pay a visit. Although the little orphan refused to let her stay, her efforts were in vain, for her neighbor simply climbed into bed for the night. The girl didn't place the bowl by the door. Later she felt the desperation of the bird as it fluttered down into the room. The lodger slept very well, and in the morning went home to report to her mother, "La Guacha sleeps alone."

"The trouble is that you surely fell asleep," answered the old lady.

"Well, of course, I couldn't help it," protested her daughter.

"Then tonight your sister will go. Let's see how she makes out."

It was just like the first time. The younger sister forced herself upon the poor orphan and stayed the night. The girl didn't place the water this time either. When the sister returned home the following day, she declared, "La Guacha sleeps alone." But her mother, not at all satisfied, ordered her not to shut her eyes the next time.

The second time, the visitor changed the hour of her arrival. Since the girl had not set the water out for two nights in a row, she had left the bowl this time in hopes of seeing her friend and telling him what was happening. Now, before the neighboring sister left for the orphan's house, her mother gave her three razor-sharp knives and said, "If you see water in the room, you must get up and say that you need to go outside. Then put the knives on the bowl with the water."

The orphan and her unwelcome guest went to sleep as usual that evening. About the time dawn was breaking, the neighbor girl heard the bird fluttering with great difficulty. She got up and saw that the room and the bowl itself were covered with blood. With that, she picked up her knives and went home to tell her mother what had happened.

When the little orphan awoke some time after, she saw the same horrible sight. Everything was smeared with blood. She vowed then and there to wander over the whole world until she found him whom she had lost. Leaving her dog alone and putting on her father's clothes, she disguised herself as a hermit and set off on the lonely road. For a weapon, she carried an ancient sword which had belonged to her father. Night came upon her as she was descending the hills, so she searched out some *patagua* shrubs and climbed into one for refuge. Nearby was a pond with some ashes on the bank.

"God only knows who's camping there," she thought, fearing that there must be some bad men about. Great was her surprise when at midnight some ducks arrived and began to wallow in the ashes. The orphan recognized them as the three neighbor women. They had kindled a fire and sat down to talk.

"What do you suppose La Guacha will say now that her little bird must be dead?" piped up the younger daughter.

"Today I was in the palace," answered the mother, "and the queen has issued a proclamation, that she will permit anyone to enter the palace who can bring the sick prince a remedy. But nobody will succeed in this."

"Mama," spoke up the older daughter, "you must know what is needed to heal the prince and cure those wounds of his."

"You've got your nose out for news," retorted her mother. "But I'm going to tell you, even though I ought not to. The prince can rise hale and hearty only if he is cured by a feather dipped in our blood. And when, pray tell, is he going to get that?"

"Let's be off to sleep," chorused the three ducks. "Day is about to break now." And letting themselves slide into the water, they swam quacking away.

Immediately the orphan girl climbed out of her bush and ran, with her heart full of vengeance, all the way to her house. A new day had already begun when she went to her room and took a very thick earthenware bottle. Then she headed straight for the house of the three neighboring witches, who always slept in one bed. She sliced off the three sleeping heads with her sword and took their blood until the bottle was filled. Following her footsteps toward home, she sat down about three in the afternoon to rest on a little log. Out of nowhere an old man approached her and asked, "Where are you going, my child?"

"My father is sick, and I'm in search of some remedy."

"He could never be sicker than the prince," answered the old man. "You should see how the king and queen are carrying on and mourning. The palace is all dark with their sadness. The prince lay dying this very morning, and there is free passage for whoever wishes to give him a remedy."

Upon hearing that, she jumped up sharply and set off at a run. From everyone she met on the road, she inquired breathlessly, "Is it true that the prince is gravely ill?" She always received the same reply, "Terribly grave. He won't live through the day." She met a boy on the road and asked him for the location of the palace.

"Do you have some medicine for him?" he asked.

"Yes, yes," she gasped, exhausted from her race.

"Then let's run faster," he replied. "You might be able to arrive while the prince is still alive."

When the girl got to the palace gate at last, everyone who saw her disguised in her father's clothes let out a shout of gladness. "There's an old man at the door who has come with a remedy for the prince." They notified the queen, who said mournfully, "It seems like a lost cause, for now he can hardly breathe. But since this is the last person and he is so old, let him come in."

Coming to the prince's bedside, the girl said in a gruff, manly voice, "Everyone go out of the room. Leave me alone with the prince." When they had all obeyed in order to see this prodigy, she took the bottle out of her jacket and dipped a feather in the blood. She began to cure the prince's wounds, especially a gaping one in his throat which practically separated his head from his trunk. As soon as the remedy was applied, his flesh drew together. The miracle was done, and the prince was healed. He sat up in bed, and looking straight at the old fellow, said, "You have saved me, old man. I shall give you whatever you ask."

"That's not important," said she. "I only ask you for the ring you have on your hand as a remembrance."

Then the prince rang a bell beside the bed. The queen and all the court came running, for the bell was rung only when the prince needed to be together with everybody. Thronged in the doorway, they found him dressed and healed of his wounds. Just at this moment, the little old man slipped unobtrusively away through the crowd. The only one to see him was the queen, who said, "You must never leave my side, for I believe that you have healed my son."

"You may pay me, madam, with that ring you are wearing on your right hand." This ring carried a portrait of the prince. The queen immediately took it off and passed it to the old man. Then she dashed off in great excitement to see her son. The queen thought that the old hermit would wait for her, but the disguised orphan girl slipped away and returned to her own cottage.

Several days passed, and she fulfilled her vow by placing the bowl of water night after night. The bird didn't come. Finally she said sadly, "He's angered with me, and the whole thing is unfair." It was a great and joyous surprise for her when she heard the fluttering of wings one night. She was sleeping with her hands resting on her breast and the two rings placed on her fingers. But this time the young man had come with his sword unsheathed and the intention of killing her in vengeance for the knives. Hearing the noise, she started up in bed, and the sparkle of jewels caught the prince's eye. He recognized his own ring and remembered the gift he had presented to the old man. Immediately he fell on his knees to beg her pardon, and she told him the whole story of the witches, whose corpses were still to be found in bed at the neighboring house.

When her innocence was proved, the prince took her up and carried her to the palace to be his wife with the king and queen's consent. The newlyweds received the crowns of the kingdom, while the old royal couple stayed on as guests at the palace. The little orphan and her prince lived happily for many years after this.

RACHEL FOUND THE GOLD
(United States, Ozarks)

ne time there was an old man up on Yocum Creek that died sudden and unexpected, without no chance to tell the folks where his money was hid. The boys hunted all over the place, but they couldn't find a penny. Nobody could sleep in the old man's room, because it seemed like there was something in bed with them, and just at midnight they would feel a cold hand on their face. So the big bed just stood there empty all the time. The folks slept in the other room, no matter if they was crowded or not.

Pretty soon a neighbor girl named Rachel come over to stay all night, and the folks told her how things was. Rachel was not afraid to sleep in the big bed, but she put a butcher knife where she could reach it. Along about midnight she felt the cold hand on her face, and there was something standing right beside the bed. Rachel figured it must be the old man's spirit. "In the name of the Father, the Son, and the Holy Ghost, follow me," says the spirit. Rachel picked up the butcher knife and followed the thing out into the orchard. "Stick that knife in the ground," says the spirit. Rachel stuck the knife right where he pointed, and when she looked up the old man's ghost was gone. So then she went back to the house and crawled in bed.

Next morning the folks says, "Well, how did you and the ghost get along?" Rachel told 'em what happened, and they all went out to the orchard. They seen the butcher knife stuck in the ground, just like she said. The boys dug right there, and found a dinner pot full of gold. It come in right handy, too, because that family was needing money the worst way.

The ghost didn't bother anybody after that. The folks just used the old man's big bed whenever they wanted to, and never had no more trouble.

MAID MALEEN
(Germany*)

There was once a young woman whose father was a great king. Maid Maleen had fallen in love with a young prince who had been faithfully courting her, but her father insisted she marry instead the son of a nearby king. Maid Maleen steadfastly refused, stating that she would marry only her chosen prince.

Maid Maleen's father became so angry that he ordered his workmen to build a tower with no windows so that not a ray of sunlight or moonlight would ever enter it. When the tower was completed, he said to his daughter, "You shall be shut up here for seven years. Then I'll come and see if you are still obstinate."

Maid Maleen and her lady-in-waiting were put in the tower with enough food and water for seven years. While they sat in total darkness, the prince who loved Maid Maleen walked round and round the tower, calling out her name. But the thick walls kept out not only the light but his voice, and he finally left, despairing for her life.

Slowly the time passed, and as the food dwindled, Maid Maleen knew that her seven years were nearly finished. They expected to hear the sound of hammers setting them free, but it was quiet. They feared they had been forgotten. When their food was nearly gone, Maid Maleen said, "We will die of hunger soon. Let us see if we can make a hole in the wall." Using the bread knife, she began to scrape at the mortar, and when she became weary, the lady-in-waiting relieved her.

After a great deal of work, they managed to loosen one stone, then a second, and finally a third. After three more days a ray of light shone into the darkness, and finally they were able to look through the opening. It was a lovely spring day with a cool breeze and a blue sky, but a dismal scene met their eyes. Her father's castle lay in ruins, and the town and countryside were destroyed for as far as the eye could see. They now understood why no one had come for them.

---

*Adapted from the Brothers Grimm.

They continued to enlarge the hole and when it was large enough they each jumped down. But where were they to go? The enemy had destroyed the kingdom, driving out or killing the people and burning the surroundings. They set out, walking on and on, seeing no one, finding no shelter, and having only nettles to eat. At last they came to a kingdom near the sea. They went from door to door, begging for work, but no one wanted them. They were even turned away at the royal palace until finally the cook said they could work as scullery maids.

Unknown to them, they had found work in the kingdom of the prince Maid Maleen had loved. He had mourned her for seven years, refusing to marry, but had at last given in to the wishes of his parents who had chosen for him a rich but unattractive and cold princess. The bride had arrived for the wedding, but she was so ashamed of her appearance that she shut herself up in her room, requiring Maid Maleen to bring up her meals from the kitchen.

When the wedding day arrived, the ugly princess said to Maid Maleen, "You are a lucky girl. I've sprained my ankle and can't walk to the church. Put on my wedding dress and take my place. It will be a great honor for you."

Maid Maleen would have nothing of it, saying, "I want no honor that is not rightly mine."

The princess entreated her to take her place and when Maid Maleen continued to refuse, she grew angry and said, "If you don't take my place, I will have the executioner remove your head."

Maid Maleen had no choice but to put on the bride's dress and jewels. As she entered the great hall, everyone was amazed at her beauty. The king announced her as his choice, and the prince thought, "She looks like my Maid Maleen! But she must be dead." He took her hand and led her toward the church. On the way they passed a nettle bush and Maid Maleen said softly,

> Oh nettle bush,
> I ate you unroasted.
> Why are you all alone?

"What did you say?" asked the prince.
"Nothing. I was only thinking."
Though he was surprised at her answer, he said nothing. When they came to the footbridge, Maid Maleen said,

> Footbridge, don't break.
> I'm not the true bride.

"What did you say?" asked the prince.
"Oh, I was just thinking of Maid Maleen," she replied.

"Do you know Maid Maleen?" he asked.

"No," she said, "I have only heard of her."

When they came to the church door, she said,

> Church door, don't break.
> I'm not the true bride.

"What did you say?" asked the prince again.

"I was only thinking of Maid Maleen," she said.

He fastened a precious necklace around her neck and they went into the church where they were married. As they returned to the palace, Maid Maleen was quiet. She rushed to the bride's room, removed the gown and all the jewels except the necklace, and put on her gray frock.

When night came and the ugly princess was to be taken to the bridegroom's room, she put on a veil so he would not realize her deceit. When they were finally alone, he asked, "What was it you said to the nettle bush on the way to the church?"

"What nettle bush? I don't talk to bushes."

"Then you must not be the true bride," he said.

After a moment's thought, she said,

> I'll have to ask my maid, you see,
> She keeps my thoughts for me.

She ran to Maid Maleen and screamed, "What did you say to the nettle bush?"

Maid Maleen said, "I only said,

> Oh nettle bush,
> I ate you unroasted.
> Why are you all alone?"

The ugly princess returned to the prince's chamber and told him the words. He then asked, "But what did you say to the footbridge?"

"Footbridge? I don't speak to footbridges."

"Then you're not my true bride."

Again she said,

> I'll have to ask my maid, you see,
> She keeps my thoughts for me.

She again ran to Maid Maleen, screaming, "What did you say to the footbridge?"

Maid Maleen answered,

> Footbridge, don't break.
> I'm not the true bride.

"That has cost you your life!" and she rushed back to the prince, repeating the words upon her arrival.

"But what did you say to the church door?" he asked.

"Church door? I don't talk to church doors."

"Then you're not my true bride."

She ran off to Maid Maleen, demanding, "What did you say to the church door?"

Maid Maleen answered, "I only said,

Church door, don't break.
I'm not the true bride."

The princess screeched, "I'll have your neck for that!" And she rushed back to the prince's chamber, again repeating the words.

"But where is the necklace I gave you?" the prince inquired.

"What necklace? You gave me no necklace."

"Indeed I did, fastening it with my own hands. If you don't know this, you are not the true bride." And he reached out and pulled the veil from her face, revealing her homely face. He jumped back in horror and said, "How did you get here? Who are you?"

"I am your betrothed, but I was afraid people would ridicule my ugliness. So I ordered my maid to go in my place."

"Bring her here. I want to see her," the prince commanded.

The ugly princess went out and told the servants that the maid had been caught stealing and was to be put to death. The servants grabbed her, but she screamed so loudly that the prince heard her, rushed out, and demanded that she be set free.

Lights were brought and he saw the gold necklace he had given her. "You are the true bride. Come with me to my chamber." When they were alone, he said, "On the way to the church, you spoke of Maid Maleen. You look so much like her that I could think she is standing before me."

"I am Maid Maleen. I suffered hunger, darkness, and thirst for seven years. Then I lived as a servant in poverty. But now I am your true wife."

They embraced, kissed, and were forever happy. The false bride was executed.

The tower where Maid Maleen had been imprisoned remained standing for many years. When the children passed it, they sang,

Ding dong the hour
Who sits in the tower?
Inside there sits a princess fair.
Nobody can see her there.
No hammer can break down the wall.
No tool can ever make it fall.
Oh Johnny, won't you come and see?
Come along and follow me.

EAST OF THE SUN AND WEST OF THE MOON
(Norway)

nce upon a time there was a poor husbandman who had many children and little to give them in the way either of food or clothing. They were all pretty, but the prettiest of all was the youngest daughter, who was so beautiful that there were no bounds to her beauty.

So once—it was late on a Thursday evening in autumn, and wild weather outside, terribly dark, and raining so heavily and blowing so hard that the walls of the cottage shook again—they were all sitting together by the fireside, each of them busy with something or other, when suddenly someone rapped three times against the windowpane. The man went out to see what could be the matter, and when he got out there stood a great big white bear.

"Good evening to you," said the White Bear.

"Good evening," said the man.

"Will you give me your youngest daughter?" said the White Bear. "If you will, you shall be as rich as you are now poor."

Truly the man would have had no objection to be rich, but he thought to himself, "I must first ask my daughter about this," so he went in and told them that there was a great white bear outside who had faithfully promised to make them all rich if he might but have the youngest daughter.

She said no, and would not hear of it; so the man went out again, and settled with the White Bear that he should come again next Thursday evening, and get her answer. Then the man persuaded her, and talked so much to her about the wealth that they would have, and what a good thing it would be for herself, that at last she made up her mind to go, and washed and mended all her rags, made herself as smart as she could, and held herself in readiness to set out. Little enough had she to take away with her.

Next Thursday evening the White Bear came to fetch her. She seated herself on his back with her bundle, and thus they departed. When they had gone a great part of the way, the White Bear said, "Are you afraid?"

"No, that I am not," said she.

"Keep tight hold of my fur, and then there is no danger," said he.

And thus she rode far, far away, until they came to a great mountain. Then the White Bear knocked on it, and a door opened, and they went into a castle where there were many brilliantly lighted rooms which shone with gold and silver, likewise a large hall in which there was a well-spread table, and it was so magnificent that it would be hard to make anyone understand how splendid it was. The White Bear gave her a silver bell, and told her that when she needed anything she had but to ring this bell, and what she wanted would appear. So after she had eaten, and night was drawing near, she grew sleepy after her journey, and thought she would like to go to bed. She rang the bell, and scarcely had she touched it before she found herself in a chamber where a bed stood ready made for her, which was as pretty as anyone could wish to sleep in. It had pillows of silk, and curtains of silk fringed with gold, and everything that was in the room was of gold or silver; but when she had lain down and put out the light a man came and lay down beside her, and behold it was the White Bear, who cast off the form of a beast during the night. She never saw him, however, for he always came after she had put out her light, and went away before daylight appeared.

So all went well and happily for a time, but then she began to be very sad and sorrowful, for all day long she had to go about alone; and she did so wish to go home to her father and mother and brothers and sisters. Then the White Bear asked what it was that she wanted, and she told him that it was so dull there in the mountain, and that she had to go about all alone, and that in her parents' house at home there were all her brothers and sisters, and it was because she could not go to them that she was so sorrowful.

"There might be a cure for that," said the White Bear, "if you would but promise me never to talk with your mother alone, but only when the others are there too; for she will take hold of your hand," he said, "and will want to lead you into a room to talk with you alone; but that you must by no means do, or you will bring great misery on both of us."

So one Sunday the White Bear came and said that they could now set out to see her father and mother, and they journeyed thither, she sitting on his back, and they went a long, long way, and it took a long, long time; but at last they came to a large white farmhouse, and her brothers and sisters were running about outside it, playing, and it was so pretty that it was a pleasure to look at it.

"Your parents dwell here now," said the White Bear; "but do not forget what I said to you, or you will do much harm both to yourself and me."

"No, indeed," said she, "I shall never forget"; and as soon as she was at home the White Bear turned round and went back again.

There were such rejoicings when she went in to her parents that it seemed as if they would never come to an end. Everyone thought that he could never be sufficiently grateful to her for all she had done for them all.

Now they had everything that they wanted, and everything was as good as it could be. They all asked her how she was getting on where she was. All was well with her too, she said; and she had everything that she could want. What other answers she gave I cannot say, but I am pretty sure that they did not learn much from her. But in the afternoon, after they had dined at midday, all happened just as the White Bear had said. Her mother wanted to talk with her alone in her own chamber. But she remembered what the White Bear had said, and would on no account go. "What we have to say can be said at any time," she answered. But somehow or other her mother at last persuaded her, and she was forced to tell the whole story. So she told how every night a man came and lay down beside her when the lights were all put out, and how she never saw him, because he always went away before it grew light in the morning, and how she continually went about in sadness, thinking how happy she would be if she could but see him, and how all day long she had to go about alone, and it was so dull and solitary. "Oh!" cried the mother, in horror, "you are very likely sleeping with a troll! But I will teach you a way to see him. You shall have a bit of one of my candles, which you can take away with you hidden in your breast. Look at him with that when he is asleep, but take care not to let any tallow drop upon him."

So she took the candle, and hid it in her breast, and when evening drew near the White Bear came to fetch her away. When they had gone some distance on their way, the White Bear asked her if everything had not happened just as he had foretold, and she could not but own that it had. "Then, if you have done what your mother wished," said he, "you have brought great misery on both of us."

"No," she said, "I have not done anything at all."

So when she had reached home and had gone to bed it was just the same as it had been before, and a man came and lay down beside her, and late at night, when she could hear that he was sleeping, she got up and kindled a light, lit her candle, let her light shine on him, and saw him, and he was the handsomest prince that eyes had ever beheld, and she loved him so much that it seemed to her that she must die if she did not kiss him that very moment. So she did kiss him; but while she was doing it she let three drops of hot tallow fall upon his shirt, and he awoke. "What have you done now?" said he. "You have brought misery on both of us. If you had but held out for the space of one year I should have been free. I have a stepmother who has bewitched me so that I am a white bear by day and a man by night; but now all is at an end between you and me, and I must leave you, and go to her. She lives in a castle that lies east of the sun and west of the moon, and there too is a princess with a nose which is three ells long, and she now is the one whom I must marry."

She wept and lamented, but all in vain, for go he must. Then she asked him if she could not go with him. But no, that could not be. "Can you tell me the way then, and I will seek you — that I may surely be allowed to do!"

"Yes, you may do that," said he, "but there is no way thither. It lies east of the sun and west of the moon, and never would you find your way there."

When she awoke in the morning both the prince and the castle were gone, and she was lying on a small green patch in the midst of a dark, thick wood. By her side lay the self-same bundle of rags which she had brought with her from her own home. So when she had rubbed the sleep out of her eyes, and wept till she was weary, she set out on her way, and thus she walked for many and many a long day, until at last she came to a great mountain. Outside it an aged woman was sitting, playing with a golden apple. The girl asked her if she knew the way to the prince who lived with his stepmother in the castle that lay east of the sun and west of the moon, and who was to marry a princess with a nose three ells long. "How do you happen to know about him?" inquired the old woman. "Maybe you are she who ought to have had him." "Yes, indeed, I am," she said. "So it is you, then?" said the old woman. "I know nothing about him but that he dwells in a castle east of the sun and west of the moon. You will be a long time in getting to it, if ever you get to it at all; but you shall have the loan of my horse, and then you can ride on it to an old woman who is a neighbor of mine: perhaps she can tell you about him. When you have got there you must just strike the horse beneath the left ear and bid it go home again; but you may take the golden apple with you."

So the girl seated herself on the horse, and rode for a long, long way, and at last she came to the mountain, where an aged woman was sitting outside with a gold carding-comb. The girl asked her if she knew the way to the castle that lay east of the sun and west of the moon; but she said what the first old woman had said: "I know nothing about it, but that it is east of the sun and west of the moon, and that you will be a long time in getting to it, if ever you get there at all; but you shall have the loan of my horse to an old woman who lives the nearest to me: perhaps she may know where the castle is, and when you have got to her you may just strike the horse beneath the left ear and bid it go home again." Then she gave her the gold carding-comb, for it might, perhaps, be of use to her, she said.

So the girl seated herself on the horse, and rode a wearisome long way onward again, and after a very long time she came to a great mountain, where an aged woman was sitting, spinning at a golden spinning wheel. Of this woman, too, she inquired if she knew the way to the prince, and where to find the castle that lay east of the sun and west of the moon. But it was only the same thing once again. "Maybe it was you who should have had the prince," said the old woman. "Yes, indeed, I should have been the one," said the girl. But this old crone knew the way no better than the others—it was east of the sun and west of the moon, she knew that, "and you will be a long time in getting to it, if ever you get to it at all," she said; "but you may have the loan of my horse, and I think you had better ride to the East Wind, and ask him: perhaps he may know where the castle is, and will blow you thither. But when you have got to him you must just strike the horse beneath the left ear, and he will come home again." And then she gave her the golden spinning wheel, saying, "Perhaps you may find that you have a use for it."

The girl had to ride for a great many days, and for a long and wearisome time, before she got there; but at last she did arrive, and then she asked the East Wind if he could tell her the way to the prince who dwelt east of the sun and west of the moon. "Well," said the East Wind, "I have heard tell of the prince, and of his castle, but I do not know the way to it, for I have never blown so far; but, if you like, I will go with you to my brother the West Wind: he may know that, for he is much stronger than I am. You may sit on my back, and then I can carry you there." So she seated herself on his back, and they did go so swiftly!

When they got there, the East Wind went in and said that the girl whom he had brought was the one who ought to have had the prince up at the castle that lay east of the sun and west of the moon, and that now she was traveling about to find him again, so he had come there with her, and would like to hear if the West Wind knew where the castle was. "No," said the West Wind; "so far as that have I never blown: but if you like I will go with you to the South Wind, for he is much stronger than either of us, and he has roamed far and wide, and perhaps he can tell you what you want to know. You may seat yourself on my back, and then I will carry you to him."

So she did this, and journeyed to the South Wind, neither was she very long on the way. When they had got there, the West Wind asked him if he could tell her the way to the castle that lay east of the sun and west of the moon, for she was the girl who ought to marry the prince who lived there. "Oh, indeed!" said the South Wind, "is that she? Well," said he, "I have wandered about a great deal in my time, and in all kinds of places, but I have never blown so far as that. If you like, however, I will go with you to my brother the North Wind; he is the oldest and strongest of all of us, and if he does not know where it is no one in the whole world will be able to tell you. You may sit upon my back, and then I will carry you there." So she seated herself on his back, and off he went from his house in great haste, and they were not long on the way.

When they came near the North Wind's dwelling, he was so wild and frantic that they felt cold gusts a long while before they got there. "What do you want?" he roared out from afar, and they froze as they heard.

Said the South Wind, "It is I, and this is she who should have had the prince who lives in the castle that lies east of the sun and west of the moon. And now she wishes to ask you if you have ever been there, and can tell her the way, for she would gladly find him again."

"Yes," said the North Wind, "I know where it is. I once blew an aspen leaf there, but I was so tired that for many days afterward I was not able to blow at all. However, if you really are anxious to go there, and are not afraid to go with me, I will take you on my back, and try if I can blow you there."

"Get there I must," said she; "and if there is any way of going I will; and I have no fear, no matter how fast you go."

"Very well then," said the North Wind, "but you must sleep here tonight, for if we are ever to get there we must have the day before us."

The North Wind woke her betimes next morning, and puffed himself up, and made himself so big and so strong that it was frightful to see him, and away they went, high up through the air, as if they would not stop until they had reached the very end of the world. Down below there was such a storm! It blew down woods and houses, and when they were above the sea the ships were wrecked by hundreds. And thus they tore on and on, and a long time went by, and then yet more time passed, and still they were above the sea, and the North Wind grew tired, and more tired, and at last so utterly weary that he was scarcely able to blow any longer, and he sank and sank, lower and lower, until at last he went so low that the crests of the waves dashed against the heels of the poor girl he was carrying. "Art thou afraid?" said the North Wind.

"I have no fear," said she; and it was true. But they were not very, very far from land, and there was just enough strength left in the North Wind to enable him to throw her onto the shore, immediately under the windows of a castle that lay east of the sun and west of the moon; but then he was so weary and worn out that he was forced to rest for several days before he could go to his own home again.

Next morning she sat down beneath the walls of the castle to play with the golden apple, and the first person she saw was the maiden with the long nose, who was to have the prince. "How much do you want for that gold apple of yours, girl?" said she, opening the window. "It can't be bought either for gold or money," answered the girl. "If it cannot be bought either for gold or money, what will buy it? You may say what you please," said the princess.

"Well, if I may go to the prince who is here, and be with him tonight, you shall have it," said the girl who had come with the North Wind.

"You may do that," said the princess, for she had made up her mind what she would do. So the princess got the golden apple, but when the girl went up to the prince's apartment that night he was asleep, for the princess had so contrived it. The poor girl called to him, and shook him, and between whiles she wept; but she could not wake him. In the morning, as soon as day dawned, in came the princess with the long nose, and drove her out again. In the daytime the girl sat down once more beneath the windows of the castle, and began to card with her golden carding-comb; and then all happened as it had happened before. The princess asked her what she wanted for it, and she replied that it was not for sale, either for gold or money, but that if she could get leave to go to the prince, and be with him during the night, she should have it. But when she went up to the prince's room he was again asleep, and, let her call him, or shake him, or weep as she would, he still slept on, and she could not put any life in him. When daylight came in the morning, the princess with the long nose came too, and once more drove her away. When day had quite come, the girl seated herself under the castle windows, to spin with her golden spinning wheel, and the princess with the long nose wanted to have that also. So she opened the window, and asked what she would take for it. The girl said what she had said on each of the former occasions—that it was not for sale either for gold or for money, but if she could get leave to go to the prince who lived there, and be with him during the night, she should have it.

"Yes," said the princess, "I will gladly consent to that."

But in that place there were some Christian folk who had been carried off, and they had been sitting in the chamber which was next to that of the prince, and had heard how a woman had been in there who had wept and called on him two nights running, and they told the prince of this. So that evening, when the princess came once more with her sleeping-drink, he pretended to drink, but threw it away behind him, for he suspected that it was a sleeping-drink. So, when the girl went into the prince's room this time he was awake, and she had to tell him how she had come there.

"You have come just in time," said the prince, "for I should have been married tomorrow; but I will not have the long-nosed princess, and you alone can save me. I will say that I want to see what my bride can do, and bid her wash the shirt that has the three drops of tallow on it. This she will consent to do, for she does not know that it is you who let them fall on it; but no one can wash them out but one born of Christian folk—it cannot be done by one of a pack of trolls—and then I will say that no one shall ever be my bride but the woman who can do this, and I know that you can." There was great joy and gladness between them all that night, but the next day, when the wedding was to take place, the prince said, "I must see what my bride can do." "That you may do," said the stepmother.

"I have a fine shirt which I want to wear as my wedding shirt, but three drops of tallow have got upon it which I want to have washed off, and I have vowed to marry no one but the woman who is able to do it. If she cannot do that, she is not worth having."

Well, that was a very small matter, they thought, and agreed to do it. The princess with the long nose began to wash as well as she could, but, the more she washed and rubbed, the larger the spots grew. "Ah! you can't wash at all," said the old troll-hag, who was her mother. "Give it to me." But she too had not had the shirt very long in her hands before it looked worse still, and, the more she washed it and rubbed it, the larger and blacker grew the spots.

So the other trolls had to come and wash, but, the more they did, the blacker and uglier grew the shirt, until at length it was as black as if it had been up the chimney. "Oh," cried the prince, "not one of you is good for anything at all! There is a beggar-girl sitting outside the window, and I'll be bound that she can wash better than any of you! Come in, you girl there!" he cried. So she came in. "Can you wash this shirt clean?" he cried.

"Oh! I don't know," she said, "but I will try." And no sooner had she taken the shirt and dipped it in the water than it was white as driven snow, and even whiter than that.

"I will marry you," said the prince.

Then the old troll-hag flew into such a rage that she burst, and the princess with the long nose and all the little trolls must have burst too, for they have never been heard of since. The prince and his bride set free all the Christian folk who were imprisoned there, and took away with them all the gold and silver that they could carry, and moved far away from the castle that lay east of the sun and west of the moon.

HOW KATE GOT A HUSBAND
(United States, Ozarks)

ne time there was a fellow going with a girl named Kate, and he promised to marry her before the baby was borned. But then one day he seen a rich girl in town, so then he thought maybe it would be better to marry the rich girl. When Kate heard about this she dressed up in a cowhide with the hairy side out, and a black mask over her head, and two gravels under her tongue. When the fellow come down the lane Kate riz up out of the brush, and groaned. The fellow was scared something terrible. She says she is Old Scratch redhot from home, come to carry him off to Hell because he has broke his promise to marry Kate. He got down on his knees and begun to beg and blubber how he will marry Kate before the moon changes if they will give him another chance.

So next morning he come to Kate's house hollering for Pete's sake hurry up, we must go to town and get married. So that is what they done, and Kate never did tell how she fooled him until after the baby come. The fellow says he knowed it was Kate all the time, and the rich girl says good riddance and it serves the darn fool right. And Kate says maybe she can't be tablecloth, but she sure don't aim to be dishrag. So they lived happy ever after, just like other married folks.

GIFTS OF LOVE
(Korea)

An old woman of Korea was dying. Her two sons and daughter sadly watched over her, knowing that her life was soon to end. Since the father had died, the family had become poorer and poorer, often not having enough to eat. This distressed the old woman; still she gave her children several small remembrances.

She gave her daughter her walking stick and a bowl made from a gourd. She gave the eldest son an ax. To the youngest son she gave her cooking pot. Then she lovingly told her children that when she died they should go away from their lonely mountain hut and search for a new life.

Her days ended and her devoted children buried her. After some discussion, they decided they would fare better if they set out alone. Thus they parted, promising to reunite in better times.

After a day's journey, the daughter decided to spend the night in a cave. She was lying down to sleep when she heard a goblin say, "Come, skeleton, come with me."

"Where are you going?" she asked timidly.

The goblin exclaimed, "You don't sound dead! Let me feel your skull."

The daughter held out the bowl made from a gourd.

"All right, there is no hair. But let me feel your arm."

So she held out the walking stick.

"All right," the goblin said, satisfied that it was indeed a skeleton. "Come with me to snatch the soul of a wealthy prince!"

"Oh, yes! That should be a wonderful adventure!" replied the daughter bravely.

They went together to the nearest palace and crept into the prince's room. The goblin stole the prince's soul, put it in a purse, and handed it to the daughter to carry. They slipped out of the palace unnoticed.

The next morning the goblin was gone. The daughter left the cave, carrying the purse, and returned to the nearby kingdom. She was dismayed to learn that the entire kingdom was grieving over the death of the prince. She pleaded to be allowed to visit with the king, who reluctantly agreed to see her.

"Your highness, I beg you to let me have just a moment alone with the body of the prince. I know I can help restore his life, if you will only let me try."

The king despaired of ever seeing his son alive again, but he agreed to let her have a few brief moments with the prince. She entered his room, cautiously closing the door to remain unobserved. She slipped over to his bed, opened his mouth, and opened the purse near his mouth. As she thought would happen, the soul flew back into his mouth and he came back to life.

The delighted king declared that the girl and his son should marry, and the wedding soon followed. It was a happy marriage, blessed with the arrival of a daughter and a son. Shortly thereafter the old king died, and the prince and princess inherited the throne.

Their happiness was nearly perfect, marred only by the queen's concern about her two brothers. Five years had now passed and she knew nothing of their lot. Her husband vowed to find her brothers and sent messengers out to nearby villages and kingdoms in search of the brothers.

Finally a messenger found a man in a far-off village who appeared to match one description the queen had provided. He entreated the farmer to return with him to the court. Their reunion was exciting, and the queen quickly convinced him to leave his poor farm and take a position in the court.

Messengers continued to search diligently for her other brother. More than a year had passed, and she began to believe he must be dead. One day a slave trader came to court, seeking to sell off some pitiable wretches. The queen was about to send them away, when she noticed a particularly haggard slave. A closer look revealed this miserable creature to be her other brother.

She immediately purchased him and with the assistance of the court physician she nursed her beloved brother back to health. After his strength had returned, he also took a position in the court.

The family flourished with happy marriages and children for everyone, enjoying their prosperity for all of their lives.

CATHERINE AND HER DESTINY
(Italy, Sicily)

Long ago there lived a rich merchant who, besides possessing more treasures than any king in the world, had in his great hall three chairs, one of silver, one of gold, and one of diamonds. But his greatest treasure of all was his only daughter, who was called Catherine.

One day Catherine was sitting in her own room when suddenly the door flew open, and in came a tall and beautiful woman holding in her hands a little wheel.

"Catherine," she said, going up to the girl, "which would you rather have—a happy youth or a happy old age?"

Catherine was so taken by surprise that she did not know what to answer, and the lady repeated, "Which would you rather have—a happy youth or a happy old age?"

Then Catherine thought to herself, "If I say a happy youth, then I shall have to suffer all the rest of my life. No, I would bear trouble now, and have something better to look forward to." She so looked up and replied, "Give me a happy old age."

"So be it," said the lady, and turned her wheel as she spoke, vanishing the next moment as suddenly as she had come.

Now this beautiful lady was the Destiny of poor Catherine.

Only a few days after this the merchant heard the news that all his finest ships, laden with the richest merchandise, had been sunk in a storm, and he was left a beggar. The shock was too much for him. He took to his bed, and in a short time he was dead of his disappointment.

So poor Catherine was left alone in the world without a penny or a creature to help her. But she was a brave girl and full of spirit, and soon made up her mind that the best thing she could do was to go to the nearest town and become a servant. She lost no time in getting herself ready, and did not take long over her journey; and as she was passing down the chief street of the town a noble lady saw her out of the window, and, struck by her sad face, said to her, "Where are you going all alone, my pretty girl?"

"Ah, my lady, I am very poor, and must go to service to earn my bread."

"I will take you into my service," said she; and Catherine served her well.

Some time after her mistress said to Catherine, "I am obliged to go out for a long while, and must lock the house door, so that no thieves shall get in."

So she went away, and Catherine took her work and sat down at the window. Suddenly the door burst open, and in came her Destiny.

"Oh! so here you are, Catherine! Did you really think I was going to leave you in peace?" And as she spoke she walked to the linen press where Catherine's mistress kept all her finest sheets and underclothes, tore everything in pieces, and flung them on the floor. Poor Catherine wrung her hands and wept, for she thought to herself, "When my lady comes back and sees all this ruin she will think it is my fault," and, starting up, she fled through the open door. Then Destiny took all the pieces and made them whole again, and put them back in the press, and when everything was tidy she too left the house.

When the mistress reached home she called Catherine, but no Catherine was there. "Can she have robbed me?" thought the old lady, and looked hastily round the house; but nothing was missing. She wondered why Catherine should have disappeared like this, but she heard no more of her, and in a few days she filled her place.

Meanwhile Catherine wandered on and on, without knowing very well where she was going, till at last she came to another town. Just as before, a noble lady happened to see her passing her window, and called out to her, "Where are you going all alone, my pretty girl?"

And Catherine answered, "Ah, my lady, I am very poor, and must go to service to earn my bread."

"I will take you into my service," said the lady; and Catherine served her well, and hoped she might now be left in peace. But, exactly as before, one day that Catherine was left in the house alone her Destiny came again and spoke to her with hard words: "What! are you here now?" And in a passion she tore up everything she saw, till in sheer misery poor Catherine rushed out of the house. And so it befell for seven years, and directly Catherine found a fresh place her Destiny came and forced her to leave it.

After seven years, however, Destiny seemed to get tired of persecuting her, and a time of peace set in for Catherine. When she had been chased away from her last house by Destiny's wicked pranks she had taken service with another lady, who told her that it would be part of her daily work to walk to a mountain that overshadowed the town, and, climbing up to the top, she was to lay on the ground some loaves of freshly baked bread, and cry with a loud voice, "O Destiny, my mistress," three times. Then her lady's Destiny would come and take away the offering. "That will I gladly do," said Catherine.

So the years went by, and Catherine was still there, and every day she climbed the mountain with her basket of bread on her arm. She was happier than she had been, but sometimes, when no one saw her, she would weep as she thought over her old life, and how different it was from the one she was now leading. One day her lady saw her, and said, "Catherine, what is it? Why are you always weeping?" And then Catherine told her story.

"I have got an idea," exclaimed the lady. "Tomorrow, when you take the bread to the mountain, you shall pray my Destiny to speak to yours, and entreat her to leave you in peace. Perhaps something may come of it!"

At these words Catherine dried her eyes, and next morning, when she climbed the mountain, she told all she had suffered, and cried, "O Destiny, my mistress, pray, I entreat you, of my Destiny that she may leave me in peace."

And Destiny answered, "Oh, my poor girl, know you not your Destiny lies buried under seven coverlids, and can hear nothing? But if you will come tomorrow I will bring her with me."

And after Catherine had gone her way her lady's Destiny went to find her sister, and said to her, "Dear sister, has not Catherine suffered enough? It is surely time for her good days to begin?"

And the sister answered, "Tomorrow you shall bring her to me, and I will give her something that may help her out of her need."

The next morning Catherine set out earlier than usual for the mountain, and her lady's Destiny took the girl by the hand and led her to her sister, who lay under the seven coverlids. And her Destiny held out to Catherine a ball of silk, saying, "Keep this—it may be useful some day;" then pulled the coverings over her head again.

But Catherine walked sadly down the hill, and went straight to her lady and showed her the silken ball, which was the end of all her high hopes.

"What shall I do with it?" she asked. "It is not worth sixpence, and it is no good to me!"

"Take care of it," replied her mistress. "Who can tell how useful it may be?"

A little while after this grand preparations were made for the king's marriage, and all the tailors in the town were busy embroidering fine clothes. The wedding garment was so beautiful nothing like it had ever been seen before, but when it was almost finished the tailor found that he had no more silk. The color was very rare, and none could be found like it, and the king made a proclamation that if anyone happened to possess any they should bring it to the court, and he would give them a large sum.

"Catherine!" exclaimed the lady, who had been to the tailors and seen the wedding garment, "your ball of silk is exactly the right color. Bring it to the king, and you can ask what you like for it."

Then Catherine put on her best clothes and went to the court, and looked more beautiful than any woman there.

"May it please your majesty," she said, "I have brought you a ball of silk of the color you asked for, as no one else has any in the town."

"Your majesty," asked one of the courtiers, "shall I give the maiden its weight in gold?"

The king agreed, and a pair of scales were brought; and a handful of gold was placed in one scale and the silken ball in the other. But lo! let the king lay in the scales as many gold pieces as he would, the silk was always heavier still. Then the king took some larger scales, and heaped up all his treasures on the one side, but the silk on the other outweighed them all. At last there was only one thing left that had not been put in, and that was his golden crown. And he took it from his head and set it on top of all, and at last the scale moved and the ball had found its balance.

"Where got you this silk?" asked the king.

"It was given me, royal majesty, by my mistress," replied Catherine.

"That is not true," said the king, "and if you do not tell me the truth I will have your head cut off this instant."

So Catherine told him the whole story, and how she had once been as rich as he.

Now there lived at the court a wise woman, and she said to Catherine, "You have suffered much, my poor girl, but at length your luck has turned, and I know by the weighing of the scales through the crown that you will die a queen."

"So she shall," cried the king, who overheard these words; "she shall die my queen, for she is more beautiful than all the ladies of the court, and I will marry no one else."

And so it fell out. The king sent back the bride he had promised to wed to her own country, and the same Catherine was queen at the marriage feast instead, and lived happy and contented to the end of her life.

THE GRATEFUL PRINCE
(Germany)

Once upon a time the king of the Goldland lost himself in a forest, and try as he would he could not find the way out. As he was wandering down one path which had looked at first more hopeful than the rest he saw a man coming toward him.

"What are you doing here, friend?" asked the stranger; "darkness is falling fast, and soon the wild beasts will come from their lairs to seek for food."

"I have lost myself," answered the king, "and am trying to get home."

"Then promise me that you will give me the first thing that comes out of your house, and I will show you the way," said the stranger.

The king did not answer directly, but after awhile he spoke: "Why should I give away my *best* sporting dog. I can surely find my way out of the forest as well as this man."

So the stranger left him, but the king followed path after path for three whole days, with no better success than before. He was almost in despair, when the stranger suddenly appeared, blocking up his way.

"Promise you will give me the first thing that comes out of your house to meet you?"

But still the king was stiff-necked and would promise nothing.

For some days longer he wandered up and down the forest, trying first one path, then another, but his courage at last gave way, and he sank wearily on the ground under a tree, feeling sure his last hour had come. Then for the third time the stranger stood before the king, and said,

"Why are you such a fool? What can a dog be to you, that you should give your life for him like this? Just promise me the reward I want, and I will guide you out of the forest."

"Well, my life is worth more than a thousand dogs," answered the king, "The welfare of my kingdom depends on me. I accept your terms, so take me to my palace." Scarcely had he uttered the words than he found himself at the edge of the wood, with the palace in the dim distance. He made all the haste he could, and just as he reached the great gates out came the nurse with the royal baby, who stretched out his arms to his father. The king shrank back, and ordered the nurse to take the baby away at once. Then his great boarhound bounded up to him, but his caresses were only answered by a violent push.

When the king's anger was spent, and he was able to think what was best to be done, he exchanged his baby, a beautiful boy, for the daughter of a peasant, and the prince lived roughly as the son of poor people, while the little girl slept in a golden cradle, under silken sheets. At the end of a year, the stranger arrived to claim his property, and took away the little girl, believing her to be the true child of the king. The king was so delighted with the success of his plan that he ordered a great feast to be got ready, and gave splendid presents to the foster parents of his son, so that he might lack nothing. But he did not dare to bring back the baby, lest the trick should be found out. The peasants were quite contented with this arrangement, which gave them food and money in abundance.

By and by the boy grew big and tall, and seemed to lead a happy life in the house of his foster parents. But a shadow hung over him which really poisoned most of his pleasure, and that was the thought of the poor innocent girl who had suffered in his stead, for his foster father had told him in secret that he was the king's son. And the prince determined that when he grew old enough he would travel all over the world, and never rest till he had set her free. To become king at the cost of a maiden's life was too heavy a price to pay. So one day he put on the dress of a farm servant, threw a sack of peas on his back, and marched straight into the forest where eighteen years before his father had lost himself. After he had walked some way he began to cry loudly, "Oh, how unlucky I am! Where can I be? Is there no one to show me the way out of the wood?"

Then appeared a strange man with a long grey beard, with a leather bag hanging from his girdle. He nodded cheerfully to the prince, and said, "I know this place well, and can lead you out of it, if you will promise me a good reward."

"What can a beggar such as I promise you?" answered the prince. "I have nothing to give you save my life; even the coat on my back belongs to my master, whom I serve for my keep and my clothes."

The stranger looked at the sack of peas, and said, "But you must possess something; you are carrying this sack, which seems to be very heavy."

"It is full of peas," was the reply. "My old aunt died last night, without leaving money enough to buy peas to give the watchers, as is the custom throughout the country. I have borrowed these peas from my master, and thought to take a short cut across the forest; but I have lost myself, as you can see."

"Then you are an orphan?" asked the stranger. "Why should you not enter my service? I want a sharp fellow in the house, and you please me."

"Why not, indeed, if we can strike a bargain?" said the other. "I was born a peasant, and strange bread is always bitter, so it is the same to me whom I serve! What wages will you give me?"

"Every day fresh food, meat twice a week, butter and vegetables, your summer and winter clothes, and a portion of land for your own use."

"I shall be satisfied with that," said the youth. "Somebody else will have to bury my aunt. I will go with you!"

Now this bargain seemed to please the old fellow so much that he spun round like a top, and sang so loud that the whole wood rang with his voice. Then he set out with his companion, and chattered so fast that he never noticed that his new servant kept dropping peas out of the sack. At night they slept under a fig tree, and when the sun rose started on their way. About noon they came to a large stone, and here the old fellow stopped, looked carefully round, gave a sharp whistle, and stamped three times on the ground with his left foot. Suddenly there appeared under the stone a secret door, which led to what looked like the mouth of a cave. The old fellow seized the youth by the arm, and said roughly, "Follow me!"

Thick darkness surrounded them, yet it seemed to the prince as if their path led into still deeper depths. After a long while he thought he saw a glimmer of light, but the light was neither that of the sun nor of the moon. He looked eagerly at it, but found it was only a kind of pale cloud, which was all the light this strange underworld could boast. Earth and water, trees and plants, birds and beasts, each was different from those he had seen before; but what most struck terror into his heart was the absolute stillness that reigned everywhere. Not a rustle or a sound could be heard. Here and there he noticed a bird sitting on a branch, with head erect and swelling throat, but his ear caught nothing. The dogs opened their mouths as if to bark, the toiling oxen seemed about to bellow, but neither bark nor bellow reached the prince. The water flowed noiselessly over the pebbles, the wind bowed the tops of the trees, flies and chafers darted about, without breaking the silence. The old greybeard uttered no word, and when his companion tried to ask him the meaning of it all he felt that his voice died in his throat.

How long this fearful stillness lasted I do not know, but the prince gradually felt his heart turning to ice, his hair stood up like bristles, and a cold chill was creeping down his spine, when at last—oh, ecstasy!—a faint noise broke on his straining ears, and this life of shadows suddenly became real. It sounded as if a troop of horses were ploughing their way over a moor.

Then the greybeard opened his mouth, and said, "The kettle is boiling; we are expected at home."

They walked on a little further, till the prince thought he heard the grinding of a sawmill, as if dozens of saws were working together, but his guide observed, "The grandmother is sleeping soundly; listen how she snores."

When they had climbed a hill which lay before them the prince saw in the distance the house of his master, but it was so surrounded with buildings of all kinds that the place looked more like a village or even a small town. They reached it at last, and found an empty kennel standing in front of the gate. "Creep inside this," said the master, "and wait while I go in and see my grandmother. Like all very old people, she is very obstinate, and cannot bear fresh faces about her."

The prince crept tremblingly into the kennel, and began to regret the daring which had brought him into this scrape.

By and by the master came back, and called him from his hiding place. Something had put out his temper, for with a frown he said, "Watch carefully our ways in the house, and beware of making any mistake, or it will go ill with you. Keep your eyes and ears open and your mouth shut, obey without questions. Be grateful if you will, but never speak unless you are spoken to."

When the prince stepped over the threshold he caught sight of a maiden of wonderful beauty, with brown eyes and fair curly hair. "Well!" the young man said to himself, "if the old fellow has many daughters like that I should not mind being his son-in-law. This one is just what I admire"; and he watched her lay the table, bring in the food, and take her seat by the fire as if she had never noticed that a strange man was present. Then she took out a needle and thread, and began to darn her stockings. The master sat at the table alone, and invited neither his new servant nor the maid to eat with him. Neither was the old grandmother anywhere to be seen. His appetite was tremendous: he soon cleared all the dishes, and ate enough to satisfy a dozen men. When at last he could eat no more he said to the girl, "Now you can pick the pieces, and take what is left in the iron pot for your own dinner, but give the bones to the dog."

The prince did not at all like the idea of dining off scraps, which he helped the girl to pick up, but, after all, he found that there was plenty to eat, and that the food was very good. During the meal he stole many glances at the maiden, and would even have spoken to her, but she gave him no encouragement. Every time he opened his mouth for the purpose she looked at him sternly, as if to say, "Silence," so he could only let his eyes speak for him. Besides, the master was stretched on a bench by the oven after his huge meal, and would have heard everything.

After supper that night, the old man said to the prince, "For two days you may rest from the fatigues of the journey, and look about the house. But the day after tomorrow you must come with me, and I will point out the work you have to do. The maid will show you where you are to sleep."

The prince thought, from this, he had leave to speak, but his master turned on him with a face of thunder and exclaimed, "You dog of a servant! If you disobey the laws of the house you will soon find yourself a head shorter! Hold your tongue, and leave me in peace."

The girl made a sign to him to follow her, and, throwing open a door, nodded to him to go in. He would have lingered a moment, for he thought she looked sad, but dared not do so, for fear of the old man's anger.

"It is impossible that she can be his daughter!" he said to himself, "for she has a kind heart. I am quite sure she must be the same girl who was brought here instead of me, so I am bound to risk my head in this mad adventure." He got into bed, but it was long before he fell asleep, and even then his dreams gave him no rest. He seemed to be surrounded by dangers, and it was only the power of the maiden who helped him through it all.

When he woke his first thoughts were for the girl, whom he found hard at work. He drew water from the well and carried it to the house for her, kindled the fire under the iron pot, and, in fact, did everything that came into his head that could be of any use to her. In the afternoon he went out, in order to learn something of his new home, and wondered greatly not to come across the old grandmother. In his rambles he came to the farmyard, where a beautiful white horse had a stall to itself; in another was a black cow with two white-faced calves, while the clucking of geese, ducks, and hens reached him from a distance.

Breakfast, dinner, and supper were as savory as before, and the prince would have been quite content with his quarters had it not been for the difficulty of keeping silence in the presence of the maiden. On the evening of the second day he went, as he had been told, to receive his orders for the following morning.

"I am going to set you something very easy to do tomorrow," said the old man when his servant entered. "Take this scythe and cut as much grass as the white horse will want for its day's feed, and clean out its stall. If I come back and find the manger empty it will go ill with you. So beware!"

The prince left the room, rejoicing in his heart, and saying to himself, "Well, I shall soon get through that! If I have never yet handled either the plough or the scythe, at least I have often watched the country people work them, and know how easy it is."

He was just going to open his door, when the maiden glided softly past and whispered in his ear, "What task has he set you?"

"For tomorrow," answered the prince, "it is really nothing at all! Just to cut hay for the horse, and to clean out his stall!"

"Oh, luckless being!" sighed the girl; "how will you ever get through with it. The white horse, who is our master's grandmother, is always hungry: it takes twenty men always mowing to keep it in food for one day, and another twenty to clean out its stall. How, then, do you expect to do it all by yourself? But listen to me, and do what I tell you. It is your only chance. When you have filled the manger as full as it will hold you must weave a strong plait of the rushes which grow among the meadow hay, and cut a thick peg of stout wood, and be sure that the horse sees what you are doing. Then it will ask you what it is for, and you will say, "With this plait I intend to bind up your mouth so that you cannot eat any more, and with this peg I am going to keep you still in one spot, so that you cannot scatter your corn and water all over the place!" After these words the maiden went away as softly as she had come.

Early the next morning he set to work. His scythe danced through the grass much more easily than he had hoped, and soon he had enough to fill the manger. He put it in the crib, and returned with a second supply, when to his horror he found the crib empty. Then he knew that without the maiden's advice he would certainly have been lost, and began to put it into practice. He took out the rushes which had somehow got mixed up with the hay, and plaited them quickly.

"My son, what are you doing?" asked the horse wonderingly.

"Oh, nothing!" replied he. "Just weaving a chin strap to bind your jaws together, in case you might wish to eat any more!"

The white horse sighed deeply when it heard this, and made up its mind to be content with what it had eaten.

The youth next began to clean out the stall, and the horse knew it had found a master; and by midday there was still fodder in the manger, and the place was as clean as a new pin. He had barely finished when in walked the old man, who stood astonished at the door.

"Is it really you who have been clever enough to do that?" he asked. "Or has someone else given you a hint?"

"Oh, I have had no help," replied the prince, "except what my poor weak head could give me."

The old man frowned, and went away, and the prince rejoiced that everything had turned out so well.

In the evening his master said, "Tomorrow I have no special task to set you, but as the girl has a great deal to do in the house you must milk the black cow for her. But take care you milk her dry, or it may be the worse for you."

"Well," thought the prince as he went away, "unless there is some trick behind, this does not sound very hard. I have never milked a cow before, but I have good strong fingers."

He was very sleepy, and was just going toward his room, when the maiden came to him and asked: "What is your task tomorrow?"

"I am to help you," he answered, "and have nothing to do all day, except to milk the black cow dry."

"Oh, you *are* unlucky," cried she. "If you were to try from morning till night you couldn't do it. There is only one way of escaping the danger, and that is, when you go to milk her, take with you a pan of burning coals and a pair of tongs. Place the pan on the floor of the stall, and the tongs on the fire, and blow with all your might, till the coals burn brightly. The black cow will ask you what is the meaning of all this, and you must answer what I will whisper to you." And she stood on tiptoe and whispered something in his ear, and then went away.

The dawn had scarcely reddened the sky when the prince jumped out of bed, and, with the pan of coals in one hand and the milk pail in the other, went straight to the cow's stall, and began to do exactly as the maiden had told him the evening before.

The black cow watched him with surprise for some time, and then said, "What are you doing, sonny?"

"Oh, nothing," answered he; "I am only heating a pair of tongs in case you may not feel inclined to give as much milk as I want."

The cow sighed deeply, and looked at the milkman with fear, but he took no notice, and milked briskly into the pail, till the cow ran dry.

Just at that moment the old man entered the stable, and sat down to milk the cow himself, but not a drop of milk could he get. "Have you really managed it all yourself, or did somebody help you?"

"I have nobody to help me," answered the prince, "but my own poor head." The old man got up from his seat and went away.

That night, when the prince went to his master to hear what his next day's work was to be, the old man said, "I have a little haystack out in the meadow which must be brought in to dry. Tomorrow you will have to stack it all in the shed, and, as you value your life, be careful not to leave the smallest strand behind." The prince was overjoyed to hear he had nothing worse to do.

"To carry a little hayrick requires no great skill," thought he, "and it will give me no trouble, for the horse will have to draw it in. I am certainly not going to spare the old grandmother."

By and by the maiden stole up to ask what task he had for the next day.

The young man laughed, and said, "It appears that I have got to learn all kinds of farmer's work. Tomorrow I have to carry a hayrick, and leave not a stalk in the meadow, and that is my whole day's work!"

"Oh, you unlucky creature!" cried she; "and how do you think you are to do it? If you had all the men in the world to help you, you could not clear off this one little hayrick in a week. The instant you have thrown down the hay at the top, it will take root again from below. But listen to what I say. You must steal out at daybreak tomorrow and bring out the white horse and some good strong ropes. Then get on the haystack, put the ropes round it, and harness the horse to the ropes. When you are ready, climb up the haystack and begin to count one, two, three. The horse will ask you what you are counting, and you must be sure to answer what I whisper to you."

So the maiden whipered something in his ear, and left the room. And the prince knew nothing better to do than to get into bed.

He slept soundly, and it was still almost dark when he got up and proceeded to carry out the instructions given him by the girl. First he chose some stout ropes, and then he led the horse out of the stable and rode it to the haystack, which was made up of fifty cartloads, so that it could hardly be called "a little one." The prince did all that the maiden had told him, and when at last he was seated on top of the rick, and had counted up to twenty, he heard the horse ask in amazement, "What are you counting up there, my son?"

"Oh, nothing," said he, "I was just amusing myself with counting the packs of wolves in the forest, but there are really so many of them that I don't think I should ever be done."

The word *wolf* was hardly out of his mouth than the white horse was off like the wind, so that in the twinkling of an eye it had reached the shed, dragging the haystack behind it. The master was dumb with surprise as he came in after breakfast and found his man's day's work quite done.

"Was it really you who were so clever?" asked he. "Or did someone give you good advice?"

"Oh, I have only myself to take counsel with," said the prince, and the old man went away, shaking his head.

Late in the evening the prince went to his master to learn what he was to do next day.

"Tomorrow," said the old man, "you must bring the white-headed calf to the meadow, and, as you value your life, take care it does not escape from you."

The prince answered nothing, but thought, "Well, most peasants of nineteen have got a whole herd to look after, so surely I can manage one." And he went toward his room, where the maiden met him.

"Tomorrow I have got an idiot's work," said he; "nothing but to take the white-headed calf to the meadow."

"Oh, you unlucky being!" sighed she. "Do you know that this calf is so swift that in a single day he can run three times round the world? Take heed to what I tell you. Bind one end of this silk thread to the left foreleg of the calf, and the other end to the little toe of your left foot, so that the calf will never be able to leave your side, whether you walk, stand, or lie." After this the prince went to bed and slept soundly.

The next morning he did exactly what the maiden had told him, and led the calf with the silken thread to the meadow, where it stuck to his side like a faithful dog.

By sunset, it was back again in its stall, and then came the master and said, with a frown, "Were you really so clever yourself, or did somebody tell you what to do?"

"Oh, I have only my own poor head," answered the prince, and the old man went away growling, "I don't believe a word of it! I am sure you have found some clever friend!"

In the evening he called the prince and said, "Tomorrow I have no work for you, but when I wake you must come before my bed, and give me your hand in greeting."

The young man wondered at this strange freak, and went laughing in search of the maiden.

"Ah, it is no laughing matter," sighed she. "He means to eat you, and there is only one way in which I can help you. You must heat an iron shovel red hot, and hold it out to him instead of your hand."

So next morning he wakened very early, and had heated the shovel before the old man was awake. At length he heard him calling, "You lazy fellow, where are you? Come and wish me good morning." But when the prince entered with the red-hot shovel his master only said, "I am very ill today, and too weak even to touch your hand. You must return this evening, when I may be better."

The prince loitered about all day, and in the evening went back to the old man's room. He was received in the most friendly manner, and, to his surprise, his master exclaimed, "I am very well satisfied with you. Come to me at dawn and bring the maiden with you. I know you have long loved each other, and I wish to make you husband and wife."

The young man nearly jumped into the air for joy, but, remembering the rules of the house, he managed to keep still. When he told the maiden, he saw to his astonishment that she had become as white as a sheet, and she was quite dumb.

"The old man has found out who was your counselor," she said when she could speak, "and he means to destroy us both. We must escape somehow, or else we shall be lost. Take an ax, and cut off the head of the calf with one blow. With a second, split its head in two, and in its brain you will see a bright red ball. Bring that to me. Meanwhile, I will do what is needful here."

And the prince thought to himself, "Better kill the calf than be killed ourselves. If we can once escape, we will go back home. The peas that I strewed about must have sprouted, so that we shall not miss the way."

Then he went into the stall, and with one blow of the ax killed the calf, and with the second split its brain. In an instant the place was filled with light, as the red ball fell from the brain of the calf. The prince picked it up, and, wrapping it round with a thick cloth, hid it in his bosom. Mercifully, the cow slept through it all, or by her cries she would have awakened the master.

He looked round, and at the door stood the maiden, holding a little bundle in her arms.

"Where is the ball?" she asked.

"Here," answered he.

"We must lose no time in escaping," she went on, and uncovered a tiny bit of the shining ball, to light them on their way.

As the prince had expected, the peas had taken root, and grown into a little hedge, so that they were sure they would not lose the path. As they fled, the girl told him that she had overheard a conversation between the old man and his grandmother, saying that she was a king's daughter, whom the old fellow had obtained by cunning from her parents. The prince, who knew all about the affair, was silent, though he was glad from his heart that it had fallen to his lot to set her free. So they went on till the day began to dawn.

The old man slept very late that morning, and rubbed his eyes till he was properly awake. Then he remembered that very soon the couple were to present themselves before him. After waiting and waiting quite a long time he said to himself, with a grin, "Well, they are not in much hurry to be married," and waited again.

At last he grew a little uneasy, and cried loudly, "Man and maid! What has become of you?"

After repeating this many times, he became quite frightened, but, call as he would, neither man nor maid appeared. At last he jumped angrily out of bed to go in search of the culprits, but only found an empty house, and beds that had never been slept in. Then he went straight to the stable, where the sight of the dead calf told him all. Swearing loudly, he opened the door of the third stall quickly, and cried to his goblin servants to go and chase the fugitives. "Bring them to me, however you may find them, for have them I must!" he said. So spake the old man, and the servants fled like the wind.

The runaways were crossing a great plain, when the maiden stopped. "Something has happened!" she said. "The ball moves in my hand, and I'm sure we are being followed!" and behind them they saw a black cloud flying before the wind. Then the maiden turned the ball thrice in her hand, and cried,

> Listen to me, my ball, my ball.
> Be quick and change me into a brook,
> And my lover into a little fish.

And in an instant there was a brook with a fish swimming in it. The goblins arrived just after, but, seeing nobody, waited for a little, then hurried home, leaving the brook and the fish undisturbed. When they were quite out of sight, the brook and the fish returned to their usual shapes and proceeded on their journey.

When the goblins, tired and with empty hands, returned, their master inquired what they had seen, and if nothing strange had befallen them.

"Nothing," said they; "the plain was quite empty, save for a brook and a fish swimming in it."

"Idiots!" roared the master; "of course it was they!" And dashing open the door of the fifth stall, he told the goblins inside that they must go and drink up the brook and catch the fish. And the goblins jumped up, and flew like the wind.

The young pair had almost reached the edge of the wood, when the maiden stopped again. "Something has happened," said she. "The ball is moving in my hand," and looking round she beheld a cloud flying toward them, large and blacker than the first, and striped with red. "Those are our pursuers," cried she, and turning the ball three times in her hand she spoke to it thus:

Listen to me, my ball, my ball.
Be quick and change us both.
Me into a wild rose bush,
And him into a rose on my stem.

And in the twinkling of an eye it was done. Only just in time too, for the goblins were close at hand, and looked round eagerly for the stream and the fish. But neither stream nor fish was to be seen; nothing but a rose bush. So they went sorrowing home, and when they were out of sight the rose bush and rose returned to their proper shapes and walked all the faster for the little rest they had had.

"Well, did you find them?" asked the old man when his goblins came back.

"No," replied the leader of the goblins, "we found neither brook nor fish in the desert."

"And did you find nothing else at all?"

"Oh, nothing but a rose tree on the edge of a wood, with a rose hanging on it."

"Idiots!" cried he. "Why, that was they." And he threw open the door of the seventh stall, where his mightiest goblins were locked in. "Bring them to me, however you find them, dead or alive!" thundered he, "for I will have them! Tear up the rose tree and the roots too, and don't leave anything behind, however strange it may be!"

The fugitives were resting in the shade of a wood, and were refreshing themselves with food and drink. Suddenly the maiden looked up. "Something has happened," said she. "The ball has nearly jumped out of my bosom! Someone is certainly following us, and the danger is near, but the trees hide our enemies from us."

As she spoke she took the ball in her hand, and said,

Listen to me, my ball, my ball.
Be quick and change me into a breeze,
And make my lover into a midge.

An instant, and the girl was dissolved into thin air, while the prince darted about like a midge. The next moment a crowd of goblins rushed up, and looked about in search of something strange, for neither a rose bush nor anything else was to be seen. But they had hardly turned their backs to go home empty-handed when the prince and the maiden stood on the earth again.

"We must make all the haste we can," said she, "before the old man himself comes to seek us, for he will know us under any disguise."

They ran on till they reached such a dark part of the forest that, if it had not been for the light shed by the ball, they could not have made their way at all. Worn out and breathless, they came at length to a large stone, and here the ball began to move restlessly. The maiden, seeing this, exclaimed,

> Listen to me, my ball, my ball.
> Roll the stone quickly to one side,
> That we may find a door.

And in a moment the stone had rolled away, and they had passed through the door to the world again.

"Now we are safe," cried she. "Here the old wizard has no more power over us, and we can guard ourselves from his spells. But, my friend, we have to part! You will return to your parents, and I must go in search of mine."

"No! No!" exclaimed the prince. "I will never part from you. You must come with me and be my wife. We have gone through many troubles together, and now we will share our joys." The maiden resisted his words for some time, but at last she went with him.

In the forest they met a woodcutter, who told them that in the palace, as well as in all the land, there had been great sorrow over the loss of the prince, and many years had now passed away during which they had found no traces of him. So, by the help of the magic ball, the maiden managed that he should put on the same clothes that he had been wearing at the time he had vanished, so that his father might know him more quickly. She herself stayed behind in a peasant's hut, so that father and son might meet alone.

But the father was no longer there, for the loss of his son had killed him; and on his deathbed he confessed to his people how he had contrived that the old wizard should carry away a peasant's child instead of the prince, wherefore his punishment had fallen upon him.

The prince wept bitterly when he heard this news, for he had loved his father well, and for three days he ate and drank nothing. But on the fourth day he stood in the presence of his people as their new king, and, calling his councillors, he told them all the strange things that had befallen him, and how the maiden had borne him safe through all.

And the councillors cried with one voice, "Let her be your wife, and our liege lady."

And that is the end of the story.

BEAUTY AND THE BEAST
(France)

Once upon a time, in a very far-off country, there lived a merchant who had been so fortunate in all his undertakings that he was enormously rich. As he had, however, six sons and six daughters, he found that his money was not too much to let them all have everything they fancied, as they were accustomed to do.

But one day a most unexpected misfortune befell them. Their house caught fire and was speedily burnt to the ground, with all the splendid furniture, the books, pictures, gold, silver, and precious goods it contained; and this was only the beginning of their troubles. Their father, who had until this moment prospered in all ways, suddenly lost every ship he had upon the sea, either by dint of pirates, shipwreck, or fire. Then he heard that his clerks in distant countries, whom he trusted entirely, had proved unfaithful; and at last from great wealth he fell into the direst poverty.

All that he had left was a little house in a desolate place at least a hundred leagues from the town in which he had lived, and to this he was forced to retreat with his children, who were in despair at the idea of leading such a different life. Indeed, the daughters at first hoped that their friends, who had been so numerous while they were rich, would insist on their staying in their houses now they no longer possessed one. But they soon found that they were left alone, and that their former friends even attributed their misfortunes to their own extravagance, and showed no intention of offering them any help. So nothing was left for them but to take their departure to the cottage, which stood in the midst of a dark forest, and seemed to be the most dismal place upon the face of the earth. As they were too poor to have any servants, the girls had to work hard, like peasants, and the sons, for their part, cultivated the fields to earn their living. Roughly clothed, and living in the simplest way, the girls regretted unceasingly the luxuries and amusements of their former life; only the youngest tried to be brave and cheerful. She had been as sad as anyone when misfortune first overtook her father, but, soon recovering her natural gaiety, she set to work to make the best of things, to amuse her father and brothers as well as she could, and to try to persuade her sisters to join her in dancing and singing. But they would do nothing of the sort, and, because she was not as doleful as themselves, they declared that this miserable life was all she was fit for. But she was really far prettier and cleverer than they were; indeed, she was so lovely that she was always called Beauty. After two years, when they were all beginning to get used to their new life, something happened to disturb their tranquillity. Their father received the news that one of his ships, which he had believed to be lost, had come safely into port with a rich cargo. All the sons and daughters at once thought that their poverty was at an end, and wanted to set out directly for the town; but their father, who was more prudent, begged them to wait a little, and, though it was harvest-time, and he could ill be spared, determined to go himself first, to make inquiries. Only the youngest daughter had any doubt but that they would soon again be as rich as they were before, or at least rich enough to live comfortably in some town where they would find amusement and gay companions once more. So they all loaded their father with commissions for jewels and dresses which it would have taken a fortune to buy; only Beauty, feeling sure that it was of no use, did not ask for anything. Her father, noticing her silence, said, "And what shall I bring for you, Beauty?"

"The only thing I wish for is to see you come home safely," she answered.

But this reply vexed her sisters, who fancied she was blaming them for having asked for such costly things. Her father, however, was pleased, but as he thought that at her age she certainly ought to like pretty presents, he told her to choose something.

"Well, dear father," she said, "as you insist upon it, I beg that you will bring me a rose. I have not seen one since we came here, and I love them so much."

So the merchant set out and reached the town as quickly as possible, but only to find that his former companions, believing him to be dead, had divided between them the goods which the ship had brought; and after six months of trouble and expense he found himself as poor as when he started, having been able to recover only just enough to pay the cost of his journey. To make matters worse, he was obliged to leave the town in the most terrible weather, so that by the time he was within a few leagues of his home he was almost exhausted with cold and fatigue. Though he knew it would take some hours to get through the forest, he was so anxious to be at his journey's end that he resolved to go on; but night overtook him, and the deep snow and bitter frost made it impossible for his horse to carry him any further. Not a house was to be seen; the only shelter he could get was the hollow trunk of a great tree, and there he crouched all the night, which seemed to him the longest he had ever known. In spite of his weariness the howling of the wolves kept him awake, and even when at last the day broke he was not much better off, for the falling snow had covered up every path, and he did not know which way to turn.

At length he made out some sort of track, and though at the beginning it was so rough and slippery that he fell down more than once, it presently became easier, and led him into an avenue of trees which ended in a splendid castle. It seemed to the merchant very strange that no snow had fallen in the avenue, which was entirely composed of orange trees, covered with flowers and fruit. When he reached the first court of the castle he saw before him a flight of agate steps, and went up them, and passed through several splendidly furnished rooms. The pleasant warmth of the air revived him, and he felt very hungry; but there seemed to be nobody in all this vast and splendid palace whom he could ask to give him something to eat. Deep silence reigned everywhere, and at last, tired of roaming through empty rooms and galleries, he stopped in a room smaller than the rest, where a clear fire was burning and a couch was drawn up cosily close to it. Thinking that this must be prepared for someone who was expected, he sat down to wait till he should come, and very soon fell into a sweet sleep.

When his extreme hunger wakened him after several hours, he was still alone; but a little table, upon which was a good dinner, had been drawn up close to him, and, as he had eaten nothing for twenty-four hours, he lost no time in beginning his meal, hoping that he might soon have an opportunity of thanking his considerate entertainer, whoever it might be. But no one appeared, and even after another long sleep, from which he awoke completely refreshed, there was no sign of anybody, though a fresh meal of dainty cakes and fruit was prepared upon the little table at his elbow. Being naturally timid, the silence began to terrify him, and he resolved to search once more through all the rooms; but it was of no use. Not even a servant was to be seen; there was no sign of life in the palace! He began to wonder what he should do, and to amuse himself by pretending that all the treasures he saw were his own, and considering how he would divide them among his children. Then he went down into the garden, and though it was winter everywhere else, here the sun shone, and the birds sang, and the flowers bloomed, and the air was soft and sweet. The merchant, in ecstasies with all he saw and heard, said to himself, "All this must be meant for me. I will go this minute and bring my children to share all these delights."

In spite of being so cold and weary when he reached the castle, he had taken his horse to the stable and fed it. Now he thought he would saddle it for his homeward journey, and he turned down the path which led to the stable. This path had a hedge of roses on each side of it, and the merchant thought he had never seen or smelt such exquisite flowers. They reminded him of his promise to Beauty, and he stopped and had just gathered one to take to her when he was startled by a strange noise behind him. Turning round, he saw a frightful Beast, which seemed to be very angry and said, in a terrible voice: "Who told you that you might gather my roses? Was it not enough that I allowed you to be in my palace and was kind to you? This is the way you show your gratitude, by stealing my flowers! But your insolence shall not go unpunished."

The merchant, terrified by these furious words, dropped the fatal rose, and, throwing himself on his knees, cried, "Pardon me, noble sir. I am truly grateful to you for your hospitality, which was so magnificent that I could not imagine that you would be offended by my taking such a little thing as a rose." But the Beast's anger was not lessened by this speech.

"You are very ready with excuses and flattery," he cried; "but that will not save you from the death you deserve."

"Alas!" thought the merchant, "if my daughter Beauty could only know what danger her rose has brought me into!"

And in despair he began to tell the Beast all his misfortunes, and the reason of his journey, not forgetting to mention Beauty's request.

"A king's ransom would hardly have procured all that my other daughters asked," he said; "but I thought that I might at least take Beauty her rose. I beg you to forgive me, for you see I meant no harm."

The Beast considered for a moment, and then he said, in a less furious tone, "I will forgive you on one condition—that is, that you will give me one of your daughters."

"Ah!" cried the merchant, "if I were cruel enough to buy my own life at the expense of one of my children's, what excuse could I invent to bring her here?"

"No excuse would be necessary," answered the Beast. "If she comes at all she must come willingly. On no other condition will I have her. See if any one of them is courageous enough, and loves you well enough to come and save your life. You seem to be an honest man, so I will trust you to go home. I give you a month to see if either of your daughters will come back with you and stay here, to let you go free. If neither of them is willing, you must come alone, after bidding them good-bye forever, for then you will belong to me. And do not imagine that you can hide from me, for if you fail to keep your word I will come and fetch you!" added the Beast grimly.

The merchant accepted this proposal, though he did not really think any of his daughters would be persuaded to come. He promised to return at the time appointed, and then, anxious to escape from the presence of the Beast, he asked permission to set off at once. But the Beast answered that he could not go until the next day.

"Then you will find a horse ready for you," he said. "Now go and eat your supper, and await my orders."

The poor merchant, more dead than alive, went back to his room, where the most delicious supper was already served on the little table which was drawn up before a blazing fire. But he was too terrified to eat, and only tasted a few of the dishes, for fear the Beast should be angry if he did not obey his orders. When he had finished he heard a great noise in the next room, which he knew meant that the Beast was coming. As he could do nothing to escape his visit, the only thing that remained was to seem as little afraid as possible; so when the Beast appeared and asked roughly if he had supped well, the merchant answered humbly that he had, thanks to his host's kindness. Then the Beast warned him to remember their agreement, and to prepare his daughter exactly for what she had to expect.

"Do not get up tomorrow," he added, "until you see the sun and hear a golden bell ring. Then you will find your breakfast waiting for you here, and the horse you are to ride will be ready in the courtyard. He will also bring you back again when you come with your daughter a month hence. Farewell. Take a rose to Beauty, and remember your promise!"

The merchant was only too glad when the Beast went away, and though he could not sleep for sadness, he lay down until the sun rose. Then, after a hasty breakfast, he went to gather Beauty's rose, and mounted his horse, which carried him off so swiftly that in an instant he had lost sight of the palace, and he was still wrapped in gloomy thoughts when it stopped before the door of the cottage.

His sons and daughters, who had been very uneasy at his long absence, rushed to meet him, eager to know the result of his journey, which, seeing him mounted upon a splendid horse and wrapped in a rich mantle, they supposed to be favorable. But he hid the truth from them at first, only saying sadly to Beauty as he gave her the rose, "Here is what you asked me to bring you; you little know what it has cost."

But this excited their curiosity so greatly that presently he told them his adventures from beginning to end, and then they were all very unhappy. The girls lamented loudly over their lost hopes, and the sons declared that their father should not return to this terrible castle, and began to make plans for killing the Beast if it should come to fetch him. But he reminded them that he had promised to go back. Then the girls were very angry with Beauty, and said it was all her fault, and that if she had asked for something sensible this would never have happened, and complained bitterly that they should have to suffer for her folly.

Poor Beauty, much distressed, said to them, "I have indeed caused this misfortune, but I assure you I did it innocently. Who could have guessed that to ask for a rose in the middle of summer would cause so much misery? But as I did the mischief it is only just that I should suffer for it. I will therefore go back with my father to keep his promise."

At first nobody would hear of this arrangement, and her father and brothers, who loved her dearly, declared that nothing should make them let her go; but Beauty was firm. As the time drew near she divided all her little possessions between her sisters, and said good-bye to everything she loved, and when the fatal day came she encouraged and cheered her father as they mounted together the horse that had brought him back. It seemed to fly rather than gallop, but so smoothly that Beauty was not frightened; indeed, she would have enjoyed the journey if she had not feared what might happen to her at the end of it. Her father still tried to persuade her to go back, but in vain. While they were talking the night fell, and then, to their great surprise, wonderful colored lights began to shine in all directions, and splendid fireworks blazed out before them; all the forest was illuminated by them, and even felt pleasantly warm, though it had been bitterly cold before. This lasted until they reached the avenue of orange trees, where there were statues holding flaming torches, and when they got nearer to the palace they saw that it was illuminated from the roof to the ground, and music sounded softly from the courtyard. "The Beast must be very hungry," said Beauty, trying to laugh, "if he makes all this rejoicing over the arrival of his prey."

But, in spite of her anxiety, she could not help admiring all the wonderful things she saw.

The horse stopped at the foot of the flight of steps leading to the terrace, and when they had dismounted her father led her to the little room he had been in before, where they found a splendid fire burning, and the table daintily spread with a delicious supper.

The merchant knew that this was meant for them, and Beauty, who was rather less frightened now that she had passed through so many rooms and seen nothing of the Beast, was quite willing to begin, for her long ride had made her very hungry. But they had hardly finished their meal when the noise of the Beast's footsteps was heard approaching, and Beauty clung to her father in terror, which became all the greater when she saw how frightened he was. But when the Beast really appeared, though she trembled at the sight of him, she made a great effort to hide her horror, and saluted him respectfully.

This evidently pleased the Beast. After looking at her he said, in a tone that might have struck terror into the boldest heart, though he did not seem to be angry, "Good evening, old man. Good evening, Beauty."

The merchant was too terrified to reply, but Beauty answered sweetly, "Good evening, Beast."

"Have you come willingly?" asked the Beast. "Will you be content to stay here when your father goes away?"

Beauty answered bravely that she was quite prepared to stay.

"I am pleased with you," said the Beast. "As you have come of your own accord, you may stay. As for you, old man," he added, turning to the merchant, "at sunrise tomorrow you will take your departure. When the bell rings get up quickly and eat your breakfast, and you will find the same horse waiting to take you home; but remember that you must never expect to see my palace again."

Then turning to Beauty, he said, "Take your father into the next room, and help him to choose everything you think your brothers and sisters would like to have. You will find two traveling-trunks there; fill them as full as you can. It is only just that you should send them something very precious as a remembrance of yourself."

Then he went away, after saying, "Good-bye, Beauty; good-bye old man"; and though Beauty was beginning to think with great dismay of her father's departure, she was afraid to disobey the Beast's orders; and they went into the next room, which had shelves and cupboards all round it. They were greatly surprised at the riches it contained. There were splendid dresses fit for a queen, with all the ornaments that were to be worn with them; and when Beauty opened the cupboards she was quite dazzled by the gorgeous jewels that lay in heaps upon every shelf. After choosing a vast quantity, which she divided between her sisters—for she had made a heap of the wonderful dresses for each of them—she opened the last chest, which was full of gold.

"I think, father," she said, "that, as the gold will be more useful to you, we had better take out the other things again, and fill the trunks with it." So they did this; but the more they put in, the more room there seemed to be, and at last they put back all the jewels and dresses they had taken out, and Beauty even added as many more of the jewels as she could carry at once; and then the trunks were not too full, but they were so heavy that an elephant could not have carried them!

"The Beast was mocking us," cried the merchant; "he must have pretended to give us all these things, knowing that I could not carry them away."

"Let us wait and see," answered Beauty. "I cannot believe that he meant to deceive us. All we can do is to fasten them up and leave them ready."

So they did this and returned to the little room, where, to their astonishment, they found breakfast ready. The merchant ate his with a good appetite, as the Beast's generosity made him believe that he might perhaps venture to come back soon and see Beauty. But she felt sure that her father was leaving her forever, so she was very sad when the bell rang sharply for the second time, and warned them that the time was come for them to part. They went down into the courtyard, where two horses were waiting, one loaded with the two trunks, the other for him to ride. They were pawing the ground in their impatience to start, and the merchant was forced to bid Beauty a hasty farewell; and as soon as he was mounted he went off at such a pace that she lost sight of him in an instant. Then Beauty began to cry, and wandered sadly back to her own room. But she soon found that she was very sleepy, and as she had nothing better to do she lay down and instantly fell asleep. And then she dreamed that she was walking by a brook bordered with trees, and lamenting her sad fate, when a young prince, handsomer than anyone she had ever seen, and with a voice that went straight to her heart, came and said to her, "Ah, Beauty! you are not so unfortunate as you suppose. Here you will be rewarded for all you have suffered elsewhere. Your every wish shall be gratified. Only try to find me out, no matter how I may be disguised, as I love you dearly, and in making me happy you will find your own happiness. Be as true-hearted as you are beautiful, and we shall have nothing left to wish for."

"What can I do, Prince, to make you happy?" said Beauty.

"Only be grateful," he answered, "and do not trust too much to your eyes. And, above all, do not desert me until you have saved me from my cruel misery."

After this she thought she found herself in a room with a stately and beautiful lady, who said to her, "Dear Beauty, try not to regret all you have left behind you, for you are destined to a better fate. Only do not let yourself be deceived by appearances."

Beauty found her dreams so interesting that she was in no hurry to awake, but presently the clock roused her by calling her name softly twelve times, and then she got up and found her dressing table set out with everything she could possibly want; and when her toilet was finished she found dinner was waiting in the room next to hers. But dinner does not take very long when you are all by yourself, and very soon she sat down cosily in the corner of a sofa, and began to think about the charming prince she had seen in her dream.

"He said I could make him happy," said Beauty to herself.

"It seems, then, that his horrible Beast keeps him a prisoner. How can I set him free? I wonder why they both told me not to trust appearances? I don't understand it. But, after all, it was only a dream, so why should I trouble myself about it? I had better go and find something to do to amuse myself."

So she got up and began to explore some of the many rooms of the palace.

The first she entered was lined with mirrors, and Beauty saw herself reflected on every side, and thought she had never seen such a charming room. Then a bracelet which was hanging from a chandelier caught her eye, and on taking it down she was greatly surprised to find that it held a portrait of her unknown admirer, just as she had seen him in her dream. With great delight she slipped the bracelet on her arm, and went on into a gallery of pictures, where she soon found a portrait of the same handsome prince, as large as life, and so well painted that as she studied it he seemed to smile kindly at her. Tearing herself away from the portrait at last, she passed through into a room which contained every musical instrument under the sun, and here she amused herself for a long while in trying some of them, and singing until she was tired. The next room was a library, and she saw everything she had ever wanted to read, as well as everything she had read, and it seemed to her that a whole lifetime would not be enough even to read the names of the books, there were so many. By this time it was growing dusk, and wax candles in diamond and ruby candlesticks were beginning to light themselves in every room.

Beauty found her supper served just at the time she preferred to have it, but she did not see anyone or hear a sound, and, though her father had warned her that she would be alone, she began to find it rather dull.

But presently she heard the Beast coming, and wondered tremblingly if he meant to eat her up now.

However, as he did not seem at all ferocious, and only said gruffly, "Good evening, Beauty," she answered cheerfully and managed to conceal her terror. Then the Beast asked her how she had been amusing herself, and she told him all the rooms she had seen.

Then he asked if she thought she could be happy in his palace; and Beauty answered that everything was so beautiful that she would be very hard to please if she could not be happy. And after about an hour's talk Beauty began to think that the Beast was not nearly so terrible as she had supposed at first. Then he got up to leave her, and said in his gruff voice, "Do you love me, Beauty? Will you marry me?"

"Oh! what shall I say?" cried Beauty, for she was afraid to make the Beast angry by refusing.

"Say yes or no without fear," he replied.

"Oh! no, Beast," said Beauty hastily.

"Since you will not, goodnight, Beauty," he said.

And she answered, "Goodnight Beast," very glad to find that her refusal had not provoked him.

After he was gone she was very soon in bed and asleep, and dreaming of her unknown prince. She thought he came and said to her, "Ah, Beauty! why are you so unkind to me? I fear I am fated to be unhappy for many a long day still." And then her dreams changed, but the charming prince figured in them all; and when morning came her first thought was to look at the portrait and see if it was really like him, and she found that it certainly was.

This morning she decided to amuse herself in the garden, for the sun shone, and all the fountains were playing; but she was astonished to find that every place was familiar to her, and presently she came to the brook where the myrtle trees were growing where she had first met the prince in her dream, and that made her think more than ever that he must be kept a prisoner by the Beast. When she was tired she went back to the palace, and found a new room full of materials for every kind of work—ribbons to make into bows, and silks to work into flowers. Then there was an aviary full of rare birds, which were so tame that they flew to Beauty as soon as they saw her, and perched upon her shoulders and her head.

"Pretty little creatures," she said, "how I wish that your cage was nearer to my room, that I might often hear you sing!" So saying she opened a door, and found to her delight that it led into her own room, though she had thought it was quite the other side of the palace.

There were more birds in a room farther on, parrots and cockatoos that could talk, and they greeted Beauty by name; indeed, she found them so entertaining that she took one or two back to her room, and they talked to her while she was at supper; after which the Beast paid her his usual visit, and asked the same questions as before, and then with a gruff goodnight he took his departure, and Beauty went to bed to dream of her mysterious prince. The days passed swiftly in different amusements, and after a while Beauty found out another strange thing in the palace, which often pleased her when she was tired of being alone. There was one room which she had not noticed particularly; it was empty, except that under each of the windows stood a very comfortable chair; and the first time she had looked out of the window it had seemed to her that a black curtain prevented her from seeing anything outside. But the second time she went into the room, happening to be tired, she sat down in one of the chairs, when instantly the curtain was rolled aside, and a most amusing pantomime was acted before her; there were dances, and colored lights, and music, and pretty dresses, and it was all so gay that Beauty was in ecstasies. After that she tried the other seven windows in turn, and there was some new and surprising entertainment to be seen from each of them, so that Beauty never could feel lonely anymore. Every evening after supper the Beast came to see her, and always before saying goodnight asked her in his terrible voice, "Beauty, will you marry me?"

And it seemed to Beauty, now she understood him better, that when she said, "No, Beast," he went away quite sad. But her happy dreams of the handsome young prince soon made her forget the poor Beast, and the only thing that at all disturbed her was to be constantly told to distrust appearances, to let her heart guide her, and not her eyes, and many other equally perplexing things, which, consider as she would, she could not understand.

So everything went on for a long time, until at last, happy as she was, Beauty began to long for the sight of her father and her brothers and sisters; and one night, seeing her look very sad, the Beast asked her what was the matter. Beauty had quite ceased to be afraid of him. Now she knew that he was really gentle in spite of his ferocious looks and his dreadful voice. So she answered that she was longing to see her home once more. Upon hearing this the Beast seemed sadly distressed, and cried miserably.

"Ah! Beauty, have you the heart to desert an unhappy Beast like this? What more do you want to make you happy? Is it because you hate me that you want to escape?"

"No, dear Beast," answered Beauty softly, "I do not hate you, and I should be very sorry never to see you anymore, but I long to see my father again. Only let me go for two months, and I promise to come back to you and stay for the rest of my life."

The Beast, who had been sighing dolefully while she spoke, now replied, "I cannot refuse you anything you ask, even though it should cost me my life. Take the four boxes you will find in the room next to your own, and fill them with everything you wish to take with you. But remember your promise and come back when the two months are over, or you may have cause to repent it, for if you do not come in good time you will find your faithful Beast dead. You will not need any chariot to bring you back. Only say good-bye to all your brothers and sisters the night before you come away, and when you have gone to bed turn this ring round upon your finger and say firmly, "I wish to go back to my palace and see my Beast again." Goodnight, Beauty. Fear nothing, sleep peacefully, and before long you shall see your father once more."

As soon as Beauty was alone she hastened to fill the boxes with all the rare and precious things she saw about her, and only when she was tired of heaping things into them did they seem to be full.

Then she went to bed, but could hardly sleep for joy. And when at last she did begin to dream of her beloved prince she was grieved to see him stretched upon a grassy bank sad and weary, and hardly like himself.

"What is the matter?" she cried.

But he looked at her reproachfully, and said, "How can you ask me, cruel one? Are you not leaving me to my death perhaps?"

"Ah! don't be so sorrowful," cried Beauty; "I am only going to assure my father that I am safe and happy. I have promised the Beast faithfully that I will come back, and he would die of grief if I did not keep my word!"

"What would that matter to you?" said the prince. "Surely you would not care?"

"Indeed I should be ungrateful if I did not care for such a kind Beast," cried Beauty indignantly. "I would die to save him from pain. I assure you it is not his fault that he is so ugly."

Just then a strange sound woke her—someone was speaking not very far away; and opening her eyes she found herself in a room she had never seen before, which was certainly not nearly so splendid as those she was used to in the Beast's palace. Where could she be? She got up and dressed hastily, and then saw that the boxes she had packed the night before were all in the room. While she was wondering by what magic the Beast had transported them and herself to this strange place she suddenly heard her father's voice, and rushed out and greeted him joyfully. Her brothers and sisters were all astonished at her appearance, as they had never expected to see her again, and there was no end to the questions they asked her. She had also much to hear about what had happened to them while she was away, and of her father's journey home. But when they heard that she had only come to be with them for a short time, and then must go back to the Beast's palace for ever, they lamented loudly. Then Beauty asked her father what he thought could be the meaning of her strange dreams, and why the prince constantly begged her not to trust to appearances. After much consideration he answered, "You tell me yourself that the Beast, frightful as he is, loves you dearly, and deserves your love and gratitude for his gentleness and kindness; I think the prince must mean you to understand that you ought to reward him by doing as he wishes you to, in spite of his ugliness."

Beauty could not help seeing that this seemed very probable; still, when she thought of her dear prince who was so handsome, she did not feel at all inclined to marry the Beast. At any rate, for two months she need not decide, but could enjoy herself with her sisters. But though they were rich now, and lived in a town again, and had plenty of acquaintances, Beauty found that nothing amused her very much; and she often thought of the palace, where she was so happy, especially as at home she never once dreamed of her dear prince, and she felt quite sad without him.

Then her sisters seemed to have got quite used to being without her, and even found her rather in the way, so she would not have been sorry when the two months were over but for her father and brothers, who begged her to stay, and seemed so grieved at the thought of her departure that she had not the courage to say good-bye to them. Every day when she got up she meant to say it at night, and when night came she put it off again, until at last she had a dismal dream which helped her to make up her mind. She thought she was wandering in a lonely path in the palace gardens, when she heard groans which seemed to come from some bushes hiding the entrance of a cave, and running quickly to see what could be the matter, she found the Beast stretched out upon his side, apparently dying. He reproached her faintly with being the cause of his distress, and at the same moment a stately lady appeared, and said very gravely, "Ah! Beauty, you are only just in time to save his life. See what happens when people do not keep their promises! If you had delayed one day more, you would have found him dead."

Beauty was so terrified by this dream that the next morning she announced her intention of going back at once, and that very night she said good-bye to her father and all her brothers and sisters, and as soon as she was in bed she turned her ring round upon her finger, and said firmly, "I wish to go back to my palace and see my Beast again," as she had been told to do.

Then she fell asleep instantly, and only woke up to hear the clock saying, "Beauty, Beauty," twelve times in its musical voice, which told her at once that she was really in the palace once more. Everything was just as before, and her birds were so glad to see her! But Beauty thought she had never known such a long day, for she was so anxious to see the Beast again that she felt as if suppertime would never come.

But when it did come and no Beast appeared she was really frightened; so, after listening and waiting for a long time, she ran down into the garden to search for him. Up and down the paths and avenues ran poor Beauty, calling him in vain, for no one answered, and not a trace of him could she find; until at last, quite tired, she stopped for a minute's rest, and saw that she was standing opposite the shady path she had seen in her dream. She rushed down it, and, sure enough, there was the cave, and in it lay the Beast—asleep, as Beauty thought. Quite glad to have found him, she ran up and stroked his head, but to her horror he did not move or open his eyes.

"Oh! he is dead; and it is all my fault," said Beauty, crying bitterly.

But then, looking at him again, she fancied he still breathed, and, hastily fetching some water from the nearest fountain, she sprinkled it over his face, and to her great delight he began to revive.

"Oh! Beast, how you frightened me!" she cried. "I never knew how much I loved you until just now, when I feared I was too late to save your life."

"Can you really love such an ugly creature as I am?" said the Beast faintly. "Ah! Beauty, you only came just in time. I was dying because I thought you had forgotten your promise. But go back now and rest, I shall see you again by and by.

Beauty, who had half expected that he would be angry with her, was reassured by his gentle voice, and went back to the palace, where supper was awaiting her; and afterward the Beast came in as usual, and talked about the time she had spent with her father, asking if she had enjoyed herself, and if they had all been very glad to see her.

Beauty answered politely, and quite enjoyed telling him all that had happened to her. And when at last the time came for him to go, and he asked, as he had so often asked before, "Beauty, will you marry me?" she answered softly, "Yes, dear Beast."

As she spoke a blaze of light sprang up before the windows of the palace; fireworks crackled and guns banged, and across the avenue of orange trees, in letters all made of fireflies, was written, "Long live the prince and his bride."

Turning to ask the Beast what it could all mean, Beauty found that he had disappeared, and in his place stood her long-loved prince! At the same moment the wheels of a chariot were heard upon the terrace, and two ladies entered the room. One of them Beauty recognized as the stately lady she had seen in her dreams; the other was also so grand and queenly that Beauty hardly knew which to greet first.

But the one she already knew said to her companion, "Well, Queen, this is Beauty, who has had the courage to rescue your son from the terrible enchantment. They love one another, and only your consent to their marriage is wanting to make them perfectly happy."

"I consent with all my heart," cried the Queen. "How can I ever thank you enough, charming girl, for having restored my dear son to his natural form?"

And then she tenderly embraced Beauty and the prince, who had meanwhile been greeting the fairy and receiving her congratulations.

"Now," said the fairy to Beauty, "I suppose you would like me to send for all your brothers and sisters to dance at your wedding?"

And so she did, and the marriage was celebrated the very next day with the utmost splendor, and Beauty and the prince lived happily ever after.

JANET AND TAM LIN
(Scotland)

Janet grew up near a Scotland forest where it was believed the fairy folk dwelled. As a child, Janet obeyed her parents' request that she never enter the forest, but as she became a young lady, she couldn't resist exploring the forest for berries and flowers.

One day as she picked berries, enjoying the coolness of the woods, she was startled by the appearance of a young man. His warm smile disarmed her and she fell into conversation with him, learning that his name was Tam Lin.

From that day on, Janet would return to the woods to stroll and visit with Tam Lin. Their friendship grew and Janet asked him to return home with her to meet her parents.

"Ah, Janet," he replied, "I must tell you my sad story. When I was a child I was stolen by the fairy folk. Though I am a mortal and I can walk the woods by day, the enchantment returns me to the fairyland by night."

"So the fairy folk do exist! Oh, Tam Lin, I am sorry that you are not free," said Janet.

Though Janet knew their friendship could only exist in the woods, she became increasingly fond of Tam Lin, and they continued to meet. One fall day Janet saw that Tam Lin was quite distressed. His eyes were sad, and his mouth was set.

"What is wrong, Tam?" asked Janet.

"Now you must learn the rest of my story. Every seven years the fairy folk must pay the teind. They draw strength from the mortal they sacrifice to the spirits, and I am to be that mortal. That time is near." said Tam Lin.

"There must be a way to break the spell!" Janet insisted.

"There is a way, but it is very difficult. The spell is lifted so that I can leave the forest to go to the circle of stones. If someone who loves me can seize me during the procession and hold me for the time of twenty-one heartbeats, I shall be free of the fairies."

"But, Tam, this is wonderful, for I do love you. I will save you!"

"Janet, I love you as well. But the danger is so great that I fear for your life. Samhain Eve* is the night of the sacrifice, and wicked spirits will be

---

*Others call this Halloween.

165

roaming about. You will be at great risk. And when you seize me, the fairies will transform me so that you will yearn to release me. I could seem terrifying and threatening to you. You will possibly be in great pain."

Janet took his hands and looked up at him with great courage and love. "I will set you free," she promised.

As the days shortened and cooled, they continued to meet, but they became more and more pensive as Samhain Eve approached.

Finally the day arrived, and as the sun set most of the people closed their homes, fearing the creatures that ruled the night. But Janet made her way unseen to the crossroads where Tam Lin was to be. There she crouched, listening to the frightening night noises. At times she felt the air move nearby, and other times she glimpsed terrible creatures, but she remained unseen.

Near midnight, aching from the wait, she finally heard the clinking of bridles, and she knew the fairy folk were coming. The procession was long, and the fairy folk were beautifully dressed for the ceremony. Finally, she spied Tam Lin, who was dressed in a white robe, walking dispiritedly between two black-robed wizards.

As he passed Janet, she sprang up and threw her arms around him. The procession halted in confusion. The wizards began to whisper their magical spells.

And Tam Lin changed. He snarled at her with the drooling fangs of the huge wolf he had become.

"It's a trick," Janet told herself, and she held fast in spite of her terror.

In a moment he had changed again. She realized her hands and arms were dripping with slime as a huge wormlike creature writhed in her grasp. She shook with horror, but she continued to hold onto the animal.

Searing heat engulfed Janet as Tam Lin turned into a glowing hot metal statue. Her teeth ached from clenching them against the pain, but she did not release Tam.

Abruptly the heat was replaced with coldness so fierce that it burned her skin like before. While Janet held on, the cold statue became a huge bat, seemingly desperate to fly away. Janet closed her eyes, clutched its beating wings, and desperately wondered how much longer she could endure the bruising punishment.

Suddenly she heard the fairies weeping and screeching. The night was lit by a flash of light, and then all was quiet. Janet slowly opened her eyes and realized that she was no longer holding terrifying monsters. She was clinging to Tam Lin, once again in his mortal form. As he gently touched her face in thanks, she realized that she had truly broken the fairies' spell.

The moon was low in the sky and the forest was now quiet. Samhain Eve was over. Janet and Tam Lin walked quietly to Janet's home. They soon were married, but they never walked again in the nearby forest.

A·T·T·E·N·D·A·N·T·S

Ingenious and Loyal

THE LEARNED SERVANT GIRL
(China)

During the difficult days of the T'ang dynasty there was an old lord who governed six districts. The Lord of Luchow had a large household and many servants. One servant, Hung-hsien (Red Cord), was an unusual girl. She had learned to read and she enjoyed reading classic literature. She also played the lute and was skilled in all sorts of the arts.

One night the lord held an elaborate feast. The otherwise quiet night hours were broken only by the steady beating of a kettledrum. Hung-hsien listened carefully to the taut drumbeats and went to her lord. "I believe the drumbeats have an edge of sadness. There seems to be something troubling the drummer."

The lord sent for the drummer who told his master that his wife had just died and he had been reluctant to request leave to return to his homeland for her burial. The lord told the drummer that he was free to make his journey home, and the drummer left with praises for the lord's benevolence. The lord reflected on the wisdom of his servant.

It soon became known to the Lord of Luchow that another nearby ruler was making plans to overthrow his territory. The Lord of Weipu had gathered a strong army, training them in the martial arts. The Lord of Luchow was a peace-loving leader, and he became so distraught over the impending attack that he was unable to eat or sleep.

Hung-hsien decided she must do something to help her lord. She slipped into her room and quietly tied up her hair into a knot. She put on dark clothes and slippers. Then she retrieved from her chest a beautifully engraved magic sword. She murmured a few magic words and then she was moving on the wind.

She flew through the black night until she could see the dying embers of the evening campfire. She hovered over the sentries, noting that they drowsed in the heavy night air. Quietly she set herself down on the ground and sneaked past the sentries until she found the tent of the Lord of Weipu.

The lord was snoring gently while Hung-hsien looked quietly around the tent. Soon she spied what she wanted. She took a golden urn that was near the bed and tucked it under her arm. She slipped out of the tent and drifted noiselessly past the guards. With the sword in her other hand, she once again murmured her magic words and flew back to the Lord of Luchow's camp.

She went straight to the lord's tent and found him still unable to sleep. "My lord, I just returned from the enemy's camp. I have taken this golden urn. If you return it by messenger tomorrow you will see that he will no longer threaten you."

The next day the Lord of Weipu received the messenger and was greatly amazed to be given the golden urn. He realized that if his enemy could remove his urn from his tent he could have also taken his life. He immediately wrote to the Lord of Luchow expressing his appreciation for the return of his urn and for the sparing of his life. He also pledged his devotion to the Lord of Luchow.

When the Lord of Luchow read the message he called Hung-hsien to him and read it to her. The lord praised her for her cleverness and devotion, and Hung-hsien rejoiced that her master would be able to once again lead his people in peace and harmony.

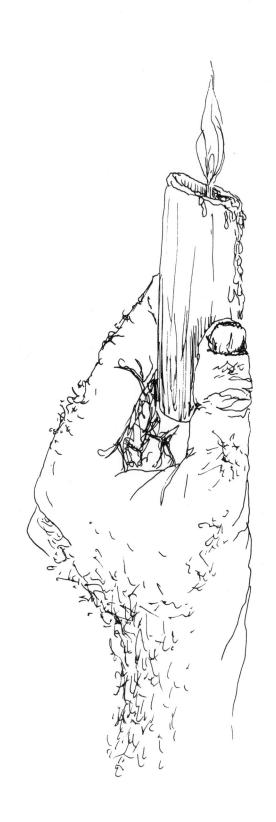

THE HAND OF GLORY
(England)

There is a stretch of land with wide open spaces of heather in the far northwestern tip of Yorkshire. When possible, travelers avoided the area, knowing that both the weather and the men were evil. Superstitions abounded, with the most gruesome being the belief in the power of the Hand of Glory.

The Hand of Glory could only be obtained from a man who had been hanged, and it had to be preserved with great care and ritual. The hand must be fresh, wrapped in a piece of a winding sheet, and then squeezed to remove the blood. Next it must be placed in a mixture of powdered salt, saltpeter, and pepper. After a fortnight it must be removed and set in the sun in a position that would support a candle when fully dried. The candle must be made in part from the fat of the dead man. When the candle was lighted in the dried hand, the owner had within his power to make all nearby persons helpless.

One evening a poor, exhausted woman arrived at an inn and asked for shelter from a threatening storm. Though she could not pay for a bed, she asked to be allowed to rest by the fire until early the next morning and asked the landlord to set out a bit of food for her early departure.

The landlord had just returned from selling sheep at a fair, and with the extra money in the inn he hesitated to let her stay. But his heart would not allow him to turn her out and he directed his serving-maid to stay up with the woman until she had had her breakfast and departed.

The woman traveler sat by the hearth and the serving-maid tried unsuccessfully to sleep on a nearby settle. The woman traveler seemed to doze, but the serving-maid sensed that all was not right, and she watched the traveler while feigning sleep. As she watched with half-closed eyes, she saw the stranger move in her chair, stretching her legs to reveal what appeared to be male breeches and boots.

Knowing they had been deceived, she thought quickly and turned over as if settling into a more comfortable position. Then she pretended to snore gently. Soon the traveler stood up and took from a pocket a dead man's dried hand, set it on the table, and fitted a candle in it. After lighting the candle, the traveler held it over the serving girl and said, "Let them sleep who are asleep, and let them who are awake stay awake."

Then he set the Hand of Glory down on the table, drew back the window curtain, and said, "Flash out the flame, Hand of Glory."

The flame doubled in size and the robber opened the door and whistled to his companions who were waiting for his signal. Quietly the brave girl jumped up from the settle, slipped up behind him, and with all her strength pushed him out the door and down the steps. She slammed and barred the door and dashed upstairs to alert her master and mistress.

When her pounding did not raise them, she opened the door, rushed to their bed, and shook them roundly. But they slept on, seemingly in a trance. She tried to raise the master's adult son, but he also lay as if dead.

She could hear the stranger and his cohorts swearing and planning to break down the door. She quickly abandoned her efforts to wake anyone, and remembering the tales of the powers of the Hand of Glory she decided to return downstairs and somehow douse the candle in its gruesome holder. Dashing into the room she spied a bowl of fresh milk and threw its contents over the hand. The candle sputtered out.

At once, the family awakened and came downstairs to find the serving-girl who told them what had happened. The landlord's son took a gun and went to the window to speak with the men who were still lurking nearby. The traveler brazenly insisted that no harm had been done and that if the innkeeper would only return the hand there would be no more trouble. But the innkeeper refused, and when his son brandished the gun, the gang headed for the moors.

The gang was never seen again. The family celebrated the bravery of their serving-maid, but never revealed the fate of the Hand of Glory.

THE WOUNDED LION
(Spain)

here was once a girl so poor that she had nothing to live on, and wandered about the world asking for charity. One day she arrived at a thatched cottage, and inquired if they could give her any work. The farmer said he wanted a cowherd, as his own had left him, and if the girl liked the place she might take it. So she became a cowherd.

One morning she was driving her cows through the meadows when she heard nearby a loud groan that almost sounded human. She hastened to the spot from which the noise came, and found it proceeded from a lion who lay stretched upon the ground.

You can guess how frightened she was! But the lion seemed in such pain that she was sorry for him, and drew nearer and nearer till she saw he had a large thorn in one foot. She pulled out the thorn and bound up the place, and the lion was grateful, and licked her hand by way of thanks with his big rough tongue.

When the girl had finished she went back to find the cows, but they had gone, and though she hunted everywhere she never found them; and she had to return home and confess to her master, who scolded her bitterly, and afterwards beat her. Then he said, "Now you will have to look after the asses."

So every day she had to take the asses to the woods to feed, until one morning, exactly a year after she had found the lion, she heard a groan which sounded quite human. She went straight to the place from which the noise came, and, to her great surprise, beheld the same lion stretched on the ground with a deep wound across his face.

This time she was not afraid at all, and ran toward him, washing the wound and laying soothing herbs upon it; and when she had bound it up the lion thanked her in the same manner as before.

After that she returned to her flock, but they were nowhere to be seen. She searched here and she searched there, but they had vanished completely!

Then she had to go home and confess to her master, who first scolded her and afterward beat her. "Now go," he ended, "and look after the pigs!"

So the next day she took out the pigs, and found them such good feeding grounds that they grew fatter every day.

Another year passed by, and one morning when the maiden was out with her pigs she heard a groan which sounded quite human. She ran to see what it was, and found her old friend the lion, wounded through and through, fast dying under a tree.

She fell on her knees before him and washed his wounds one by one, and laid healing herbs upon them. And the lion licked her hands and thanked her, and asked if she would not stay and sit by him. But the girl said she had her pigs to watch, and she must go and see after them.

So she ran to the place where she had left them, but they had vanished as if the earth had swallowed them up. She whistled and called, but only the birds answered her.

Then she sank down on the ground and wept bitterly, not daring to return home until some hours had passed away.

And when she had had her cry out she got up and searched all up and down the wood. But it was no use; there was not a sign of the pigs.

At last she thought that perhaps if she climbed a tree she might see further. But no sooner was she seated on the highest branch than something happened which put the pigs quite out of her head. This was a handsome young man who was coming down the path; and when he had almost reached the tree he pulled aside a rock and disappeared behind it.

The maiden rubbed her eyes and wondered if she had been dreaming. Next she thought, "I will not stir from here till I see him come out, and discover who he is." Accordingly she waited, and at dawn the next morning the rock moved to one side and a lion came out.

When he had gone quite out of sight the girl climbed down from the tree and went to the rock, which she pushed aside, and entered the opening before her. The path led to a beautiful house. She went in, swept and dusted the furniture, and put everything tidy. Then she ate a very good dinner, which was on a shelf in the corner, and once more clambered up to the top of her tree.

As the sun set she saw the same young man walking gaily down the path, and, as before, he pushed aside the rock and disappeared behind it.

Next morning out came the lion. He looked sharply about him on all sides, but saw no one, and then vanished into the forest.

The maiden then came down from the tree and did exactly as she had done the day before. Thus three days went by, and every day she went and tidied up the palace. At length, when the girl found she was no nearer to discovering the secret, she resolved to ask him, and in the evening when she caught sight of him coming through the wood she came down from the tree and begged him to tell her his name.

The young man looked very pleased to see her, and said he thought it must be she who had secretly kept his house for so many days. And he added that he was a prince enchanted by a powerful giant, but was only allowed to take his own shape at night, for all day he was forced to appear as the lion whom she had so often helped; and, more than this, it was the giant who had stolen the oxen and the asses and the pigs in revenge for her kindness.

And the girl asked him, "What can I do to disenchant you?"

But he said he was afraid it was very difficult, because the only way was to get a lock of hair from the head of a king's daughter, to spin it, and to make from it a cloak for the giant, who lived up on the top of a high mountain.

"Very well," answered the girl, "I will go to the city, and knock at the door of the king's palace, and ask the princess to take me as a servant."

So they parted, and when she arrived at the city she walked about the street crying, "Who will hire me for a servant? Who will hire me for a servant?" But, though many people liked her looks, for she was clean and neat, the maiden would listen to none, and still continued crying, "Who will hire me for a servant? Who will hire me for a servant?"

At last there came the waiting-maid of the princess.

"What can you do?" she said; and the girl was forced to confess that she could do very little.

"Then you will have to do scullion's work, and wash up dishes," said she; and they went straight back to the palace.

Then the maiden dressed her hair afresh, and made herself look very neat and smart, and everyone admired and praised her, till by and by it came to the ears of the princess. And she sent for the girl, and when she saw her, and how beautifully she had dressed her hair, the princess told her she was to come and comb out hers.

Now the hair of the princess was very thick and long, and shone like the sun. And the girl combed it and combed it till it was brighter than ever. And the princess was pleased, and bade her come every day and comb her hair, till at length the girl took courage, and begged leave to cut off one of the long, thick locks.

The princess, who was very proud of her hair, did not like the idea of parting with any of it, so she said no. But the girl could not give up hope, and each day she entreated to be allowed to cut off just one tress. At length the princess lost patience, and exclaimed, "You may have it, then, on condition that you shall find the handsomest prince in the world to be my bridegroom!"

And the girl answered that she would, and cut off the lock, and wove it into a coat that glittered like silk, and brought it to the young man, who told her to carry it straight to the giant—but that she must be careful to cry out a long way off what she had with her, or else he would spring upon her and run her through with his sword.

So the maiden departed and climbed up the mountain, but before she reached the top the giant heard her footsteps, and rushed out breathing fire and flame, having a sword in one hand and a club in the other. But she cried loudly that she had brought him the coat, and then he grew quiet, and invited her to come into his house.

He tried on the coat, but it was too short, and he threw it off, and declared it was no use. And the girl picked it up sadly, and returned quite in despair to the king's palace.

The next morning, when she was combing the princess's hair, she begged leave to cut off another lock. At first the princess said no, but the girl begged so hard that at length she gave in on condition that she should find her a prince as bridegroom.

The maiden told her that she had already found him, and spun the lock into shining stuff, and fastened it onto the end of the coat. And when it was finished she carried it to the giant.

This time it fitted him, and he was quite pleased, and asked her what he could give her in return. And she said that the only reward he could give her was to take the spell off the lion and bring him back to his own shape.

For a long time the giant would not hear of it, but in the end he gave in, and told her exactly how it must all be done. She was to kill the lion herself and cut him up very small; then she must burn him, and cast his ashes into the water, and out of the water the prince would come free from enchantment for ever.

But the maiden went away weeping, lest the giant should have deceived her, and that after she had killed the lion she would find she had also slain the prince.

Weeping she came down the mountain, and weeping she joined the prince, who was awaiting her at the bottom; and when he had heard her story he comforted her, and bade her be of good courage, and to do the bidding of the giant.

And the maiden believed what the prince told her; and in the morning when he put on his lion's form she took a knife and slew him, and cut him up very small, and burnt him, and cast his ashes into the water, and out of the water came the prince, beautiful as the day, and as glad to look upon as the sun himself.

Then the young man thanked the maiden for all she had done for him, and said she should be his wife and none other. But the maiden only wept sore, and answered that that she could never be, for she had given her promise to the princess when she cut off her hair that the prince should wed her and her only.

But the prince replied, "If it is the princess, we must go quickly. Come with me."

So they went together to the king's palace. And when the king and queen and princess saw the young man a great joy filled their hearts, for they knew him for the eldest son, who had long ago been enchanted by a giant and lost to them.

And he asked his parents' consent that he might marry the girl who had saved him, and a great feast was made, and the maiden became a princess, and in due time a queen, and she richly deserved all the honors showered upon her.

THE FORTY THIEVES
(Arabia)

In a town in Persia there dwelt two brothers, one named Cassim, the other Ali Baba. Cassim was married to a rich wife and lived in plenty, while Ali Baba had to maintain his wife and children by cutting wood in a neighboring forest and selling it in the town. One day, when Ali Baba was in the forest, he saw a troop of men on horseback, coming toward him in a cloud of dust. He was afraid they were robbers, and climbed into a tree for safety. When they came up to him and dismounted, he counted forty of them. They unbridled their horses and tied them to trees. The finest man among them, whom Ali Baba took to be their captain, went a little way among some bushes, and said, "Open, Sesame!" so plainly that Ali Baba heard him. A door opened in the rocks, and having made the troop go in, he followed them, and the door shut again of itself. They stayed some time inside, and Ali Baba, fearing they might come out and catch him, was forced to sit patiently in the tree. At last the door opened again, and the forty thieves came out. As the captain went in last he came out first, and made them all pass by him; he then closed the door, saying, "Shut, Sesame!" Every man bridled his horse and mounted, the captain put himself at their head, and they returned as they came.

Then Ali Baba climbed down and went to the door concealed among the bushes, and said, "Open, Sesame!" and it flew open. Ali Baba, who expected a dull, dismal place, was greatly surprised to find it large and well lighted, and hollowed by the hand of man in the form of a vault, which received the light from an opening in the ceiling. He saw rich bales of merchandise—silk, stuff-brocades all piled together, and gold and silver in heaps, and money in leather purses. He went in and the door shut behind him. He did not look at the silver, but brought out as many bags of gold as he thought his asses, which were browsing outside, could carry, loaded them with the bags, and hid it all with fagots. With "Shut, Sesame!" he closed the door and went home.

Then he drove his asses into the yard, shut the gates, carried the money bags to his wife, and emptied them out before her. He bade her keep the secret, and he would go and bury the gold. "Let me first measure it," said his wife. "I will go borrow a measure of someone, while you dig the hole." So she ran to the wife of Cassim and borrowed a measure.

Knowing Ali Baba's poverty, the sister was curious to find out what sort of grain his wife wished to measure, and artfully put some suet at the bottom of the measure. Ali Baba's wife went home and set the measure on the heap of gold, and filled it and emptied it often, to her great content. She then carried it back to her sister, without noticing that a piece of gold was sticking to it, which Cassim's wife perceived directly her back was turned. She grew very curious, and said to Cassim when he came home, "Cassim, your brother is richer than you. He does not count his money, he measures it." He begged her to explain this riddle, which she did by showing him the piece of money and telling him where she found it. Then Cassim grew so envious that he could not sleep, and went to his brother in the morning before sunrise. "Ali Baba," he said, showing him the gold piece, "you pretend to be poor and yet you measure gold." By this Ali Baba perceived that through his wife's folly Cassim and his wife knew their secret, so he confessed all and offered Cassim a share. "That I expect," said Cassim; "but I must know where to find the treasure, otherwise I will discover all, and you will lose all." Ali Baba, more out of kindness than fear, told him of the cave, and the very words to use. Cassim left Ali Baba, meaning to be beforehand with him and get the treasure for himself. He rose early next morning, and set out with ten mules loaded with great chests. He soon found the place, and the door in the rock. He said, "Open, Sesame!" and the door opened and shut behind him. He could have feasted his eyes all day on the treasures, but he now hastened to gather together as much of it as possible; but when he was ready to go he could not remember what to say for thinking of his great riches. Instead of "Sesame," he said, "Open, Barley!" and the door remained fast. He named several different sorts of grain, all but the right one, and the door still stuck fast. He was so frightened at the danger he was in that he had as much forgotten the word as if he had never heard it.

About noon the robbers returned to their cave, and saw Cassims' mules roving about with great chests on their backs. This gave them the alarm: they drew their sabers, and went to the door, which opened on their captain's saying, "Open, Sesame!" Cassim, who had heard the trampling of their horses' feet, resolved to sell his life dearly, so when the door opened he leaped out and threw the captain down. In vain, however, for the robbers with their sabers soon killed him. On entering the cave they saw all the bags laid ready, and could not imagine how anyone had got in without knowing their secret. They cut Cassim's body into four quarters, and nailed them up inside the cave, in order to frighten anyone who should venture in, and went away in search of more treasure.

As night drew on Cassim's wife grew very uneasy, and ran to her brother-in-law, and told him where her husband had gone. Ali Baba did his best to comfort her, and set out to the forest in search of Cassim. The first thing he saw on entering the cave was his dead brother. Full of horror, he put the body on one of his asses, and bags of gold on the other two, and, covering all with some fagots, returned home. He drove the two asses laden with gold into his own yard, and led the other to Cassim's house. The door was opened by the slave Morgiana, whom he knew to be both brave and cunning. Unloading the ass, he said to her, "This is the body of your master, who has been murdered, but whom we must bury as though he had died in his bed. I will speak with you again, but now tell your mistress I am come." The wife of Cassim, on learning the fate of her husband, broke out into cries and tears, but Ali Baba offered to take her to live with him and his wife if she would promise to keep his counsel and leave everything to Morgiana; whereupon she agreed, and dried her eyes.

Morgiana, meanwhile, sought an apothecary and asked him for some lozenges. "My poor master," she said, "can neither eat nor speak, and no one knows what his distemper is." She carried home the lozenges and returned next day weeping, and asked for an essence only given to those just about to die. Thus, in the evening, no one was surprised to hear the wretched shrieks and cries of Cassim's wife and Morgiana, telling everyone that Cassim was dead. The day after Morgiana went to an old cobbler near the gates of the town who opened his stall early, put a piece of gold in his hand, and bade him follow her with his needle and thread. Having bound his eyes with a handkerchief, she took him to the room where the body lay, pulled off the bandage, and bade him sew the quarters together, after which she covered his eyes again and led him home. Then they buried Cassim, and Morgiana his slave followed him to the grave, weeping and tearing her hair, while Cassim's wife stayed at home uttering lamentable cries. Next day she went to live with Ali Baba, who gave Cassim's shop to his eldest son.

The forty thieves, on their return to the cave, were much astonished to find Cassim's body gone and some of their moneybags. "We are certainly discovered," said the captain, "and shall be undone if we cannot find out who it is that knows our secret. Two men must have known it; we have killed one, we must now find the other. To this end one of you who is bold and artful must go into the city dressed as a traveler, and discover whom we have killed, and whether men talk of the strange manner of his death. If the messenger fails he must lose his life, lest we be betrayed." One of the thieves started up and offered to do this, and after the rest had highly commended him for his bravery he disguised himself, and happened to enter the town at daybreak, just by Baba Mustapha's stall. The thief bade him good-day, saying, "Honest man, how can you possibly see to stitch at your old age?"

"Old as I am," replied the cobbler, "I have very good eyes, and you will believe me when I tell you that I sewed a dead body together in a place where I had less light than I have now."

The robber was overjoyed at his good fortune, and, giving him a piece of gold, desired to be shown the house where he stitched up the dead body. At first Mustapha refused, saying that he had been blindfolded;

but when the robber gave him another piece of gold he began to think he might remember the turnings if blindfolded as before. This means succeeded; the robber partly led him, and was partly guided by him, right in front of Cassim's house, the door of which the robber marked with a piece of chalk. Then, well pleased, he bade farewell to Baba Mustapha and returned to the forest. By and by Morgiana, going out, saw the mark the robber had made, quickly guessed that some mischief was brewing, and fetching a piece of chalk marked two or three doors on each side, without saying anything to her master or mistress.

The thief, meantime, told his comrades of his discovery. The captain thanked him, and bade him show him the house he had marked. But when they came to it they saw that five or six of the houses were chalked in the same manner. The guide was so confounded that he knew not what answer to make, and when they returned he was at once beheaded for having failed. Another robber was dispatched, and, having won over Baba Mustapha, marked the house in red chalk; but Morgiana being again too clever for them, the second messenger was put to death also. The captain now resolved to go himself, but, wiser than the others, he did not mark the house, but looked at it so closely that he could not fail to remember it. He returned, and ordered his men to go into the neighboring villages and buy nineteen mules, and thirty-eight leather jars, all empty, except one which was full of oil. The captain put one of his men, fully armed, into each, rubbing the outside of the jars with oil from the full vessel. Then the nineteen mules were loaded with thirty-seven robbers in jars, and the jar of oil, and reached the town by dusk. The captain stopped his mules in front of Ali Baba's house, and said to Ali Baba, who was sitting outside for coolness, "I have brought some oil from a distance to sell at tomorrow's market, but it is now so late that I know not where to pass the night, unless you will do me the favor to take me in." Though Ali Baba had seen the captain of the robbers in the forest, he did not recognize him in the disguise of an oil merchant. He bade him welcome, opened his gates for the mules to enter, and went to Morgiana to bid her prepare a bed and supper for his guest. He brought the stranger into his hall, and after they had supped went again to speak to Morgiana in the kitchen, while the captain went into the yard under pretense of seeing after his mules, but really to tell his men what to do. Beginning at the first jar and ending at the last, he said to each man, "As soon as I throw some stones from the window of the chamber where I lie, cut the jars open with your knives and come out, and I will be with you in a trice." He returned to the house, and Morgiana led him to his chamber. She then told Abdallah, her fellow slave, to set on the pot to make some broth for her master, who had gone to bed.

"Do not be uneasy," said Abdallah; "go into the yard and take some out of one of those jars."

Morgiana thanked him for his advice, took the oil pot, and went into the yard. When she came to the first jar the robber inside said softly, "Is it time?"

Any other slave but Morgiana, on finding a man in the jar instead of the oil she wanted, would have screamed and made a noise; but she, knowing the danger her master was in, bethought herself of a plan, and answered quietly, "Not yet, but presently." She went to all the jars, giving the same answer, till she came to the jar of oil. She now saw that her master, thinking to entertain an oil merchant, had let thirty-eight robbers into his house. She filled her oil pot, went back to the kitchen, and, having lit her lamp, went again to the oil jar and filled a large kettle full of oil. When it boiled she went and poured enough oil into every jar to stifle and kill the robber inside. When this brave deed was done she went back to the kitchen, put out the fire and the lamp, and waited to see what would happen.

In a quarter of an hour the captain of the robbers awoke, got up, and opened the window. As all seemed quiet he threw down some little pebbles which hit the jars. He listened, and as none of his men seemed to stir he grew uneasy, and went down into the yard. On going to the first jar and saying, "Are you asleep?" he smelt the hot boiled oil, and knew at once that his plot to murder Ali Baba and his household had been discovered. He found all the gang were dead, and, missing the oil out of the last jar, became aware of the manner of their death. He then forced the lock of a door leading into a garden, and climbing over several walls made his escape. Morgiana heard and saw all this, and, rejoicing at her success, went to bed and fell asleep.

At daybreak Ali Baba arose, and, seeing the oil jars there still, asked why the merchant had not gone with his mules. Morgiana bade him look in the first jar and see if there was any oil. Seeing a man, he started back in terror. "Have no fear," said Morgiana; "the man cannot harm you: he is dead." Ali Baba, when he had recovered somewhat from his astonishment, asked what had become of the merchant. "Merchant!" said she, "he is no more a merchant than I am!" and she told him the whole story, assuring him that it was a plot of the robbers of the forest, of whom only three were left, and that the white and red chalk marks had something to do with it. Ali Baba at once gave Morgiana her freedom, saying that he owed her his life. They then buried the bodies in Ala Baba's garden, while the mules were sold in the market by his slaves.

The captain returned to his lonely cave, which seemed frightful to him without his lost companions, and firmly resolved to avenge them by killing Ali Baba. He dressed himself carefully, and went into the town, where he took lodgings in an inn. In the course of a great many journeys to the forest he carried away many rich stuffs and much fine linen, and set up a shop opposite that of Ali Baba's son. He called himself Cogia Hassan, and as he was both civil and well dressed he soon made friends with Ali

Baba's son, and through him with Ali Baba, whom he was continually asking to sup with him. Ali Baba, wishing to return his kindness, invited him into his house and received him smiling, thanking him for his kindness to his son. When the merchant was about to take his leave Ali Baba stopped him, saying, "Where are you going, sir, in such haste? Will you not stay and sup with me?" The merchant refused, saying that he had a reason; and, on Ali Baba's asking him what that was, he replied, "It is, sir, that I can eat no victuals that have any salt in them." "If that is all," said Ali Baba, "let me tell you that there shall be no salt in either the meat or the bread that we eat tonight." He went to give this order to Morgiana, who was much surprised. "Who is this man," she said, "who eats no salt with his meat?" "He is an honest man, Morgiana," returned her master; "therefore do as I bid you." But she could not withstand a desire to see this strange man, so she helped Abdallah to carry up the dishes, and saw in a moment that Cogia Hassan was the robber captain, and carried a dagger under his garment. "I am not surprised," she said to herself, "that this wicked man, who intends to kill my master, will eat no salt with him; but I will hinder his plans."

She sent up the supper by Abdallah, while she made ready for one of the boldest acts that could be thought on. When the dessert had been served, Cogia Hassan was left alone with Ali Baba and his son, whom he thought to make drunk and then to murder them. Morgiana, meanwhile, put on a headdress like a dancing-girl's, and clasped a girdle round her waist, from which hung a dagger with a silver hilt, and said to Abdallah, "Take your tabor, and let us go and divert our master and his guest." Abdallah took his tabor and played before Morgiana until they came to the door, where Abdallah stopped playing and Morgiana made a low curtsy.

"Come in, Morgiana," said Ali Baba, "and let Cogia Hassan see what you can do"; and, turning to Cogia Hassan, he said, "She's my slave and my housekeeper." Cogia Hassan was by no means pleased, for he feared that his chance of killing Ali Baba was gone for the present; but he pretended great eagerness to see Morgiana, and Abdallah began to play and Morgiana to dance. After she had performed several dances she drew her dagger and made passes with it, sometimes pointing it at her own breast, sometimes as her master's, as if it were part of the dance. Suddenly, out of breath, she snatched the tabor from Abdallah with her left hand, and, holding the dagger in her right hand, held out the tabor to her master. Ali Baba and his son put a piece of gold into it, and Cogia Hassan, seeing that she was coming to him, pulled out his purse to make her a present, but while he was putting his hand into it Morgiana plunged the dagger into his heart.

"Unhappy girl!" cried Ali Baba and his son, "what have you done to ruin us?"

"It was to preserve you, master, not to ruin you," answered Morgiana. "See here," opening the false merchant's garment and showing the dagger;

"see what an enemy you have entertained! Remember, he would eat no salt with you, and what more would you have? Look at him! He is both the false oil merchant and the captain of the forty thieves."

Ali Baba was so grateful to Morgiana for thus saving his life that he offered her to his son in marriage, who readily consented, and a few days after the wedding was celebrated with great splendor. At the end of a year Ali Baba, hearing nothing of the two remaining robbers, judged they were dead, and set out to the cave. The door opened on his saying, "Open, Sesame!" He went in, and saw that nobody had been there since the captain left it. He brought away as much gold as he could carry, and returned to town. He told his son the secret of the cave, which his son handed down in his turn, so the children and grandchildren of Ali Baba were rich to the end of their lives.

THE MASTER-MAID
(Norway)

O nce upon a time there was a king who had many sons. I do not exactly know how many there were, but the youngest of them could not stay quietly at home, and was determined to go out into the world and try his luck, and after a long time the king was forced to give him leave to go. When he had traveled about for several days, he came to a giant's house, and hired himself to the giant as a servant. In the morning the giant had to go out to pasture his goats, and as he was leaving the house he told the king's son that he must clean out the stable. "And after you have done that," he said, "you need not do any more work today, for you have come to a kind master, and that you shall find. But what I set you to do must be done both well and thoroughly, and you must on no account go into any of the rooms which lead out of the room in which you slept last night. If you do, I will take your life."

"Well, to be sure, he is an easy master!" said the prince to himself as he walked up and down the room humming and singing, for he thought there would be plenty of time left to clean out the stable; "but it would be amusing to steal a glance into his other rooms as well," thought the prince, "for there must be something that he is afraid of my seeing, as I am not allowed to enter them." So he went into the first room. A cauldron was hanging from the walls; it was boiling, but the prince could see no fire under it. "I wonder what is inside it," he thought, and dipped a lock of his hair in, and the hair became just as if it were all made of copper. "That's a nice kind of soup. If anyone were to taste that his throat would be gilded," said the youth, and then he went into the next chamber. There, too, a cauldron was hanging from the wall, bubbling and boiling, but there was no fire under this either. "I will just try what this is like too," said the prince, thrusting another lock of his hair into it, and it came out silvered over. "Such costly soup is not to be had in my father's palace," said the prince; "but everything depends on how it tastes," and then he went into the third room. There, too, a cauldron was hanging from the wall, boiling, exactly the same as in the two other rooms, and the prince took pleasure in trying this also, so he dipped a lock of hair in, and it came out so brightly gilded that it shone again. "Some talk about going from bad to worse," said the prince; but this is better and better. If he boils gold here, what can

191

he boil in there?" He was determined to see, and went through the door into the fourth room. No cauldron was to be seen there, but on a bench someone was seated who was like a king's daughter, but, whosoever she was, she was so beautiful that never in the prince's life had he seen her equal.

"Oh! in heaven's name what are you doing here?" said she who sat upon the bench.

"I took the place of servant here yesterday," said the prince.

"May you soon have a better place, if you have come to serve here!" said she.

"Oh! but I think I have got a kind master," said the prince. "He has not given me hard work to do today. When I have cleaned out the stable I shall be done."

"Yes, but how will you be able to do that?" she asked again. "If you clean it out as other people do, ten pitchforksful will come in for every one you throw out. But I will teach you how to do it: you must turn your pitchfork upside down, and work with the handle, and then all will fly out of its own accord."

"Yes, I will attend to that," said the prince, and stayed sitting where he was the whole day, for it was soon settled between them that they would marry each other, he and the king's daughter; so the first day of his service with the giant did not seem long to him. But when evening was drawing near she said that it would now be better for him to clean out the stable before the giant came home. When he got there he had a fancy to try if what she had said were true, so he began to work in the same way that he had seen the stable-boys doing in his father's stables, but he soon saw that he must give up that, for when he had worked a very short time he had scarcely room left to stand. So he did what the princess had taught him, turned the pitchfork round, and worked with the handle, and in the twinkling of an eye the stable was as clean as if it had been scoured. When he had done that, he went back again into the room in which the giant had given him leave to stay, and there he walked backward and forward on the floor, and began to hum and to sing.

Then came the giant home with the goats. "Have you cleaned the stable?" asked the giant.

"Yes, now it is clean and sweet, master," said the king's son.

"I shall see about that," said the giant, and went round to the stable, but it was just as the prince had said.

"You have certainly been talking to my master-maid, for you never got that out of your own head," said the giant.

"Master-maid! What kind of a thing is that, master?" said the prince, making himself look as stupid as an ass; "I should like to see that."

"Well, you will see her quite soon enough," said the giant.

On the second morning the giant had again to go out with his goats, so he told the prince that on that day he was to fetch home his horse, which was out on the mountainside, and when he had done that he might rest himself for the remainder of the day, "for you have come to a kind master, and that you shall find," said the giant once more. "But do not go into any of the rooms that I spoke of yesterday, or I will wring your head off," said he, and then went away with his flock of goats.

"Yes, indeed, you are a kind master," said the prince; "but I will go in and talk to the master-maid again; perhaps before long she may like better to be mine than yours."

So he went to her. Then she asked him what he had to do that day.

"Oh! not very dangerous work, I fancy," said the king's son. "I have only to go up the mountainside after his horse."

"Well, how do you mean to set about it?" asked the master-maid.

"Oh! there is no great art in riding a horse home," said the king's son. "I think I must have ridden friskier horses before now."

"Yes, but it is not so easy a thing as you think to ride the horse home," said the master-maid; "but I will teach you what to do. When you go near it, fire will burst out of its nostrils like flames from a pine torch: but be very careful, and take the bridle which is hanging by the door there, and fling the bit straight into its jaws, and then it will become so tame that you will be able to do what you like with it." He said he would bear this in mind, and then he again sat in there the whole day by the master-maid, and they chatted and talked of one thing and another, but the first thing and the last now was, how happy and delightful it would be if they could but marry each other, and get safely away from the giant; and the prince would have forgotten both the mountainside and the horse if the master-maid had not reminded him of them as evening drew near, and said that now it would be better if he went to fetch the horse before the giant came. So he did this, and took the bridle which was hanging on a crook, and strode up the mountainside, and it was not long before he met with the horse, and fire and red flames streamed forth out of its nostrils. But the youth carefully watched his opportunity, and just as it was rushing at him with open jaws he threw the bit straight into its mouth, and the horse stood as quiet as a young lamb, and there was no difficulty at all in getting it home to the stable. Then the prince went back into his room again, and began to hum and to sing.

Toward evening the giant came home. "Have you fetched the horse back from the mountainside?" he asked.

"That I have, master; it was an amusing horse to ride, but I rode him straight home, and put him in the stable too," said the prince.

"I will see about that," said the giant, and went out to the stable, but the horse was standing there just as the prince had said. "You have certainly been talking with my master-maid, for you never got that out of your own head," said the giant again.

"Yesterday, master, you talked about this master-maid, and today you are talking about her; ah! heaven bless you, master, why will you not show me the thing? for it would be a real pleasure to me to see it," said the prince, who again pretended to be silly and stupid.

"Oh! you will see her quite soon enough," said the giant.

On the morning of the third day the giant again had to go into the wood with the goats. "Today you must go underground and fetch my taxes," he said to the prince. "When you have done this, you may rest for the remainder of the day, for you shall see what an easy master you have come to," and then he went away.

"Well, however easy a master you may be, you set me very hard work to do," thought the prince; "but I will see if I cannot find your master-maid; you say she is yours, but for all that she may be able to tell me what to do now," and he went to her. So, when the master-maid asked him what the giant had set him to do that day, he told her that he was to go underground and get the taxes.

"And how will you set about that?" said the master-maid.

"Oh! you must tell me how to do it," said the prince, "for I have never yet been underground, and even if I knew the way I do not know how much I am to demand."

"Oh! yes, I will soon tell you that; you must go to the rock there under the mountainridge, and take the club that is there, and knock on the rocky wall," said the master-maid. "Then someone will come out who will sparkle with fire: you shall tell him your errand, and when he asks you how much you want to have you are to say, 'As much as I can carry.' "

"Yes, I will keep that in mind," said he, and then he sat there with the master-maid the whole day, until night drew near, and he would gladly have stayed there till now if the master-maid had not reminded him that it was time to be off to fetch the taxes before the giant came.

So he set out on his way, and did exactly what the master-maid had told him. He went to the rocky wall, and took the club, and knocked on it. Then came one so full of sparks that they flew both out of his eyes and his nose. "What do you want?" said he.

"I was to come here for the giant, and demand the tax for him," said the king's son.

"How much are you to have then?" said the other.

"I ask for no more than I am able to carry with me," said the prince.

"It is well for you that you have not asked for a horse-load." said he who had come out of the rock. "But now come in with me."

This the prince did, and what a quantity of gold and silver he saw! It was lying inside the mountain like heaps of stones in a waste place, and he got a load that was as large as he was able to carry, and with that he went his way. So in the evening, when the giant came home with the goats, the prince went into the chamber and hummed and sang again as he had done on the other two evenings.

"Have you been for the tax?" said the giant.

"Yes, that I have, master," said the prince.

"Where have you put it then?" said the giant again.

"The bag of gold is standing there on the bench," said the prince.

"I will see about that," said the giant, and went away to the bench, but the bag was standing there, and it was so full that gold and silver dropped out when the giant untied the string.

"You have certainly been talking with my master-maid!" said the giant, "and if you have I will wring your neck."

"Master-maid?" said the prince; "yesterday my master talked about this master-maid, and today he is talking about her again, and the first day of all it was talk of the same kind. I do wish I could see the thing myself," said he.

"Yes, yes, wait till tomorrow," said the giant, "and then I myself will take you to her."

"Ah! master, I thank you—but you are only mocking me," said the king's son.

Next day the giant took him to the master-maid. "Now you shall kill him, and boil him in the great big cauldron you know of, and when you have got the broth ready give me a call," said the giant; then he lay down on the bench to sleep, and almost immediately began to snore so that it sounded like thunder among the hills.

So the master-maid took a knife, and cut the prince's little fingers, and dropped three drops of blood upon a wooden stool; then she took all the old rags, and shoe soles, and all the rubbish she could lay hands on, and put them in the cauldron; and then she filled a chest with gold dust, and a lump of salt, and a water flask which was hanging by the door, and she also took with her a golden apple, and two gold chickens; and then she and the prince went away with all the speed they could, and when they had gone a little way they came to the sea, and then they sailed, but where they got the ship from I have never been able to learn.

Now, when the giant had slept a good long time, he began to stretch himself on the bench on which he was lying. "Will it soon boil?" said he.

"It is just beginning," said the first drop of blood on the stool.

So the giant lay down to sleep again, and slept for a long, long time. Then he began to move about a little again. "Will it soon be ready now?" said he, but he did not look up this time any more than he had done the first time, for he was still half asleep.

"Half done!" said the second drop of blood, and the giant believed it was the master-maid again, and turned himself on the bench, and lay down to sleep once more. When he had slept again for many hours, he began to move and stretch himself. "Is it not done yet?" said he.

"It is quite ready," said the third drop of blood. Then the giant began to sit up, and rub his eyes, but he could not see who it was who had spoken to him, so he asked for the master-maid, and called her. But there was no one to give him an answer.

"Ah! well, she has just stolen out for a little," thought the giant, and he took a spoon, and went off to the cauldron to have a taste; but there was nothing in it but shoe soles, and rags, and such trumpery as that, and all was boiled up together, so that he could not tell whether it was porridge or milk pottage. When he saw this, he understood what had happened, and fell into such a rage that he hardly knew what he was doing. Away he went after the prince and the master-maid, so fast that the wind whistled behind him, and it was not long before he came to the water, but he could not get over it. "Well, well, I will soon find a cure for that: I have only to call my river-sucker," said the giant, and he did call him. So his river-sucker came and lay down, and drank one, two, three draughts, and with that the water in the sea fell so low that the giant saw the master-maid and the prince out on the sea in their ship. "Now you must throw out the lump of salt," said the master-maid, and the prince did so, and it grew up into such a great high mountain right across the sea that the giant could not come over it, and the river-sucker could not drink any more water. "Well, well, I will soon find a cure for that," said the giant, so he called to his hill-borer to come and bore through the mountain so that the river-sucker might be able to drink up the water again. But just as the hole was made, and the river-sucker was beginning to drink, the master-maid told the prince to throw one or two drops out of the flask, and when he did this the sea instantly became full of water again, and before the river-sucker could take one drink they reached the land and were in safety. So they determined to go home to the prince's father, but the prince would on no account permit the master-maid to walk there, for he thought that it was unbecoming either for her or for him to go on foot.

"Wait here the least little bit of time, while I go home for the seven horses that stand in my father's stable," said he; "it is not far-off, and I shall not be long away, but I will not let my betrothed bride go on foot to the palace."

"Oh! no, do not go, for if you go home to the king's palace you will forget me, I foresee that."

"How could I forget you? We have suffered so much evil together, and love each other so much," said the prince; and he insisted on going home for the coach with the seven horses, and she was to wait for him there, by the seashore. So at last the master-maid had to yield, for he was so absolutely determined to do it. "But when you get there you must not even give yourself time to greet anyone, but go straight into the stable, and take the horses, and put them in the coach, and drive back as quickly as you can. For they will all come round about you; but you must behave just as if you did not see them, and on no account must you taste anything, for if you do it will cause great misery both to you and to me," said she; and this he promised.

But when he got home to the king's palace one of his brothers was just going to be married, and the bride and all her kith and kin had come to the palace; so they all thronged round him, and questioned him about this and that, and wanted him to go in with them; but he behaved as if he did not see them, and went straight to the stable, and got out the horses and began to harness them. When they saw that they could not by any means prevail on him to go in with them, they came out to him with meat and drink, and the best of everything that they had prepared for the wedding; but the prince refused to touch anything, and would do nothing but put the horses in as quickly as he could. At last, however, the bride's sister rolled an apple across the yard to him, and said, "As you won't eat anything else, you may like to take a bite of that, for you must be both hungry and thirsty after your long journey." And he took up the apple and bit a piece out of it. But no sooner had he got the piece of apple in his mouth than he forgot the master-maid and that he was to go back in the coach to fetch her.

"I think I must be mad! What do I want with this coach and horses?" said he; and then he put the horses back into the stable, and went into the king's palace, and there it was settled that he should marry the bride's sister, who had rolled the apple to him.

The master-maid sat by the seashore for a long, long time, waiting for the prince, but no prince came. So she went away, and when she had walked a short distance she came to a little hut which stood all alone in a small wood, hard by the king's palace. She entered it and asked if she might be allowed to stay there. The hut belonged to an old crone, who was also an ill-tempered and malicious troll. At first she would not let the master-maid remain with her; but at last, after a long time, by means of good words and good payment, she obtained leave. But the hut was as dirty and black inside as a pigsty, so the master-maid said that she would smarten it up a little, that it might look a little more like what other people's houses looked inside. The old crone did not like this either. She scowled, and was very cross, but the master-maid did not trouble herself about that. She took out her chest of gold, and flung a handful of it or so into the fire, and the gold boiled up and poured out over the whole of the hut, until every part of it both inside and out was gilded. But when the gold began to bubble up the old hag grew so terrified that she fled away as if the Evil One himself were pursuing her, and she did not remember to stoop down as she went through the doorway, and so she split her head and died. Next morning the sheriff came traveling by there. He was greatly astonished when he saw the gold hut shining and glittering there in the copse, and he was still more astonished when he went in and caught sight of the beautiful young maiden who was sitting there; he fell in love with her at once, and straightway on the spot he begged her, both prettily and kindly, to marry him.

"Well, but have you a great deal of money?" said the master-maid.

"Oh! yes; so far as that is concerned, I am not ill off," said the sheriff. So now he had to go home to get the money, and in the evening he came back, bringing with him a bag with two bushels in it, which he set down on the bench. Well, as he had such a fine lot of money, the master-maid said she would have him, so they sat down to talk.

But scarcely had they sat down together before the master-maid wanted to jump up again. "I have forgotten to see to the fire," she said.

"Why should you jump up to do that?" said the sheriff; "I will do that!" So he jumped up, and went to the chimney in one bound.

"Just tell me when you have got hold of the shovel," said the master-maid.

"Well, I have hold of it now," said the sheriff.

"Then may you hold the shovel, and the shovel you, and pour red-hot coals over you, till day dawns," said the master-maid. So the sheriff had to stand there the whole night and pour red-hot coals over himself, and, no matter how much he cried and begged and entreated, the red-hot coals did not grow the colder for that. When the day began to dawn, and he had power to throw down the shovel, he did not stay long where he was, but ran away as fast as he possibly could; and everyone who met him stared and looked after him, for he was flying as if he were mad, and he could not have looked worse if he had been both flayed and tanned, and everyone wondered where he had been, but for very shame he would tell nothing.

The next day the attorney came riding by the place where the master-maid dwelt. He saw how brightly the hut shone and gleamed through the wood, and he too went into it to see who lived there, and when he entered and saw the beautiful young maiden he fell even more in love with her than the sheriff had done, and began to woo her at once. So the master-maid asked him, as she had asked the sheriff, if he had a great deal of money, and the attorney said he was not ill off for that, and would at once go home to get it; and at night he came with a great big sack of money—this time it was a four-bushel sack—and set it on the bench by the master-maid. So she promised to have him, and he sat down on the bench by her to arrange about it, but suddenly she said that she had forgotten to lock the door of the porch that night, and must do it.

"Why should you do that?" said the attorney; "sit still, I will do it."

So he was on his feet in a moment, and out in the porch.

"Tell me when you have got hold of the door latch," said the master-maid.

"I have hold of it now," cried the attorney.

"Then may you hold the door, and the door you, and may you go between wall and wall till day dawns."

What a dance the attorney had that night! He had never had such a waltz before, and he never wished to have such a dance again. Sometimes he was in front of the door, and sometimes the door was in front of him, and it went from one side of the porch to the other, till the attorney was well-nigh beaten to death. At first he began to abuse the master-maid, and then to beg and pray, but the door did not care for anything but keeping him where he was till break of day.

As soon as the door let go its hold of him, off went the attorney. He forgot who ought to be paid off for what he had suffered, he forgot both his sack of money and his wooing, for he was so afraid lest the house door should come dancing after him. Everyone who met him stared and looked after him, for he was flying like a madman, and he could not have looked worse if a herd of rams had been butting at him all night long.

On the third day the bailiff came by, and he too saw the gold house in the little wood, and he too felt that he must go and see who lived there; and when he caught sight of the master-maid he became so much in love with her that he wooed her almost before he greeted her.

The master-maid answered him as she had answered the other two, that if he had a great deal of money she would have him. "So far as that is concerned, I am not ill off," said the bailiff; so he was at once told to go home and fetch it, and this he did. At night he came back, and he had a still larger sack of money with him than the attorney had brought; it must have been at least six bushels, and he set it down on the bench. So it was settled that he was to have the master-maid. But hardly had they sat down together before she said that she had forgotten to bring in the calf, and must go out to put it in the byre.

"No, indeed, you shall not do that," said the bailiff; "I am the one to do that." And, big and fat as he was, he went out as briskly as a boy.

"Tell me when you have got hold of the calf's tail," said the master-maid.

"I have hold of it now," cried the bailiff.

"Then may you hold the calf's tail, and the calf's tail hold you, and may you go round the world together till day dawns!" said the master-maid. So the bailiff had to bestir himself, for the calf went over rough and smooth, over hill and dale, and, the more the bailiff cried and screamed, the faster the calf went. When daylight began to appear, the bailiff was half dead; and so glad was he to leave loose of the calf's tail that he forgot the sack of money and all else.

He walked more slowly—more slowly than the sheriff and the attorney had done, but, the slower he went, the more time had everyone to stare and look at him; and they used it too, and no one can imagine how tired out and ragged he looked after his dance with the calf.

On the following day the wedding was to take place in the king's palace, and the elder brother was to drive to church with his bride, and the brother who had been with the giant with her sister. But when they had seated themselves in the coach and were about to drive off from the palace one of the trace-pins broke, and, though they made one, two, and three to put in its place, that did not help them, for each broke in turn, no matter what kind of wood they used to make them of. This went on for a long time, and they could not get away from the palace, so they were all in great trouble. Then the sheriff said (for he too had been bidden to the wedding at Court): "Yonder away in the thicket dwells a maiden, and if you can but get her to lend you the handle of the shovel that she uses to make up her fire I know very well that it will hold fast." So they sent off a messenger to the thicket, and begged so prettily that they might have the loan of her shovel-handle of which the sheriff had spoken that they were not refused; so now they had a trace-pin which would not snap in two.

But all at once, just as they were starting, the bottom of the coach fell in pieces. They made a new bottom as fast as they could, but, no matter how they nailed it together, or what kind of wood they used, no sooner had they got the new bottom into the coach and were about to drive off than it broke again, so that they were still worse off than when they had broken the trace-pin. Then the attorney said, for he too was at the wedding in the palace: "Away there in the thicket dwells a maiden, and if you could but get her to lend you one-half of her porch-door I am certain that it will hold together." So they again sent a messenger to the thicket, and begged so prettily for the loan of the gilded porch-door of which the attorney had told them that they got it at once. They were just setting out again, but now the horses were not able to draw the coach. They had six horses already, and now they put in eight, and then ten, and then twelve, but the more they put in, and the more the coachman whipped them, the less good it did; and the coach never stirred from the spot. It was already beginning to be late in the day, and to church they must and would go, so everyone who was in the palace was in a state of great distress. Then the bailiff spoke up and said: "Out there in the gilded cottage in the thicket dwells a girl, and if you could but get her to lend you her calf I know it could draw the coach, even if it were as heavy as a mountain." They all thought that it was ridiculous to be drawn to church by a calf, but there was nothing else for it but to send a messenger once more, and beg as prettily as they could, on behalf of the king, that she would let them have the loan of the calf that the bailiff had told them about. The master-maid let them have it immediately — this time also she would not say "no."

Then they harnessed the calf to see if the coach would move; and away it went, over rough and smooth, over stock and stone, so that they could scarcely breathe, and sometimes they were on the ground, and sometimes up in the air; and when they came to the church the coach began to go round and round like a spinning wheel, and it was with the utmost difficulty and danger that they were able to get out of the coach and into the church. And when they went back again the coach went quicker still, so that most of them did not know how they got back to the palace at all.

When they had seated themselves at the table the prince who had been in service with the giant said that he thought they ought to have invited the maiden who had lent them the shovel handle, and the porch door, and the calf up to the palace, "for," said he, "if we had not got these three things, we should never have got away from the palace."

The king also thought that this was both just and proper, so he sent five of his best men down to the gilded hut, to greet the maiden courteously from the king, and to get her to be so good as to come up to the palace to dinner at midday.

"Greet the king, and tell him that, if he is too good to come to me, I am too good to come to him," replied the master-maid.

So the king had to go himself, and the master-maid went with him immediately, and, as the king believed that she was more than she appeared to be, he seated her in the place of honor by the youngest bridegroom. When they had sat at table for a short time, the master-maid took out the cock, and the hen, and the golden apple which she had brought away with her from the giant's house, and set them on the table in front of her, and instantly the cock and the hen began to fight with each other for the golden apple.

"Oh! look how those two there are fighting for the golden apple," said the king's son.

"Yes, and so did we two fight to get out that time when we were in the mountain," said the master-maid.

So the prince knew her again, and you may imagine how delighted he was. He ordered the troll-witch who had rolled the apple to him to be torn in pieces between four-and-twenty horses, so that not a bit of her was left, and then for the first time they began really to keep the wedding, and, weary as they were, the sheriff, the attorney, and the bailiff kept it up too.

UBAZAKURA
(Japan)

Three hundred years ago, in the village called Asamimura, in the district called Onsengori, in the province of Iyo, there lived a good man named Tokubei. This Tokubei was the richest person in the district and headman of the village as well. In most matters he was fortunate, but he had reached the age of forty without knowing the happiness of becoming a father. Therefore he and his wife, in the affliction of their childlessness, addressed many prayers to the divinity Fudo-Sama, who had a famous temple called Saihoji in Asamimura. At last their prayers were heard. The wife of Tokubei gave birth to a daughter. The child was very pretty, and she received the name of O-Tsuyu. A nurse called O-Sodé was hired for the little one.

O-Tsuyu grew up to be a very beautiful girl, but at the age of fifteen she fell ill and the doctors thought she was going to die. The nurse O-Sodé, who loved O-Tsuyu with a real mother's love, went to the temple Saihoji and fervently prayed to Fudo-Sama on behalf of the girl. Every day for twenty-one days she went to the temple and prayed, and at the end of that time O-Tsuyu suddenly and completely recovered. There was great rejoicing in the house of Tokubei, and he gave a feast to all his friends in celebration of the happy event. But on the night of the feast the nurse O-Sodé was suddenly taken ill, and on the following morning, the doctor who had been summoned to attend her announced that she was dying.

The family in great sorrow gathered about her bed to bid her farewell. But she said to them, "It is time that I should tell you something. My prayer has been heard. I besought Fudo-Sama that I might be permitted to die in the place of O-Tsuyu, and this great favor has been granted to me. Therefore you must not grieve for my death; but I have one request to make. I promised Fudo-Sama that I would have a cherry tree planted in the garden of Saihoji for an offering of thanks and a commemoration. Now I shall not be able to plant the tree there myself, so I must ask you to fulfill that vow for me. Goodbye, dear friends, and remember that I was happy to die for O-Tsuyu's sake."

After the funeral of O-Sodé, a young cherry tree, the finest that could be found, was planted in the garden of Saihoji by the parents of O-Tsuyu. The tree grew and flourished, and on the sixteenth day of the second month of the following year, the anniversary of O'Sodé's death, it blossomed in a wonderful way. And so it continued to blossom every year on this same date for two hundred and fifty-four years, always upon the sixteenth day of the second month, and its flowers, pink and white, were the most beautiful ever seen.

The people called it *Ubazakura*, the Cherry Tree of the Nurse.

W·I·V·E·S A·N·D M·O·T·H·E·R·S
Devoted and Cunning

KUMBA AND KAMBILI
(Africa)

Each night when the sky turned dark, the Malinke people cowered in their huts. An evil magician who nightly transformed into a lion was creeping into villages, killing and devouring the people.

Messengers from each village appealed to the great warrior Kambili to find and kill the lion-man before he could claim more victims.

"Great Kambili, save our people. Find this terrible lion-man and kill him. You are brave and can succeed!"

Kambili responded, "It shall be done."

Though renowned as a warrior, Kambili first had to determine the identity of the lion-man, and obtaining such knowledge required magic. Kumba, his clever and resourceful wife, was skilled in all manner of magic. At Kambili's request she cast her spells and sang her questing songs to the unseen spirits. Her efforts were rewarded and the spirits murmured their answers into her ear. She shared these with her husband.

"I have learned who the dreadful lion-man is, but he will not be easily killed. He is a wizard of great power and it will take far greater magic than mine to slay him."

Kambili thoughtfully considered her words. Then he said, "We must go ask Bari, the Truth Seeker, what to do. He is the finest magician, with great wisdom. He will guide us."

The ancient Truth Seeker listened carefully to Kumba and Kambili and then told them what to do.

"You will need to obtain hair from the lion-man's head and a sandal from his foot and bury both deep in the earth before the idol of Nya-ji. Nya-ji will then tell you how to vanquish the lion-man."

Kambili was dismayed at the thought of trying to obtain the hair and sandal, but Kumba had thought of a plan. "I will go to his hut and tell him I have fallen in love with him. I will offer to cook his dinner and then slip into his food a potion that will make him sleep. Then I will remove a lock of his hair, take a sandal, and return to you."

Kambili became even more disheartened at the thought of Kumba being in such danger. But Kumba assured him that she would take great care. Soon she left in search of the magician.

Kumba found the evil magician sitting outside his hut. She told him, "Although you never realized it, I have seen you and grown to love you. My greatest desire is to be the wife of such a noble and mighty man. May I cook for you? You will then know what a fine wife I could be."

The evil magician was flattered at this beautiful woman's attentions and rose to let her enter his hut. Kumba made herself busy preparing an attractive feast, adding the sleeping potion to the most tempting portion. As he ate, he praised her skills and promised that indeed she would be his bride.

In time he became drowsy and soon after he fell into a deep sleep. Kumba cautiously trimmed off a strand of hair, removed a sandal, and slipped out of the hut to return to Kambili.

As Kumba greeted Kambili she showed him the sandal and hair, and they rejoiced at her success and safe return. Kambili took his spear along to prepare a deep hole in front of the idol of Nya-ji, a figure of a man carved out of a tree trunk. After setting the hair and sandal in the hole, he filled the hole with the earth.

As they finished, the idol spoke in a deep voice. "To slay this man you must lure him to the grove of trees near the village of Jimini. Only there can you successfully slay him." The voice spoke no more.

Kambili turned to Kumba and asked, "What would bring the lion-man to that grove? We must think of what to do."

"Hunters in search of a lion lure it by tying a young goat to a tree and awaiting the lion. Since the lion-man seeks human flesh, we must use human bait. We will go to the grove and I will entice him with my enchanted song. You will hide and when he approaches you can kill him."

Kambili was gravely distressed. "I cannot risk your life. The danger is too great."

"But you will be the one at risk. You will have to slay this ruthless lion. If you are bold enough to fight this beast, I am brave enough to set the trap."

After some thought, Kambili saw no alternative and agreed to the plan. They went directly to the grove near Jimini, arriving at sunset. Kumba leaned against a tree while Kambili hid himself in the bushes.

As they waited for nightfall they watched the sky transform from a hazy blue to a blushing pink. Finally a dusky black was lightened by a radiant moon and shimmering stars.

Knowing that the lion-man would soon be about, Kumba began to sing a magical song about her solitary presence in the grove. The enchantment stirred the air, and the song drifted to where the beast prowled. The melody told the lion of a delectable morsel, readily taken in the grove of trees.

The lion crept across the plain, drooling in his greed, but taking care to send ahead a magic spell of sleep. Kumba's song of magic provided her with protection, but Kambili could not resist the heaviness that swept over him. As a cloud drifted across the moon, his head dropped on his chest, and he was lost in sleep.

Kumba sensed that the lion was near, and as the moonlight returned she saw him lurking between the trees. His eyes glistened as he watched her ravenously.

Kumba called softly to alert Kambili, and as she stopped singing she realized the tremendous strength of the lion-man's spell. As the lion's tail lazily swung back and forth, Kumba knew that Kambili was lost to her unless she could break the spell of sleep. As the lion crouched for its attack, Kumba sang a spell to awaken Kambili.

As Kambili's eyes opened he was jolted awake by the sight of the lion who was preparing to leap upon Kumba. Kambili bounded from the bushes, howling in rage, and threw himself in front of Kumba. As Kambili raised his spear, the ravenous beast seemed to hover above him, teeth dripping and claws spread to tear at its prey. Unable to check itself, the lion's leap gave Kambili the advantage, and he thrust his spear through the lion's chest and into its heart. The immense beast thudded to the ground and lay still. As Kumba and Kambili anxiously watched, the lion's body returned to the form of the feared evil magician, now also dead.

Wearily, Kambili and Kumba returned to their village to announce that the villagers could once again sleep without fear. They honored both Kambili and Kumba, for without Kumba's skill and cleverness the brave Kambili could not have slain the dreaded lion-man.

PRINCESS SIVATRA
(India)

There was once a noble and honorable king of a region of India. Ahapati was beloved by the people he ruled. His happiness would have been complete, except that he had no children. The goddess Siva took pity on him, however, and she came to King Ahapati telling him that he and his wife would be blessed with a daughter by the year's end.

The year passed quickly, made pleasant by the anticipation of the royal birth. When the baby arrived, the king named her Sivatra in honor of the goddess Siva. Sivatra's childhood was happy, and she basked in the love of her parents.

Soon Sivatra was eighteen and it was time for her to journey into the forest to learn from those who lived among nature in peace and harmony. When Sivatra returned from her sojourn, she went to her father in the palace.

"My dear father," Sivatra said, "while I was in the forest I met the exiled king Yumatsena. His enemies left him poor and blind. He lives with his son Sayavan. I have fallen in love with him."

The king knew this unfortunate, though admirable, royal family and was delighted that his daughter had chosen so worthy a husband. But before he offered his blessing, he called his advisor to him, asking him if he thought the match was wise.

"My noble king," the counselor replied, "I regret what I must tell you. Last night the goddess Siva came to me in a dream. Sayavan has but one year to live. Sivatra is doomed to grief if she makes this match."

The king said to Sivatra, "Dear daughter of mine, I want your life to be happy. You are too young to become a widow. Find yourself a healthy man."

But Sivatra was unyielding. "Father, it matters not to me how much time we have together. An hour of happiness with my love is worth more to me than a lifetime with another."

From the day of Sivatra's birth, the king had only wanted her to be happy, and he could not deny her the right to marry Sayavan. In a short time they were wed in the beauty of the forest where they had met.

211

At the time of their marriage a year seemed very far away, but the days and nights of happiness passed all too quickly. They lived simply, and though Sivatra treasured each fleeting hour the year was drawing to a close. Soon there were only four days left. Sivatra decided to appeal to the gods for mercy.

She went to the forest where she had met her love and stood quietly in prayerful meditation. Several hours passed. Sayavan came in search of her and upon finding her asked why she was standing in the forest.

"My love, I cannot tell you more than this. I will be standing here for four days and nights. It is something I must do in offering to the gods. I will tell you no more."

Sayavan was dismayed and pleaded with her to share with him why she had taken on such a futile task, but her determination and silence were unwavering.

Night fell, and Sivatra continued to stand. She whispered to the gods that she would continue her vigil until her prayers were answered. The sunrise was beautiful. Still Sivatra continued to wait for her miracle. Soon it was the last sunrise.

Not realizing that his last day on earth had arrived, Sayavan came to Sivatra. "My dear wife, you have not had rest or food for these past four days and nights. Please let me take you home to rest. Then I will gather some sweet fruit for you to eat."

"Dear husband," said Sivatra, "my only wish is to have this day with you. Let me come with you and we will gather fruit together."

Seeing that she would have no other way, Sayavan allowed her to come with him. As they walked through the forest they listened to the soft quietness and enjoyed the early morning sunshine. After collecting enough fruit for their meal, Sayavan persuaded Sivatra to rest while he gathered some firewood. As she listened to him chop the wood she prayed that her fears were groundless.

Suddenly Sayavan turned to her and whispered, "My dear, I can hardly see you. My head hurts dreadfully. I must rest." And he fell into a deep sleep.

Sivatra knew that the year was now truly drawing to a close. She trembled as she lifted her beloved's head onto her lap and stroked his forehead.

A moment later she looked up to see a frightful figure looming over him. She eased Sayavan's head onto the ground and stood to face the intruder.

"Who are you? You are not of this world, are you?" she demanded bravely.

"Your bravery is foolish, but you are correct. I am Yama, the god of the dead and I am here for your husband."

As Sivatra watched, her beloved took his last breath. As Yama turned to leave with Sayavan's soul, Sivatra ran past him and stood in front of his path.

"Be gone with you," he roared. "Return to your home. His life is done."

"I will not go home. My life is with Sayavan. I will follow him—and you—wherever you go."

Yama knew of her four-day sacrifice and was not untouched by her devotion. "I cannot give back Sayavan's life, but I can give you a wish. What would it be?"

"Sayavan's father is blind. Can you give him back his sight?"

"It is done. Now go," said Yama.

But Sivatra held her ground in front of Yama.

"I will grant you another wish. Then you must go."

"Sayavan's father has been exiled for years. Give him back his empire."

"Consider it done. Now move away," said Yama.

But Sivatra would not leave, though fatigue pulled at her.

"Make a third wish," said Yama. "Then leave me to my task."

"My father has no son. Give him a son."

"It is done," said Yama.

Though she swayed with exhaustion, Sivatra continued to stand in Yama's path.

Yama was annoyed by her determination, but he admired her strength.

"You may have a fourth wish," he offered indifferently.

"I want a son," Sivatra stated.

"So you shall have a son. But now you must let me by and you must return to your home."

He pushed her aside and set off down the path. Sivatra wept with dismay and weariness, but she followed along behind him, pleading that he grant her a last wish. Yama became so distracted and distraught at her grief that he stopped and faced her.

"Your devotion is beyond my understanding. I will grant you one last wish, any that you desire."

"Give my husband back to me," she cried.

"It is done," he said, and disappeared.

Sivatra ran back to her husband, and cradled him in her arms. The color began to return to his face and his eyes fluttered open.

"What has happened? Have I been asleep?"

Sivatra's eyes filled with tears. "You were only resting a bit. Let us go home, my dear."

Sayavan rose and joined Sivatra as they walked slowly through the darkening forest. As they returned to their home they were greeted by Yumatsena with the joyous news that he could once again see. Within a short time a messenger arrived to announce that the enemy king had been overthrown and Yumatsena was expected to resume his rightful rule.

"This is truly a night of miracles!" the king proclaimed.

Sivatra thought of all that had happened and knew that even though she had not lost Sayavan as foretold, she would continue to treasure each passing moment with her beloved.

THE SPRIG OF ROSEMARY
(Spain)

Once there was a man who made his daughter work very hard all day long. He sent her out into the woods one day to gather kindling, and as she was collecting leaves and twigs she happened upon a rosemary plant. She decided it would brighten up her home and pulled at a sprig of it. But the plant resisted her efforts until she used all her strength and pulled up the entire plant.

"Why did you come to steal my firewood?" asked a voice.

She turned to see a handsome young man standing by her and was so bewildered that she could only mumble a few words about her father sending her out to gather kindling.

He bade her to follow him and led her through the opening made by the uprooted rosemary plant. They traveled underground, visiting about this and that, till they came to a splendid palace. Then he told her that he was a lord and that he would be pleased if she would marry him. Realizing that her life would be much better than her former miserable existence and that this young lord was quite congenial, she agreed to his proposal. Soon they were married.

The lord had a housekeeper who gave the girl the keys to the house, cautioning her that she was to never use one particular key to open a chest. If she did it would be the ruination of them all. The girl promised, but the presence of the key tugged at her mind. One day she could no longer resist the need to learn what was in the chest and she inserted the key and carefully lifted the lid.

Inside she found a serpent's skin. She naturally did not know that her husband was a magician who used the skin for his sorcery. The sight of the skin made her feel ill, but before she could close the chest, the earth trembled, the palace vanished, and she found herself in the middle of a field.

By this time she had fallen deeply in love with the young lord, and she reviled herself for having been so foolish. Seeing a rosemary bush nearby, she broke off a sprig and decided she would never rest until she had found her husband, given him the sprig, and asked his forgiveness for her foolishness.

She set out, walking until she came to a small house. She asked if they could use a servant and was told she could stay with them. Her sadness became so obvious that her mistress asked her why she grieved. The girl told her what had happened and how she intended to search the world until she found her husband.

The mistress of the house said, "You must go to the sun, the moon, and the wind and ask them where he is. They go everywhere and know what is happening in the world."

The girl set out again, walking until she came to the golden castle of the sun. She knocked on the door, saying "Oh sun, I have come to ask for your help. Through my own foolishness I have lost my husband." And she told him her story.

The sun could not tell her where to find her husband, but he did give her a nut, telling her to open it only when she was in great need.

The girl thanked him and left, searching for the castle of the moon. When she arrived, an old woman answered her knock and the girl told her of her quest. The moon came out and listened to her story, though she had watched her at night and knew of her plight. She was also unable to tell her where to find her husband, but she gave her an almond to open when she was in great need.

The girl left in search of the wind and after much walking came to his castle. She told him her story, and the wind was sorry for her. He could not help her except to give her a walnut to use when she was in great need.

The wind seemed to be her last chance and her disappointment overwhelmed her. She sat down and began to weep. The wind was so distressed that he told her he would set out and try to learn something that might help her. With a great bluster he departed, and in the blink of an eye he was back.

"I have learned something of great importance," he announced with glee. "Your husband has been hidden in the palace of a king who intends to marry him to his ill-tempered daughter tomorrow. He is under a spell that has made him forget his past."

"Can you help me, dear wind? Would you do all you can to delay the wedding? Then perhaps I can rescue my dear husband."

The wind whisked off to the palace, arriving much faster than the girl. He blew into the room where the tailors prepared the wedding costumes. He scattered all the laces and trims out through the windows. The tailors tried to recover them, but it was soon clear that they would have to begin again.

The king decided that his daughter would have to marry in whatever sort of dress could be pieced together, but the result was so dismal that he agreed to delay the ceremony.

Meanwhile the girl had arrived at the castle. Before knocking she cracked the nut and drew out of it the most beautiful veil ever created.

When the door was opened she asked, "Ask the princess if she would like this veil for her wedding."

Upon seeing the veil, the princess was elated because hers had been destroyed by the wind's prank. She asked how much the girl wanted for the veil and willingly paid her a handsome sum.

When the princess left, the girl cracked open the almond and drew out from it the most splendid petticoats ever seen. She knocked again, asking if the princess would like to buy her petticoats.

As soon as the princess saw the petticoats she asked what the girl wanted for them. The girl named an even more costly sum, but the princess was delighted to pay it for the petticoats.

When the princess had departed, the girl cracked open her walnut and out came a dress of great brilliance and beauty. She knocked at the door once again, inquiring as to whether the princess wished to buy this glorious dress.

The princess was thrilled with the dress, and she immediately asked the girl what her price was.

This time the girl did not ask for gold. Instead she stated that she wanted to see the groom. This did not please the princess, but she so wanted the dress that she decided it was an easy request to fulfill.

Thus the girl was led to the room where her husband was held. She found him sleeping and touched him with the sprig of rosemary she still carried. The spell was broken and he woke and recognized her. He called for the king, telling him that she was his true wife. They went back to the girl's home where they were happy through their old age.

KING LINDORM
(Sweden)

There once lived a king and a queen who ruled over a very great kingdom. They had large revenues, and lived happily with each other; but, as the years went past, the king's heart became heavy, because the queen had no children. She also sorrowed greatly over it, because, although the king said nothing to her about this trouble, yet she could see that it vexed him that they had no heir to the kingdom; and she wished every day that she might have one.

One day a poor old woman came to the castle and asked to speak with the queen. The royal servants answered that they could not let such a poor beggar-woman go in to their royal mistress. They offered her a penny, and told her to go away. Then the woman desired them to tell the queen that there stood at the palace gate one who would help her secret sorrow. This message was taken to the queen, who gave orders to bring the old woman to her. This was done, and the old woman said to her, "I know your secret sorrow, O queen, and am come to help you in it. You wish to have a son; you shall have two if you follow my instructions."

The queen was greatly surprised that the old woman knew her secret wish so well, and promised to follow her advice.

"You must have a bath set in your room, O queen," said she, "and filled with running water. When you have bathed in this you will find under the bath two red onions. These you must carefully peel and eat, and in time your wish will be fulfilled."

The queen did as the poor woman told her; and after she had bathed she found the two onions under the bath. They were alike in size and appearance. When she saw these she knew that the woman had been something more than she seemed to be, and in her delight she ate up one of the onions, skin and all. When she had done so she remembered that the woman had told her to peel them carefully before she ate them. It was now too late for the one of them, but she peeled the other and then ate it too.

In due time it happened as the woman had said; but the first that the queen gave birth to was a hideous lindorm, or serpent. No one saw this but her waiting-woman, who threw it out of the window into the forest beside the castle. The next that came into the world was the most beautiful little prince, and he was shown to the king and queen, who knew nothing about his brother the lindorm.

221

There was now joy in all the palace and over the whole country on account of the beautiful prince; but no one knew that the queen's first-born was a lindorm, and lay in the wild forest. Time passed with the king, the queen, and the young prince in all happiness and prosperity, until he was twenty years of age. Then his parents said to him that he should journey to another kingdom and seek for himself a bride, for they were beginning to grow old, and would fain see their son married before they were laid in their grave. The prince obeyed, had his horses harnessed to his gilded chariot, and set out to woo his bride. But when he came to the first crossroads there lay a huge and terrible lindorm right across the road, so that his horses had to come to a standstill.

"Where are you driving to?" asked the lindorm with a hideous voice.

"That does not concern you," said the prince. "I am the prince, and can drive where I please."

"Turn back," said the lindorm. "I know your errand, but you shall get no bride until I have got a mate and slept by her side."

The prince turned home again, and told the king and the queen what he had met at the crossroads; but they thought that he should try again on the following day, and see whether he could not get past it, so that he might seek a bride in another kingdom.

The prince did so, but got no further than the first crossroads; there lay the lindorm again, who stopped him in the same way as before.

The same thing happened on the third day when the prince tried to get past: the lindorm said, with a threatening voice, that before the prince could get a bride he himself must find a mate.

When the king and queen heard this for the third time they could think of no better plan than to invite the lindorm to the palace, and they would find him a mate. They thought that a lindorm would be quite well satisfied with anyone that they might give him, and so they would get some slave-woman to marry the monster. The lindorm came to the palace and received a bride of this kind, but in the morning she lay torn in pieces. So it happened every time that the king and queen compelled any woman to be his bride.

The report of this soon spread over all the country. Now it happened that there was a man who had married a second time, and his wife heard of the lindorm with great delight. Her husband had a daughter by his first wife who was more beautiful than all other maidens, and so gentle and good that she won the hearts of all who knew her. His second wife, however, had also a grown-up daughter, who by herself would have been ugly and disagreeable enough, but beside her good and beautiful stepsister seemed still more ugly and wicked, so that all turned from her with loathing.

The stepmother had long been annoyed that her husband's daughter was so much more beautiful than her own, and in her heart she conceived a bitter hatred for her stepdaughter. While she now heard that there was in the king's palace a lindorm which tore in pieces all the women that were married to him, and demanded a beautiful maiden for his bride, she went to the king, and said that her stepdaughter wished to wed the lindorm, so that the country's only prince might travel and seek a bride. At this the king was greatly delighted, and gave orders that the young girl should be brought to the palace.

When the messengers came to fetch her she was terribly frightened, for she knew that it was her wicked stepmother who in this way was aiming at her life. She begged that she might be allowed to spend another night in her father's house. This was granted her, and she went to her mother's grave. There she lamented her hard fate in being given over to the lindorm, and earnestly prayed to her mother for counsel. How long she lay there by the grave and wept one cannot tell, but sure it is that she fell asleep and slept until the sun rose. Then she rose up from the grave, quite happy at heart, and began to search about in the fields. There she found three nuts, which she carefully put away in her pocket.

"When I come into very great danger I must break one of these," she said to herself. Then she went home, and set out quite willingly with the king's messengers.

When these arrived at the palace with the beautiful young maiden everyone pitied her fate; but she herself was of good courage, and asked the queen for another bridal chamber than the one the lindorm had had before. She got this, and then she requested them to put a pot full of strong lye on the fire and lay down three new scrubbing brushes. The queen gave orders that everything should be done as she desired; and then the maiden dressed herself in seven clean snow-white shirts, and held her wedding with the lindorm.

When they were left alone in the bridal chamber the lindorm, in a threatening voice, ordered her to undress herself.

"Undress yourself first!" said she.

"None of the others bade me do that," said he in surprise.

"But I bid you," said she.

Then the lindorm began to writhe, and groan, and breathe heavily; and after a little he had cast his outer skin, which lay on the floor, hideous to behold. Then his bride took off one of her snow-white shirts, and cast it on the lindorm's skin. Again he ordered her to undress, and again she commanded him to do so first. He had to obey, and with groaning and pain cast off one skin after another, and for each skin the maiden threw off one of her shirts, until there lay on the floor seven lindorm skins and six snow-white shirts; the seventh she still had on. The lindorm now lay before her as a formless, slimy mass, which she with all her might began to scrub with the lye and new scrubbing brushes.

When she had nearly worn out the last of these there stood before her the loveliest youth in the world. He thanked her for having saved him from his enchantment, and told her that he was the king and queen's eldest son, and heir to the kingdom. Then he asked her whether she would keep the promise she had made to the lindorm, to share everything with him. To this she was well content to answer yes.

Each time that the lindorm had held his wedding one of the king's retainers was sent next morning to open the door of the bridal chamber and see whether the bride was alive. This next morning also he peeped in at the door, but what he saw there surprised him so much that he shut the door in a hurry, and hastened to the king and queen, who were waiting for his report. He told them of the wonderful sight he had seen. On the floor lay seven lindorm skins and six snow-white shirts, and beside these three worn-out scrubbing brushes, while in the bed a beautiful youth was lying asleep beside the fair young maiden.

The king and queen marveled greatly what this could mean; but just then the old woman who was spoken of in the beginning of the story was again brought in to the queen. She reminded her how she had not followed her instructions, but had eaten the first onion with all its skins, on which account her first-born had been a lindorm. The waiting-woman was then summoned, and admitted that she had thrown it out through the window into the forest. The king and queen now sent for their eldest son and his young bride. They took them both in their arms, and asked him to tell about his sorrowful lot during the twenty years he had lived in the forest as a hideous lindorm. This he did, and then his parents had it proclaimed over the whole country that he was their eldest son, and along with his spouse should inherit the country and kingdom after them.

Prince Lindorm and his beautiful wife now lived in joy and prosperity for a time in the palace; and when his father was laid in the grave, not long after this, he obtained the whole kingdom. Soon afterward his mother also departed from this world.

Now it happened that an enemy declared war against the young king; and, as he foresaw that it would be three years at the least before he could return to his country and his queen, he ordered all his servants who remained at home to guard her most carefully. That they might be able to write to each other in confidence, he had two seal rings made, one for himself and one for his young queen, and issued an order that no one, under pain of death, was to open any letter that was sealed with one of these. Then he took farewell of his queen, and marched out to war.

The queen's wicked stepmother had heard with great grief that her beautiful stepdaughter had prospered so well that she had not only preserved her life, but had even become queen of the country. She now plotted continually how she might destroy her good fortune. While King Lindorm was away at the war the wicked woman came to the queen, and spoke fair to her, saying that she had always foreseen that her stepdaughter was destined to be something great in the world, and that she had on this account secured that she should be the enchanted prince's bride. The queen, who did not imagine that any person could be so deceitful, bade her stepmother welcome, and kept her beside her.

Soon after this the queen had two children, the prettiest boys that anyone could see. When she had written a letter to the king to tell him of this her stepmother asked leave to comb her hair for her, as her own mother used to do. The queen gave her permission, and the stepmother combed her hair until she fell asleep. Then she took the seal ring off her neck, and exchanged the letter for another, in which she had written that the queen had given birth to two whelps.

When the king received this letter he was greatly distressed, but he remembered how he himself had lived for twenty years as a lindorm, and had been freed from the spell by his young queen. He therefore wrote back to his most trusted retainer that the queen and her two whelps should be taken care of while he was away.

The stepmother, however, took this letter as well, and wrote a new one, in which the king ordered that the queen and the two little princes should be burnt at the stake. This she also sealed with the queen's seal, which was in all respects like the king's.

The retainer was greatly shocked and grieved at the king's orders, for which he could discover no reason; but, as he had not the heart to destroy three innocent beings, he had a great fire kindled, and in this he burned a sheep and two lambs, so as to make people believe that he had carried out the king's commands. The stepmother had made these known to the people, adding that the queen was a wicked sorceress.

The faithful servant, however, told the queen that it was the king's command that during the years he was absent in the war she should keep herself concealed in the castle, so that no one but himself should see her and the little princes.

The queen obeyed, and no one knew but that both she and her children had been burned. But when the time came near for King Lindorm to return home from the war the old retainer grew frightened because he had not obeyed his orders. He therefore went to the queen, and told her everything, at the same time showing her the king's letter containing the command to burn her and the princes. He then begged her to leave the palace before the king returned.

The queen now took her two little sons, and wandered out into the wild forest. They walked all day without finding a human habitation, and became very tired. The queen then caught sight of a man who carried some venison. He seemed very poor and wretched, but the queen was glad to see a human being, and asked him whether he knew where she and her little children could get a house over their heads for the night.

The man answered that he had a little hut in the forest, and that she could rest there; but he also said that he was one who lived entirely apart from men, and owned no more than the hut, a horse, and a dog, and supported himself by hunting.

The queen followed him to the hut and rested there overnight with her children, and when she awoke in the morning the man had already gone out hunting. The queen then began to put the room in order and prepare food, so that when the man came home he found everything neat and tidy, and this seemed to give him some pleasure. He spoke but little, however, and all that he said about himself was that his name was Peter.

Later in the day he rode out into the forest, and the queen thought that he looked very unhappy. While he was away she looked about her in the hut a little more closely, and found a tub full of shirts stained with blood, lying among water. She was surprised at this, but thought that the man would get the blood on his shirt when he was carrying home venison. She washed the shirts, and hung them up to dry, and said nothing to Peter about the matter.

After some time had passed she noticed that every day he came riding home from the forest he took off a blood-stained shirt and put on a clean one. She then saw that it was something other than the blood of the deer that stained his shirts, so one day she took courage and asked him about it.

At first he refused to tell her, but she then related to him her own story, and how she had succeeded in delivering the lindorm. He then told her that he had formerly lived a wild life, and had finally entered into a written compact with the Evil Spirit. Before this contract had expired he had repented and turned from his evil ways, and withdrawn himself to this solitude. The Evil One had then lost all power to take him, but so long as he had the contract he could compel him to meet him in the forest each day at a certain time, where the evil spirits then scourged him till he bled.

Next day, when the time came for the man to ride into the forest, the queen asked him to stay at home and look after the princes, and she would go to meet the evil spirits in his place. The man was amazed, and said that this would not only cost her her life, but would also bring upon him a greater misfortune than the one he was already under. She bade him be of good courage, looked to see that she had the three nuts that she had found beside her mother's grave, mounted her horse, and rode out into the forest. When she had ridden for some time the evil spirits came forth and said, "Here comes Peter's horse and Peter's hound; but Peter himself is not with them."

Then at a distance she heard a terrible voice demanding to know what she wanted.

"I have come to get Peter's contract," said she.

At this there arose a terrible uproar among the evil spirits, and the worst voice among them all said, "Ride home and tell Peter that when he comes tomorrow he shall get twice as many strokes as usual."

The queen then took one of her nuts and cracked it, and turned her horse about. At this sparks of fire flew out of all the trees, and the evil spirits howled as if they were being scourged back to their abode.

The next day at the same time the queen again rode out into the forest; but on this occasion the spirits did not dare to come so near her. They would not, however, give up the contract, but threatened both her and the man. Then she cracked her second nut, and all the forest behind her seemed to be in fire and flames, and the evil spirits howled even worse than on the previous day; but the contract they would not give up.

The queen had only one nut left now, but even that she was ready to give up in order to deliver the man. This time she cracked the nut as soon as she came near the place where the spirits appeared, and what then happened to them she could not see, but amid wild screams and howls the contract was handed to her at the end of a long branch. The queen rode happily home to the hut, and happier still was the man, who had been sitting there in great anxiety, for now he was freed from all the power of the evil spirits.

Meanwhile King Lindorm had come home from the war, and the first question he asked when he entered the palace was about the queen and the whelps. The attendants were surprised: they knew of no whelps. The queen had had two beautiful princes; but the king had sent orders that all these were to be burned.

The king grew pale with sorrow and anger, and ordered them to summon his trusted retainer, to whom he had sent the instructions that the queen and the whelps were to be carefully looked after. The retainer, however, showed him the letter in which there was written that the queen and her children were to be burned, and everyone then understood that some great treachery had been enacted.

When the king's trusted retainer saw his master's deep sorrow he confessed to him that he had spared the lives of the queen and the princes, and had only burned a sheep and two lambs, and had kept the queen and her children hidden in the palace for three years, but had sent her out into the wild forest just when the king was expected home. When the king heard this his sorrow was lessened, and he said that he would wander out into the forest and search for his wife and children. If he found them he would return to his palace; but if he did not find them he would never see it again, and in that case the faithful retainer who had saved the lives of the queen and the princes should be king in his stead.

The king then went forth alone into the wild forest, and wandered there the whole day without seeing a single human being. So it went with him the second day also, but on the third day he came by roundabout ways to the little hut. He went in there, and asked for leave to rest himself for a little on the bench. The queen and the princes were there, but she was poorly clad and so sorrowful that the king did not recognize her, neither did he think for a moment that the two children, who were dressed only in rough skins, were his own sons.

He lay down on the bench, and, tired as he was, he soon fell asleep. The bench was a narrow one, and as he slept his arm fell down and hung by the side of it.

"My son, go and lift your father's arm up on the bench," said the queen to one of the princes, for she easily knew the king again, although she was afraid to make herself known to him. The boy went and took the king's arm, but, being only a child, he did not lift it up very gently on to the bench.

The king woke at this, thinking at first that he had fallen into a den of robbers, but he decided to keep quiet and pretend that he was asleep until he should find out what kind of folk were in the house. He lay still for a little, and, as no one moved in the room, he again let his arm glide down off the bench. Then he heard a woman's voice say, "My son, go you and lift your father's arm up on the bench, but don't do it so roughly as your brother did." Then he felt a pair of little hands softly clasping his arm; he opened his eyes, and saw his queen and her children.

He sprang up and caught all three in his arms, and afterward took them, along with the man and his horse and his hound, back to the palace with great joy. The most unbounded rejoicing reigned there then, as well as over the whole kingdom, but the wicked stepmother was burned.

King Lindorm lived long and happily with his queen, and there are some who say that if they are not dead now they are still living to this day.

PRINCESS MAYA
(India)

There was an old king whose wife had died. He was no longer wealthy, but he did rejoice in his two daughters, Madri and Maya. Born as twins, they were alike in their beauty, but not in their manner. Madri was content to stay at home, chatting with her friends about things of the court. Maya preferred to travel and study, an unusual pastime for a princess. Her studies were broad, including the learning of the language of animals.

Maya's father indulged her studies, but she greatly annoyed him with her morning salutation, "Good morning, dear father. Your deserts!"

One day he lost his temper with her when her laughter woke him from his afternoon nap. "What has happened!" he demanded. "Can't a man enjoy his sleep in peace? Or was it my snores!"

"I did not laugh at your snores, father."

"What was it then?"

"I overheard the two ants speaking as they crawled on your couch."

"Now tell me. What did these ants have to say?"

At first Maya was reluctant to tell what she had overheard, but finally he persuaded her. She told them that they were discussing how both of them had daughters with no suitors. They were in hopes that the king would give a wedding banquet for one of his daughters and that they would then find grooms for their daughters.

Maya went on, "But what made me laugh is that one of them wondered how the king could sleep in peace with two unmarried daughters under his roof."

"Hm," the king muttered as he turned over on his couch. He said no more, but thought about what she had said.

The next morning he told his chief advisor that Maya needed to change her ways. "There is something definitely wrong with her. What do you think?"

His advisor was reluctant to speak, but when pressed, said, "If the queen were alive she could have explained it to you. You see, your daughters are of an age for marriage. They are no longer children."

"Without money for their dowries it will be difficult to find them husbands. Anyway, I don't understand why Maya is so different from Madri. They are identical, yet Maya is so independent. Why can't she be like Madri?"

The king's advisor answered, "I think Maya is an intelligent young woman who would benefit from having a suitable husband, even if he were poor."

The king pondered his advisor's words and decided that he was right. The next morning he called her to him and said, "Maya, you will have your own deserts today. By evening you will have a husband. Last night I decided that the first available man I saw this morning would be your husband. You are to be married to a beggar from Avanti."

Maya was stunned into silence by her father's proclamation. But she decided to make the best of it. Her father was so distraught that he didn't even attend the wedding. When he asked after the couple his advisor told him that they had left happily, with Maya saying,

> Better to have a beggar as spouse
> Than dwell alone in a great king's house.

"So be it," said the king. "It sounds as if she learned that from her studies. I hope it serves her well."

As the beggar and Maya left, he said he had a story to tell. "I am not really a beggar. I travel because I am too embarrassed to stay in any one place. Once when I had gone hunting, I had fallen asleep by an anthill. From that day to this, no matter how much I eat, I am constantly hungry and the food does not nourish me. My father hired many doctors, but I was so ashamed of my greediness that I ran away."

"There must be a cure," said Maya. "We should not give up hope. Let me think about this."

After some deliberation, Maya suggested they return to the anthill where he had once slept, reasoning that perhaps she would get an idea about what to do. When they arrived, her husband looked tired so she encouraged him to rest while she went into town for food. He sat down under a mango tree to sleep while she hurried to the town.

When she returned to the mango tree, she saw her husband still asleep. But as she got closer she saw that the head of a snake was emerging from his mouth. Another snake was slithering out of the anthill. As she hid behind the tree she listened to their conversation.

The snake from the anthill hissed, "You have become the lowest of them all. Your host will soon die of starvation because you eat all he consumes. Then what will you do?"

"Say nothing about me," hissed the other snake. "You lie on that anthill keeping others from the treasures below it. They do you no good, yet you hoard them. You are merely jealous because I am fat from my frequent feedings."

"I am hardly jealous! Someone will realize that a bit of black mustard seed will be the end of you."

"And if that happens, I hope you are drowned in a bucket of vinegar."

Maya had understood all they said and she wasted no time in killing the snakes. Her husband was cured and they retrieved the treasure, an appropriate dowry for Maya to offer to her husband. They returned to his home, where he resumed his position as a prince. Thus Maya got her deserts as well as a happy life.

THE BASIL PLANT
(Chile)

There was once a woman who had three very pretty and industrious daughters. They all lived across from the king's palace, where they had a garden with the very best and finest basil plants. Now this king was accustomed to come out every day at dawn to see the daughters, for they pleased him very much. One day he called down to one of them from his balcony, "Listen, you tricky girl, how many leaves does your basil plant have?" She looked up and chanted back,

Shut your mouth, you king so sly.
How many stars are there in the sky?

The king went fuming inside, mumbling, "She'll pay for this." He hired a man and a mule and filled the saddlebags with oranges. He ordered the man to sell the fruit, being sure to go by the girls' house. Sure enough, they called him over. "Orange vendor, come back. How much are they a hundred?"

"For you, miss, I'll leave them all for a little kiss," he replied.

The oldest daughter, who had called him, was enraged and bustled into the house, slamming the door behind her. The next day the same thing happened to the second sister, who was equally enraged. "Get along, you old pig!" she yelled from the door. "Imagine offering me oranges for a kiss." She too flew into the house all flustered and hot.

"Didn't you buy any oranges?" asked the youngest daughter.

"No, of course not. Didn't you hear what he wanted for them?"

"You mean to say you didn't kiss him?" said the youngest, infuriated. "Why, we would have had all the oranges we could have eaten. If he comes again, I'm going to go out."

As soon as the man passed again, she dashed out, calling, "Come back, orange man, come back."

"How could I resist a lady as lovely as you? If you'll just give me one little kiss, the oranges are yours."

"Can it be true?" she said. "Go on and unload the fruit."

When he had finished unpacking, she gave him a kiss on the lips, and away he went.

235

The next morning, the king got up especially early and went out on his balcony to see the girl. "How many leaves does your basil plant have?" he called merrily. She looked up and taunted back,

> Shut your mouth, you king so sly.
> How many stars are there in the sky?

"Shut your own mouth, you deceiving girl," laughed the king. "How many kisses did you give the old orange vendor?"

"Well, that was a nice trick," she said to herself, "but the king isn't going to win." Immediately she got herself a black costume, a little bell, and a gentle little burro. Early the next day, she rode forth ringing the bell, "Ting-a-ling, ting-a-ling." She was dressed in the black suit with very long fingers so as to appear especially skinny. The girl rode around to the palace gate and rang the bell, but the guards wouldn't let her through, wanting to know who on earth she was. With a long face and the very black costume, she told them she was Death come to visit the king. They promptly let her in, trembling as they opened the gates. She trotted right up to the front door. "Ting-a-ling, ting-a-ling, I've come to fetch the king."

Inside the palace, the king leaped up in his nightshirt, begging her not to carry him off. "My dear little, lovely little Death, don't, oh, please don't, not yet!"

"Ting-a-ling, ting-a-ling, I've come to take my king," and she rang the bell over and over. He begged and insisted so that she finally said in a low, hollow voice, "Under one condition will I leave you: that you give the burro three kisses on his backside." The king promptly lifted the burro's tail and kissed him three times. Then Death rode away. "Ting-a-ling, ting-a-ling, now I won't take my king."

When the king had recovered from his shock the following morning, he went out to see the girl and called down, "Listen, you deceitful creature, how many leaves does the basil plant have?" She jeered up from below,

> Shut your mouth, you king so sly.
> How many stars are there in the sky?

"Quiet down yourself," he shouted back. "How many kisses did you give the grimy old orange vendor?"

"You pipe down," she returned. "How many times did you kiss the burro's behind?"

The king rushed into his palace, muttering to himself, "What the devil! Now I have to call for this girl and marry her." So he commanded the mother with her three daughters to appear before him. She was greatly frightened by the summons and was sure the king was going to kill all of them. But the daughters weren't very upset. "For eating so many oranges," they laughed.

"These are your three daughters, are they not?" asked the king when the old woman appeared trembling in the throne room.

"Yes, sir, that they are."

"Well, then, I'm going to ask you for the youngest."

"But how can you, sire? I'm so very poor!" sobbed the old woman.

"That doesn't matter," answered the king. "Tomorrow will be the wedding, and don't worry about its doing you any harm."

After the ceremony, the king told his new bride emphatically to keep her nose out of the justice he meted out in his kingdom. (Don't you see how he thought she was a devilish person?) The new queen agreed to this request with the reservation that the king must promise to grant her one favor before she died, whenever she should ask him for it. Soon, petitions and complaints began to come in to the king from his people. The first case was that of a man who had ridden into town on a mare followed by a newborn colt. While he was shopping in town, another man had ridden off on a stallion followed by the first man's colt. When the owner of the colt rode out to round it up, the second man had claimed that it belonged to his horse. They had argued for a long time and finally decided to bring their case before the king.

"Let's see," said the ruler, "both of you stand over there. The one whom the colt follows will be the owner." The two men joined together and set their horses to walking, but the colt, being so young, staggered unsurely behind the stallion, whereupon the king declared in favor of the owner of the stallion. The man with the mare went to seek the queen and tell her his troubles, for she was known as a merciful person. She told him to keep mum and come back in the afternoon for further instructions.

A few days later, two more men came before the king with a complaint. One had said that whenever he stayed out in the cold, he froze. The other had mocked him and said that he dared to stay out in the coldest night. The king appointed a board of judges, who asked the man who stayed out all night what he had seen. He answered that there had been a tiny little fire above him in the hills. The judges answered that he had surely warmed himself there and thus avoided being frozen. But the two were not content and continued to squabble over this question until the king ruled the same as his judges. The loser left the court in low spirits and went straight to the queen.

"Don't worry about it," she counseled. "Tomorrow I'm going to see to it that the king learns how to dispense justice."

When the man returned the next day for more advice, the queen told him to go and wait in a pasture where the king was going to ride by. He should go with a bag of barley and a big pot to cook it in. "Then," she continued, "when the king comes by, he's going to ask you what you are doing. You must tell him you're cooking the barley in order to sow it. When he asks you how in the world such a thing can be, you must answer,

'Your Majesty, since you say that stallions can bear colts, why can't this cooked barley grow?' "

When the king arose early the next day to set out on his trip, he ordered the queen to put on the pot for breakfast and throw plenty of wood on the fire. After waiting for a while, the king became impatient and noticed that the pot was sitting in the doorway.

"I thought I told you to be quick," he said to the queen. "How is that pot going to boil sitting in the doorway?" At that moment, one of the disputants came in and said, "Your Majesty, you said the other man hadn't been frozen because there was a tiny fire on the hillside; why then can't your pot boil in the doorway with such a big fire in the stove?"

The king went off to the country in a very bad humor, thinking angrily about the queen, for he knew that these tricks were of her doing. Soon he and his retinue came upon the man who was cooking barley in a field alongside the road.

"Man, what are you up to there with that pot? Why on earth are you cooking barley?" asked the king.

"To sow it, sire," he answered.

"But whatever makes you think it's going to come up?"

"Why not?" answered the man. "If stallions can bear colts, why can't this barley sprout?"

The king stormed away, fuming to himself, "This is the queen's doing and I'll make her pay for it. I warned her before not to stick her nose into my affairs." When he returned to the castle at lunchtime, he said to his wife, "It's just about time to settle our accounts for all this meddling around of yours." He stamped outside and lit an enormous bonfire, but the queen said it really didn't matter to her, for we are all born to die. She was very calm at the prospect of being roasted. When the bonfire was crackling high in the air, the king took her up in his coach and said, "You must amend your ways and prepare to die."

"So be it," said she, "for I'm not afraid of death."

Arriving at the site of the burning, the royal couple got down from the coach and strolled up and down, arm in arm, until the hour came and the king beckoned to the executioner. Just as the fire was piping hot to receive the queen, she cried, "Wait, all of you!" She beckoned to the king. "Do you remember that I am entitled to ask for a favor before dying?"

"Why, yes, I do recall something like that," answered the king.

"Then come over here." As he approached, she embraced him and hugged tight. "There you are, my love."

"That's enough, enough," groaned the king, trying to pull away.

"No, this is the request," replied the queen. "If you wish to burn me, we'll burn together." Realizing that she wasn't going to loosen her grip, the king gave in, and said, "Why should the two of us fry together? In this case, I'll pardon you, but never try your tricks again. Now let's be off to the house."

"I'm at your command, my dear," answered the queen smiling.

"From this day on," declared the king, "I'm not going to dispense any more justice. You're the one who has to do it." And that was how the queen came to be judge at the royal court.

THE LUTE PLAYER

(Russia)

nce upon a time there were a king and a queen who lived happily and comfortably together. They were very fond of each other and had nothing to worry them, but at last the king grew restless. He longed to go out into the world, to try his strength in battle against some enemy, and to win all kinds of honor and glory.

So he called his army together and gave orders to start for a distant country where a heathen king ruled who mistreated or tormented everyone he could lay his hands on. The king then gave his parting orders and wise advice to his ministers, took a tender leave of his wife, and set off with his army across the seas.

I cannot say whether the voyage was short or long; but at last he reached the country of the heathen king and marched on, defeating all who came in his way. But this did not last long, for in time he came to a mountain pass, where a large army was waiting for him, who put his soldiers to flight, and took the king himself prisoner.

He was carried off to the prison where the heathen king kept his captives, and now our poor friend had a very bad time indeed. All night long the prisoners were chained up, and in the morning they were yoked together like oxen and had to plough the land till it grew dark.

This state of things went on for three years before the king found any means of sending news of himself to his dear queen, but at last he contrived to send this letter: "Sell all our castles and palaces, and put all our treasures in pawn and come and deliver me out of this horrible prison."

The queen received the letter, read it, and wept bitterly as she said to herself, "How can I deliver my dearest husband? If I go myself and the heathen king sees me he will just take me to be one of his wives. If I were to send one of the ministers! — but I hardly know if I can depend on them."

She thought, and thought, and at last an idea came into her head. She cut off all her beautiful long brown hair and dressed herself in boy's clothes. Then she took her lute and, without saying anything to anyone, she went forth into the wide world.

She traveled through many lands and saw many cities, and went through many hardships before she got to the town where the heathen king lived. When she got there she walked all round the palace and at the back she saw the prison. Then she went into the great court in front of the palace, and taking her lute in her hand, she began to play so beautifully that one felt as though one could never hear enough.

After she had played for some time she began to sing, and her voice was sweeter than the lark's:

> I come from my own country far
>   Into this foreign land,
> Of all I own I take alone
>   My sweet lute in my hand.
>
> Oh! who will thank me for my song,
>   Reward my simple lay?
> Like lover's sighs it still shall rise
>   To greet thee day by day.
>
> I sing of blooming flowers
>   Made sweet by sun and rain;
> Of all the bliss of love's first kiss,
>   And parting's cruel pain.
>
> Of the sad captive's longing
>   Within his prison wall,
> Of hearts that sigh when none are nigh
>   To answer to their call.
>
> My songs begs for your pity,
>   And gifts from out your store,
> And as I play my gentle lay
>   I linger near your door.
>
> And if you hear my singing
>   Within your palace, sire,
> Oh! give, I pray, this happy day,
>   To me my heart's desire.

No sooner had the heathen king heard this touching song sung by such a lovely voice, than he had the singer brought before him.

"Welcome, O lute player," said he. "Where do you come from?"

"My country, sire, is far away across many seas. For years I have been wandering about the world and gaining my living by my music."

"Stay here then a few days, and when you wish to leave I will give you what you ask for in your song—your heart's desire."

So the lute player stayed on in the palace and sang and played almost all day long to the king, who could never tire of listening and almost forgot to eat or drink or to torment people. He cared for nothing but the music, and nodded his head as he declared, "That's something like playing and singing. It makes me feel as if some gentle hand had lifted every care and sorrow from me."

After three days the lute player came to take leave of the king.

"Well," said the king, "what do you desire as your reward?"

"Sire, give me one of your prisoners. You have so many in your prison, and I should be glad of a companion on my journeys. When I hear his happy voice as I travel along I shall think of you and thank you."

"Come along then," said the king, "choose whom you will." And he took the lute player through the prison himself.

The queen walked about among the prisoners, and at length she picked out her husband and took him with her on her journey. They were long on their way, but he never found out who she was, and she led him nearer and nearer to his own country.

When they reached the frontier the prisoner said, "Let me go now, kind lad; I am no common prisoner, but the king of this country. Let me go free and ask what you will as your reward."

"Do not speak of reward," answered the lute player. "Go in peace."

"Then come with me, dear boy, and be my guest."

"When the proper time comes I shall be at your palace," was the reply, and so they parted.

The queen took a short way home, got there before the king and changed her dress.

An hour later all the people in the palace were running to and fro and crying out, "Our king has come back! Our king has returned to us."

The king greeted every one very kindly, but he would not so much as look at the queen.

Then he called all his council and ministers together and said to them, "See what sort of a wife I have. Here she is falling on my neck, but when I was pining in prison and sent her word of it she did nothing to help me."

And his council answered with one voice, "Sire, when news was brought from you the queen disappeared and no one knew where she went. She only returned today."

Then the king was very angry and cried, "Judge my faithless wife! Never would you have seen your king again, if a young lute player had not delivered him. I shall remember him with love and gratitude as long as I live."

While the king was sitting with his council, the queen found time to disguise herself. She took her flute, and slipping into the court in front of the palace she sang, clear and sweet:

I sing the captive's longing
    Within his prison wall,
Of hearts that sigh when none are nigh
    To answer to their call.

My song begs for your pity,
    And gifts from out your store,
And as I play my gentle lay
    I linger near your door.

And if you hear my singing
    Within your palace, sire,
Oh! give, I pray, this happy day,
    To me my heart's desire.

As soon as the king heard this song he ran out to meet the lute player, took him by the hand and led him into the palace.

"Here," he cried, "is the boy who released me from my prison. And now, my true friend, I will indeed give you your heart's desire."

"I am sure you will not be less generous than the heathen king was, sire. I ask of you what I asked and obtained from him. But this time I don't mean to give up what I get. I want *you* — yourself!"

And as she spoke she threw off her long cloak and everyone saw it was the queen.

Who can tell how happy the king was? In the joy of his heart he gave a great feast to the whole world, and the whole world came and rejoiced with him for a whole week.

I was there too, and ate and drank many good things. I shan't forget that feast as long as I live.

THE LEGEND OF TCHI-NIU
(China)

Tong-Yong's mother died while he was yet an infant, and when he became a youth of nineteen years his father also passed away, leaving him utterly alone in the world and without resources of any sort. Being a very poor man, Tong's father had put himself in great straits to educate the lad, and had not been able to lay by even one copper coin of his earnings. Tong lamented greatly to find himself so destitute that he could not honor the memory of that good father by having the customary rites of burial performed and a carved tomb erected on a propitious site. Only the poor are friends of the poor, and among all those Tong knew no one was able to assist him in defraying the expenses of the funeral. In one way alone could the youth obtain money. This was by selling himself as a slave to some rich landowner, and this he at last decided to do. In vain, his friends did their utmost to dissuade him; they attempted to delay his sacrifice by making him beguiling promises of future aid, but to no purpose. Tong only replied that he would sell his freedom a hundred times if it were possible, rather than suffer his father's memory to remain unhonored even for a brief season. Furthermore, confident in his youth and strength, he determined to put a high price on his servitude, a price that would enable him to build a handsome tomb but would also be well-nigh impossible for him ever to repay.

Accordingly he repaired to the broad public place where slaves and debtors were exposed for sale, and seated himself upon a bench of stone, having affixed to his shoulders a placard inscribed with the terms of his servitude and the list of his qualifications as a laborer. Many who read the characters on the placard smiled disdainfully at the price asked and passed on without a word. Others lingered only to question him out of simple curiosity. Some commended him with hollow praise, some openly mocked his unselfishness and laughed at his childish piety. Thus many hours wearily passed, and Tong had almost despaired of finding a master when there rode by a high official of the province, a grave and handsome man, lord of a thousand slaves and owner of vast estates. Reining in his Tartar horse, the official halted to read the placard. He did not smile or advise or ask any questions, but having observed the price asked and the fine strong limbs of the youth, he purchased him without further ado, merely ordering his attendant to pay the sum and see that the necessary papers were made out.

Thus Tong found himself enabled to fulfill the wish of his heart, to have a monument built which, although of small size, would delight the eyes of all who beheld it because it would be designed by cunning artists and executed by skillful sculptors. The pious rites were performed, the silver coin was placed in the mouth of the dead, the white lanterns were hung at the door, the holy prayers were recited, and paper shapes of all things the departed might need in the land of the genii were consumed in consecrated fire. After the geomancers and the necromancers had chosen a burial spot that no unlucky star could shine upon, a place of rest that no demon or dragon might ever disturb, the beautiful *chih* was built. Phantom money was strewn along the way, the funeral procession departed from the dwelling of the dead, and with prayers and lamentations the mortal remains of Tong's good father were borne to the tomb. Then Tong entered the service of his purchaser, who allotted him a little hut to dwell in, and there Tong carried with him those wooden tablets bearing the ancestral names before which filial piety must daily burn the incense of prayer and perform the tender duties of family worship.

Spring perfumed the land with flowers, and three times had been celebrated the festival of the dead called *Siu-fan-ti*, and three times had Tong swept and garnished his father's tomb and presented his fivefold offering of fruits and meats. The period of mourning passed, yet he did not cease to mourn. The years revolved with their many moons, bringing him no hour of joy, no day of happy rest. Yet he never lamented his servitude or failed to perform the rites of ancestral worship, until at last one day the fever of the rice fields overcame him, and he could not arise from his bed. His fellow laborers thought him destined to die. There was no one to care for his needs, inasmuch as the slaves and servants were busy with the duties of the household and the labor of the fields, departing to toil at sunrise and returning weary only after sundown.

Now while the sick youth slumbered one sultry noon in the fitful sleep of exhaustion, he dreamed that a strange and beautiful woman stood beside him and touched his forehead with the long, fine fingers of her shapely hand. At her cool touch a strange sweet shock passed through him, and all his veins tingled as if thrilled by new life. Opening his eyes in wonder, he saw bending over him the charming being of whom he had dreamed, and he knew that her hand really caressed his throbbing forehead. The flame of the fever was gone, a delicious coolness penetrated every fiber of his body, and the thrill of which he had dreamed still tingled in his blood. Even at the same moment, the eyes of the gentle visitor met his own, and he saw they were singularly beautiful, shining like splendid black jewels under brows curved like the wings of the swallow. Yet their calm gaze seemed to pass through him as light through crystal. A vague awe came upon him, so that the question that had risen to his lips found no utterance.

Then she, still caressing him, smiled and said, "I have come to restore your strength and to be your wife. Arise and worship with me."

Her clear voice had tones melodious as a bird's song, but in her gaze there was an imperious power which Tong felt he dare not resist. Rising from his bed, he was astounded to find his strength wholly restored. The cool, slender hand which held his own led him away so swiftly that he had little time for amazement. He would have given years of existence for courage to speak of his misery, to declare his utter inability to maintain a wife, but something irresistible in the long dark eyes of his companion forbade him to speak.

As though his inmost thought had been discerned by that wondrous gaze, she said to him in the same clear voice, "I will provide."

Shame made him blush at the thought of his wretched aspect and tattered apparel until he observed that she also was poorly attired, like a woman of the people, wearing no ornament of any kind, not even shoes on her feet. Before he had yet spoken to her, they came before the ancestral tablets, and there she knelt with him and they prayed and pledged their faith in a cup of wine, brought he knew not from where. Thus together they worshiped Heaven and Earth and thus she became his wife.

It was a mysterious marriage, for neither on that day nor at any future time could Tong venture to ask his wife the name of her family or of the place whence she came, nor could he answer any of the curious questions that his fellow laborers asked him concerning her. And she, moreover, never uttered a word about herself, except to say that her name was Tchi. Yet, although Tong had such awe of her that while her eyes were upon him he was as one having no will of his own, he loved her utterly, and the thought of his serfdom ceased to weigh upon him from the hour of his marriage. As through magic, the little dwelling was transformed. Its misery was masked with charming paper devices, with dainty decorations created out of nothing by that pretty jugglery of which only woman knows the secret.

Each morning the young husband found a well-prepared and ample meal awaiting him, and each evening also when he returned from the fields. The wife sat all day at her loom, weaving silk after a fashion unlike anything that had ever been seen before in that province. For as she wove, the silk flowed from the loom like a slow current of glossy gold, bearing upon its undulations strange forms of violet and crimson and jewel-green, shapes of ghostly horsemen riding on horses and of phantom chariots dragon-drawn, and of standards of trailing cloud. In every dragon's heart glimmered a mystic pearl, in every rider's helmet sparkled a precious gem. And each day Tchi would weave a great piece of this figured silk until the fame of her weaving spread abroad. From far and near people thronged to see the marvelous work. Silk merchants of great cities heard of it, and they sent messengers to Tchi, asking her to weave for them and teach them her secret. Then she wove for them, as they desired, in return for the silver pieces they brought her, but when they begged her to teach them, she only laughed.

"Assuredly, I could never teach you," she said, "for no one among you has fingers like mine."

And indeed no man could discern her fingers when she wove any more than he might behold the wings of a bee vibrating in swift flight. The seasons passed, and Tong never knew want, so well did his beautiful wife fulfill her promise, "I will provide." The coins of bright silver brought by the silk merchants were piled up higher and higher in the great carved chest that Tchi had bought for the storage of the household goods.

One morning when Tong, having finished his repast, was about to depart for the fields, Tchi unexpectedly bade him remain. Opening the great chest, she took out and gave him a document written in the official characters called *li-shu*. And Tong, looking at it, cried out for joy, for it was the certificate of his manumission. Tchi had secretly purchased her husband's freedom with the price of her wondrous silks!

"You shall labor no more for any master," she said, "but for your own sake only. And I have also bought this dwelling, with all it contains, and the tea fields to the south, and the mulberry groves close by, all of which are yours."

Tong, beside himself for gratefulness, would have prostrated himself in worship before her, but she would not permit it. Thus he was made free, and prosperity came to him with his freedom. Whatsoever he gave to the sacred earth was returned to him centupled. His servants loved him and blessed the beautiful Tchi, so silent and yet so kindly to all about her. The loom soon remained untouched, for Tchi gave birth to a son, a boy so beautiful that Tong wept with delight when he looked upon him. Thereafter the wife devoted herself wholly to the care of the child.

It soon became manifest that the boy was not less wonderful than his wonderful mother. In the third month of his life he could speak, in the seventh month he could repeat by heart the proverbs of the sages and recite the holy prayers. Before the eleventh month he could use the writing brush with skill and copy in shapely characters the precepts of Lao-tse. Even the priests of the temples came to behold the child and to converse with him, and they marveled at his charm and the wisdom of what he said.

They blessed Tong, saying, "Surely this son is a gift from the Master of Heaven, a sign that the immortals love you. May your eyes behold a hundred happy summers!"

It was now in the period of the eleventh moon. The flowers had withered, the perfume of the summer had vanished, the winds were growing chill, and in Tong's home the evening fires were lighted. Long the husband and wife sat in the mellow glow, he speaking much of his hopes and joys, and of his son who was to be so grand a man, and of many other paternal thoughts, while she, speaking little, listened to his words and often turned her wonderful eyes upon him with an answering smile. Never had she seemed so beautiful, and Tong, watching her face, did not mark how the night waned, nor how the fire sank low, nor how the wind sang in the leafless trees outside.

Suddenly Tchi arose, and in silence she took his hand in hers and led him gently as on that strange wedding morning to the cradle where their boy slumbered, faintly smiling in his dreams. In that moment there came upon Tong the same strange fear that he had felt when Tchi's eyes had first met his own, the vague fear that love and trust had calmed but had never wholly cast out, like the fear of the gods. Unknowingly, as one yielding to that pressure of mighty invisible hands, he bowed himself low before her, kneeling as to a divinity. When he lifted his eyes again to her face, he closed them forthwith in awe, for she towered before him taller than any mortal woman, and there was a glow about her as of sunbeams, and the light of her limbs shone through her garments.

Her sweet voice came to him with all the tenderness of other hours, saying, "Oh, my beloved, the moment has come when I must forsake you, for I was never of mortal born, and the Invisible may incarnate themselves for a time only. Yet I leave the pledge of our love, this fair son, who shall ever be as faithful and as fond as you have been. Know, my beloved, that I was sent to you by the Master of Heaven in reward for your filial piety, and that I must now return to the glory of His house. I am the Goddess Tchi-Niu."

Even as she ceased to speak, the great glow faded and Tong, opening his eyes again, knew that she had vanished forever, mysteriously as pass the winds of heaven, irrevocably as the light of a flame blown out. Yet all the doors were barred, all the windows unopened, and still the child slept, smiling in his sleep. Outside, the darkness was breaking, the sky brightened swiftly, the night was past. With splendid majesty the east threw open high gates of gold for the coming of the sun, and, illuminated by the glory of his coming, the vapors of morning wrought themselves into marvelous shapes of shifting color, into forms as strangely beautiful as the silken dreams woven in the loom of Tchi-Niu.

THE TIGER WITH THE WHITE EARS
(Korea)

igh in a mountain pass there stood a small house. The man who lived there with his wife spent many hours collecting the magic herb of wild ginseng. For many years they had lived alone, rarely seeing another person because of the remoteness of the pass.

One day a man named Gim arrived at the village at the foot of the mountain. He told some villagers that he wanted some ginseng and asked where he might purchase some. The villagers pointed toward the pass where the man and his wife lived but told Gim that no one had ever gone there.

A dense mountain forest lay between the village and the high pass. Gim began to work his way through the forest, stopping often to rest. The way was difficult and the thick trees often shut out the sun. But Gim continued his efforts until he came to the small house at the top of the pass.

"Hello!" he called out. He was surprised to be greeted by a woman about forty years of age. When he told her his purpose she told him her husband had gone to market on the other side of the mountain.

"He has been gone since early this morning and thus he should be back soon. Please sit down and rest yourself until he returns."

Gim rested while the woman continued with her routine chores. Soon several hours had passed and it had become dark.

"I am afraid that something has happened to delay him," the woman said. "Would you come with me while I search for him?"

Gim agreed to accompany her and they took torches and began to walk down a path on the other side of the mountain. They had walked for some time when the woman stopped. She bent down and retrieved something white from the ground.

"No!" she exclaimed. "This is my husband's handkerchief! There is blood on the ground. He must have been killed!"

They followed the trail of blood into some bushes and were confronted with the sight of a huge tiger tearing the flesh from a dead man. Seeing that it was the body of her husband, the woman rushed at the tiger, brandishing her torch in its face. The tiger turned to leave, but it used its huge jaws to drag the body after it. The woman howled with anger and continued her pursuit. Finally the tiger dropped the body and watched while the woman lifted the cold corpse onto her back.

Gim held the torches while she carried the body up the path to her home. When they arrived she placed the body in the back storeroom of the house. She suggested that Gim rest for the night and he accepted gratefully. He was exhausted from the dreadful experience and lay down to try to recover.

He had barely begun to relax when he heard a vicious roar followed by a loud crash. He heard the woman calling to him to come out, and when he found her she was standing by the door to the storeroom. At her feet lay the huge yellow tiger.

"I knew the tiger would not give up that easily. I waited behind the door to the storeroom and when it came in search of my husband's body I killed it with this ax. Look at its ears. This is the white-eared tiger that has tormented the villagers. For years if a man went into the woods for only a moment he risked being killed by this tiger. It would even dig up graves to retrieve bodies. It was rarely seen, though occasionally the villagers would see it playing with a body. The white ears were always mentioned. This is that evil tiger."

By this time it was nearly dawn and the woman asked Gim to share breakfast with her. After they had eaten and rested some, she offered Gim some mountain ginseng in appreciation for his help throughout the night.

Gim made his way down the mountain, telling the villagers what had happened the night before. That evening he and many others returned to pay their respects to the woman who had lost her husband and killed the fearful tiger. But when they arrived they found that she had joined her husband in death, burning down the house, the torn body of her husband, and herself.

WHAT CANDY ASHCRAFT DONE
(United States, Ozarks)

One time there was a man and woman come a-traveling through the country with a good team and a brand-new Springfield wagon. They was Yankees, and both of them loved money. So they got a fine coffin with silver handles and put it in the wagon. Whenever they come to a big house the woman would rub whitening on her face and then lay in the coffin like she was dead.

The man would go to the door and ask the people if he could sleep in the barn, and then he wanted to put the corpse in the house till morning. He is used to sleeping in barns himself, but he don't want it said that his poor sister has laid a corpse in no barn, because they come of a good family back home and it would break his mother's heart. So the folks would help carry the coffin into the house, and everybody says it is a handsome corpse. Away in the night the woman would get up out of the coffin and unbar the door, so the man could come in. And then they would rob the house and maybe kill all the people besides.

When they come to the old Ashcraft place it was a fine big house, but there wasn't nobody living there only Lige Ashcraft and his wife Candy. They didn't like Yankees much, but no Ashcraft could turn down travelers, and it was coming on to rain anyhow. So they helped carry the coffin into the big hall. They give the fellow a good supper and offered to let him sleep in the spare room. But he says no, as he is all dirty from traveling. And his poor sister's jewelry and keepsakes are packed in the wagon, so he will sleep out there in the wagonshed, he says.

Lige and Candy give him the lantern, and then they barred the door and went to bed. After they laid there awhile Candy says, "Listen, Lige, there's something funny about them people." Lige he just grunted. Pretty soon Candy says, "Lige, I could swear I seen that corpse's eye-winker move, right after we set the coffin on them chairs." Lige says it is all foolishness, because he seen thousands of dead Yankees in the War, and their eye-winkers never moved a gosh-darn bit. "You better go to sleep," he says, "because we got to get up early. That poor fellow wants to get a soon start in the mornin', and we must give him a good breakfast." And then Lige he rolled over and begun to snore.

257

Candy laid there and thought about it awhile, and then she got up easy and went downstairs barefooted. She picked up a hatchet by the kitchen stove, and then she slipped into the hall and hunkered down close to the coffin. After while there come a little noise, and the woman in the coffin set up. She had a gun in her hand, so Candy just swung the hatchet. The Yankee woman fell back in the coffin, and Candy set down on the floor because she was kind of dizzy. Candy hadn't never killed anybody before, and she felt like maybe she was going to faint.

Pretty soon she went back and woke up Lige. When she told him what happened he says she must have dreamed it. But he slipped down to the hall and seen how things was. Then he picked up the hatchet and motioned for Candy to unbar the door. Soon as it swung open the other Yankee come a-sneaking in. Lige just split his head open like it was a pumpkin. The fellow never knowed what hit him.

After Lige lit the lamp, him and Candy just set there awhile, looking at them corpses. Both of the Yankees had pistols and knives under their clothes. The man was wearing a money-belt full of gold, and the woman had three diamond rings in a little sack round her neck. There was big bundle of greenbacks and silver in the coffin, too. Soon as it got light enough, Lige dug a big hole out in the cornfield and buried the corpses and the coffin with the silver handles. Then he drove off down the road, and after while he come back afoot. Lige never did say what he done with them fine horses and the Springfield wagon, and Candy had sense enough not to ask no questions. She just scrubbed the hall right good and washed the hatchet. Lige wrapped the money and the rings up in a piece of rawhide and put it in a safe place. He showed Candy where the stuff was hid, so she could find it if anything happened to him. And then him and her set down and eat their dinner, just like they always done.

Lige and Candy talked some about going out West, but they never done it. They raised a big family right there on the old farm. The kids all went to school, and one of the boys made a lawyer, and finally he got to be prosecuting attorney. After Lige died Aunt Candy just visited around amongst the children. Whenever they give a party the old lady would dress up just as fine as anybody. She had three gold rings, too, with big diamonds in them.

THE HUSBAND AND WIFE
(Norway)

Once upon a time there was a hardworking man who thought his wife spent her days at home idling away the time. One evening during the haying season he came home, grumbling and complaining about his work.

"There, there, my good man. Don't fret so," his wife said soothingly. "Tomorrow let's trade work. You stay home and mind the house and babe, and I will go into the fields with the mowers."

That proposal sounded just fine to the husband and he told her he would be happy to stay at home. He knew it would be a day of ease.

Early the next morning the wife took a scythe and went out to the hayfield, while the husband stayed behind to do the housework. He decided to first churn some butter. After a bit of churning he got thirsty, so he went down to the cellar to tap a barrel of ale. Just as he was putting the tap into the barrel, he heard the pig come into the kitchen. Up the stairs he ran, tap in hand, to make sure the pig didn't upset the churn. But alas, the churn was already overturned, and the pig was snuffling in the cream that was all over the floor. He was so furious that he forgot about the barrel of ale and chased the pig out of the house, kicking the animal hard, and leaving it for dead in front of the house. He saw the tap in his hand and ran downstairs as quick as he could, but the ale had all run out of the barrel.

He hurried to the barn for more cream, filled the churn, and began to churn so they would have butter for their supper. Soon he remembered that the cow was still shut up and needed to be taken to the meadow. It had gotten so late that he didn't have time to go all the way to the meadow. The house was against a hill with a sod roof, and it had a fine patch of grass growing on it. So the husband decided that if he could fix a plank across the back, he could easily get the cow up to the roof to graze.

Their baby was crawling around on the floor, so he took the churn with him so it wouldn't be upset once again. He first went to the well to get the cow a bucket of water, and as he leaned over to draw out the water the cream ran out of the churn and into the well. He prodded the cow up onto the roof and it began to graze.

261

Now it was nearly dinnertime and there was still no butter, so he thought he would at least make some porridge. He filled the pot with water and hung it over the fire. Then he realized that the cow might fall off the front of the roof, so he climbed up and tied a rope around the cow's neck. He let the rope down through the chimney and when he went into the cottage he tied it to his leg so the cow couldn't fall down.

He hurried to grind the oatmeal, for the water was boiling in the pot. But while he was grinding, the cow slid off the roof, dragging the husband up the chimney.

Shortly after this, the wife came home for her dinner and found the cow hanging by its neck from the roof. She ran up and cut the rope with her scythe. She heard her husband yell and hurried into the house. There she found him covered with soot from the chimney, with the house in disarray, the child crying, and no dinner prepared.

The next day the husband happily went off to his fields, never again complaining about the idle days of his wife.

THE FOOLISH HUSBANDS
(Scotland)

A young man lived with his young wife at her parents' farm. They were quite contented, working together at all sorts of tasks.

Soon the weather turned cool and the family went to the moors to cut peat for the winter fires. After working for several hours, the young wife returned home to feed the horses and return with the family's dinner. When she went into the stables, she noticed the saddle of the mare hanging above her head and began to think to herself that if that saddle had fallen she would have been killed. She was so distraught at this thought that she sat down and wept.

The rest of the family continued to work, becoming quite hungry as they waited for her to return. Finally the mother decided she would go to their farm to make certain that no harm had befallen the young wife. She looked through the home, and finally began to search the other buildings. When she came to the stable she heard her daughter weeping.

"Whatever is the matter, my dear?" she asked, entering the stable.

"I came in here to feed the horses and saw the saddle above my head. I realized that if it had fallen I would be killed, and the thought of it made me sad."

The mother said, "You are right! It surely would have killed you. And what would I have done without my daughter?" And she sat down and joined her daughter in crying.

The father was getting quite anxious and annoyed at their absence, and he soon returned to the farm. Finding them in the stable he asked why they were weeping. When they told him, he joined them, declaring that his life would be ruined if his daughter had been lost to him.

Finally evening arrived and the young husband came in search of his family. He found them all in the stable, sharing their grief. "What has happened? Why are you all weeping?" he asked.

"When your wife came into the stable she saw the saddle above her head and realized that if it had fallen she surely would have died. We are all upset at the thought," answered the father.

"But this is foolish. It didn't fall and she is fine," the young husband said. And he went into the house to get his dinner.

The next morning he got up and said to them, "I am leaving in search of three people as foolish as you." And he left.

As he approached the next town he saw the door of a cottage standing open. Some women were spinning in the front room. He asked if they were from the town.

"We do not come from this town, but are married to some men within it," they responded.

"Well, is it a good place to live?" he asked.

The women looked at each other and chuckled. "The men of this town are so foolish that we can make them believe anything," they said.

"I would like to see that," he said. "I am wearing a gold ring. It is for the woman who can make her husband look the most foolish."

That day when the first husband came home his wife said to him, "You look sick!"

"I do?" he asked.

"Yes, you do," she answered. "You need to take off your clothes and get into bed."

The husband got into bed, feeling that he must look terribly ill. His wife soon came to his bedside.

"You look near dead," she said.

"I do?" he asked, becoming quite worried.

"Oh dear God, he is dead," she said as she reached over and closed his eyes.

He lay there feeling quite certain that he must be dead.

Meanwhile the second husband came home and his wife said, "You are not my husband!"

"What do you mean? I am not your husband?" he asked.

"No it isn't you at all," she insisted. And he left to sleep in the woods.

When the third husband came home his wife gave him his supper and he went to bed. The next morning a messenger came to tell him that he needed to attend the burial of the first husband. He began to get up, but his wife told him there was no need to hurry. As he lay in bed he soon heard the funeral passing by the house.

"Now you must hurry," called the wife. He got out of bed and looked around for his clothes.

"Where are my clothes?" he asked.

"Why you are wearing them," she answered.

"I am?" he asked.

"Yes, and you need to hurry lest you miss the burying."

He ran off down the road, not wanting to miss the burial of his friend. As the mourners saw a man in his nightshirt running toward them they ran away in fright.

The third husband was standing all alone at the head of the coffin when the second husband came out of the wood.

"Why are you out here looking as if you haven't slept?" asked the man in his nightshirt.

"Because I am not who I am. But may I ask why you are in your nightshirt?" he inquired.

"I am not in my nightshirt. My wife told me I had on all my clothes."

Suddenly the first husband sat up in the coffin and said, "And my wife told me that I was dead!"

The other two husbands were so terrified that they ran all the way home. The first husband got out of the coffin and went home. His wife got the gold ring, as he had been the most foolish of all.

BOLSTER
(England)

T here once lived a giant named Bolster who could tolerate a wife for only a single year. At the end of a year of matrimony he would dispose of his present wife and replace her with a new one. In order to rid himself of a wife he would take her to the top of St. Agnes's hill and stone her to death with huge rocks and boulders.

Bolster felt the need to cleanse himself for this strenuous annual ritual, so on the morning of the planned day, he would walk to an unused mine shaft, open a vein, and bleed himself until the mine shaft was full of his blood. Then he would seal the vein and return home to kill his wife, feeling rested and refreshed.

Since Bolster had lived for a great long time he had at last taken his thousandth wife. She had been a loving and hardworking wife, but she did not think her wifely duties extended to serving as a giant's sacrifice. Further, she could not imagine that St. Agnes was pleased with Bolster's hilltop sport.

As her marriage year drew to a close, she appealed to St. Agnes for advice, and St. Agnes appeared to her in person. The two women talked together and made their plans. Bolster's wife returned home, declaring that she was ready for his ritual.

The next morning she cheerfully prepared Bolster's breakfast and accompanied him lightheartedly to the hill. When they neared St. Agnes's hill, she asked to rest a bit and since he needed to let blood, he agreed to stop.

"There is a mine shaft right here," she said. "Would it suffice?"

"It matters not which mine shaft it is," said Bolster. And he sat down, cut open the vein on his wrist, draped it over the opening, and lay back thinking of the sport that was to come. Occasionally he looked into the shaft, but it wasn't full, so he lay back contentedly.

As he bled he was lulled to sleep by his wife's soft songs, the sun's warmth, and the waves of the nearby sea. While he drowsed she sang on until she saw the sea become streaked with red. Still she sang until he woke, feeling strangely weak. He looked out to the sea, seeing that it was no longer blue, but was blood red. Realizing that the mine shaft led to the sea, he stood up to murder his devious wife. But the loss of blood made him dizzy, and his legs fell out from under him. He collapsed on the ground and in moments was dead. As his wife departed, she thanked St. Agnes for her gracious help.

HOW TOODIE FIXED OLD GRUNT
(United States, Ozarks)

ne time there was a farmer and his wife lived in a little old cabin, right at the edge of the big timber. They had three daughters that was the prettiest girls for miles around. But the folks was awful poor, because the old man couldn't work much, and it was mighty hard for them to keep their skillet greasy.

An old bachelor named Grunt lived down the road a piece. He says he was tired of living by himself, so he married the oldest girl. She didn't want to marry old Grunt, but the folks talked her into it. He had a good farm and a fine big house, and money in the bank besides.

Things went along all right for about a year, and then all of a sudden old Grunt was raising hell all over the neighborhood, because he says his wife has run off with a peddler from Missouri. So then he married the next-to-the-oldest girl. She didn't want to marry old Grunt, but the folks talked her into it. He had a good farm and a fine big house, and money in the bank besides.

Things went along all right for about a year, and then old Grunt's second wife showed up missing, and he says she has run off with a cowboy from Oklahoma. So then he married the youngest girl. She didn't want to marry old Grunt, but the folks talked her into it. He had a good farm and a fine house, and money in the bank besides.

The youngest girl was named Toodie, and she had a boyfriend name of Jack. When old Grunt and Toodie went uptown to get married, Jack searched Grunt's house, and he found where the two sisters was killed and throwed in a old cistern. So Jack hid in the bushes, and when Toodie come back he told her, "Old Grunt killed your sisters, look out he don't kill you."

Pretty soon Toodie and old Grunt had words about something, and he says, "You're my wife now, an' you got to mind whatever I say." Toodie she sassed him right back, and old Grunt says, "You better look out, or I will do you the same as I done them other fool girls," and he pulled out his big old knife. "I'm goin' to kill you right now," he says, "an' put you down the cistern!"

Toodie was fixed for him with both hands full of pepper, and all of a sudden she threw it right in old Grunt's eyes. Old Grunt begun to beller and slash around, but he couldn't see nothing because his eyes was blinded with pepper. Jack come out from where he was a-hiding, and hit old Grunt with a stick of wood. And then him and Toodie wrastled old Grunt down and cut his head plumb off. It served him right, too. So they threw him down the cistern, and worked pretty near all night a-filling the whole thing up with rocks. And then they put dirt on top, and Toodie planted flowers, so you couldn't tell if there had ever been a cistern on the place.

About three weeks after that Toodie told everybody her husband has run off and left her. She says she can't stay in a big house like that all by herself, and she got the old folks to move in with her. Then after awhile they needed a hired man to help with the work, and so Jack he moved in too.

Things went along all right for a while, and then the old folks died off. Toodie had a good farm and a fine big house now, and money in the bank besides. So her and Jack got married, and raised a big family, and they all lived happy ever after.

THE FLYING HEAD
(United States, Native American)

Many years ago tribes still roamed freely across the land. When nights grew dark and stormy, evil monsters and spirits also would prowl the land. There were many monsters, but the most feared was the horrible Flying Head. This one had no body or legs, but was a huge head with wings protruding from its cheeks. It could fly as high as the eagle searching for its prey and then dive down faster than a hawk. Victims were unable to defend themselves because the head had thick skin to protect it. Once seized, its victims quickly fell prey to its ripping fangs. No man, woman, child, or animal was safe from the Flying Head.

One night there was a great storm. A howling wind whipped tree branches back and forth, and the rain beat against all without shelter. It was just the sort of night in which ghouls and monsters like to emerge to hunt for hapless victims. Everyone had sought hiding places to keep safe from the fiends.

But there was one woman who did not hide. She was alone with her baby in a longhouse. She knew that it had been many moons since the Flying Head had appeared, and she suspected it would seize the opportunity presented by the stormy night to prowl the earth. But she also decided that it was time someone stopped the monster from further killing.

She fed her baby and hid it well. Then she made a huge fire in the hearth, heating many large stones till they were red and glowing. Then she waited, pretending that she was busy with her evening cooking.

Suddenly the Flying Head was in the doorway. Seeing her, it drooled and leered, anticipating its feast. But the woman ignored the beast, keeping her back to it and pretending to continue with her cooking. She took a forked stick and picked up a glowing stone and pretended to eat it.

"This is delicious," she said, picking up another stone. "What a feast my family is missing. What wonderful food!" And she continued to pick up the hot stones, passing them by her mouth and then onto the floor.

The monster could not resist the thought of a great hot feast, and it rushed into the longhouse. It pushed the woman aside and swallowed in one bite the entire pile of red-hot rocks. In a moment there was a screech that was heard by all the surrounding tribes. The monster flew out of the longhouse and above the trees, howling until branches broke and the earth shook. The screams continued for several minutes, but at last they faded and were heard no more.

The young woman picked up her baby and went to the door and looked out on the now quiet night. Her people came to hear what had occurred and were amazed at her cunning. The Flying Head never returned and the people lived in peace.

THE TWELVE MONTHS
(Greece)

nce upon a time there was a widow woman who had five children, but she was so poor she hadn't so much as a brass farthing. She could find no work to do except once a week, when a gentlewoman of the neighborhood had her in to bake her bread. But for her trouble she did not give her even the corner of a loaf to take for her children to eat, but the poor woman went home with the dough on her hands and there she washed them in clean water and this water she boiled and made gruel and this the children ate. And with this gruel they were satisfied the whole week till their mother went again to make bread at the gentlewoman's house and returned, with hands unwashed, to make them gruel again.

The gentlewoman's children, for all the food they had, so much and so rich, and for all the fresh bread they fed on, were like dried mackerel. But the poor woman's children were filled out and chubby, like plump red mullet. Even the gentlewoman was amazed and spoke about it to her friends.

Her friends said, "The poor woman's children are filled out and chubby because she takes away your children's luck on her hands and gives it to her own children. That is why they get fat and yours grow thinner and dwindle away."

The gentlewoman believed this and when the day came again for making bread, she did not let the poor woman leave with her hands unwashed, but made her wash them clean, so that the luck should stay in her house. And the poor woman came home with tears in her eyes. When her children saw her and saw that she had no dough on her hands, they began to cry. On the one hand, the children wept, and on the other, the mother.

At last, like a grown woman, she steeled herself and calmed her tears, and said to her children, "Dry your eyes, my children, and weep no more, and I'll find a piece of bread for you to eat."

And she went from door to door and barely found someone to give her a stale corner of bread. She dipped it well in water and shared it among her children, and when they had eaten, she put them to bed and they fell asleep. And at midnight she left the house without looking back lest she see her children dying of hunger.

As she walked through the wilderness in the night, she saw a light shining on a high place, and went up toward it. And when she drew close to it, she saw it was a tent, and from the center hung a great candelabra with twelve candles, and underneath it hung a round thing like a ball. She went into the tent and saw twelve young men who were talking over what to do about a certain matter. The tent was round and to the right of the entrance sat three young men with their collars open, and in their hands they carried tender grass and tree blossoms. Next to these young men sat another three, with their sleeves rolled up, and coatless, carrying in their hands dry ears of wheat. Next to these sat another three young men, each with a bunch of grapes in his hand. Next to these sat another three young men, each huddled over himself and wearing a long fur from the neck to the knee.

When the young men saw the woman, they said, "Greetings, good Aunt, be seated."

And after greeting them, the woman sat down. And when she was seated, they asked her how it was she had come to that place. And the poor widow told them of her plight and her troubles. Seeing that the poor woman was hungry, one of those who wore furs got up and laid the table for her to eat, and she saw that he was lame. When the woman had eaten her fill, the young men began to ask her all kinds of things about the country, and the woman answered as well as she could.

At last the three young men that had their collars open said to her, "Now, good Aunt, how do you get on with the months of the year? How do you like March, April, and May?"

"I like them well, my lads," answered the widow, "and indeed, when these months come, the mountains and fields grow green, the earth is gay with all kinds of flowers, and from them comes scent, so that a body feels revived. All the birds begin to sing. The husbandmen see that their fields are green and rejoice in their hearts and make their granaries ready. So we have no complaints against March, April, and May, otherwise God would send fire to burn us for our ingratitude."

Then the next three young men that had their sleeves rolled up and ears of wheat in their hands, asked, "Well, and what have you to say to June, July, and August?"

"Nor can we complain over those three months, because, with the warmth they bring, they ripen the crops and all the fruits. Then the husbandmen reap what they have sown and the gardeners gather their fruit. And indeed the poor are made happy by these months, for they do not need many and costly clothes."

Then the next three young men that carried grapes, "How do you get on with the months of September, October, and November?"

"In those months," answered the woman, "folk gather grapes and make them into wine. And they are good besides in that they tell us that winter is coming, and folk set about getting in wood, coals, and heavy clothing, so as to keep warm."

Then the three young men in furs asked her, "Now, how do you get on with December, January, and February?"

"Ah, those are the months that care for us greatly," said the poor woman, "and we love them very much. And will you ask for why? Here's why! Because folk are by nature insatiable and would like to work the whole year round, so as to earn much, but those winter months come and cause us to draw into a corner and rest ourselves after the summer's labors. Folk love these months because, with their rains and snows, they cause all the seeds and grasses to grow. So, my lads, all the months are good and worthy and each one does his work, may God preserve them. It is us folk who are not good."

Then eleven of the young men made a sign to the first of those who carried grapes, and he went out and very shortly came back with a stoppered jar in his arms and he gave it to the woman, saying, "Come now, Auntie, and take this jar home with you to raise your children on."

Joyfully the woman took the jar on her shoulder, and said to the young men, "May your years be many, my lads."

"May the hour be good to you, good Aunt," they answered, and she went.

Just as dawn was breaking, she came back home and found her children still asleep. She spread out a cloth and emptied the jar onto it. When she saw that it was full of gold pieces she all but went out of her mind for joy. When it was well and truly light, she went to the baker's and bought five or six loaves and an *oka* of cheese and woke her children, washed and tidied them, set them to say their prayers, and then gave them bread and cheese, and the little dears ate until they were truly full. Then she bought a kilo of wheat and took it to the mill and had it ground, made it into dough, and took the loaves to the bakery to bake. And just as she was returning from the bakery, with the board laden with bread on her shoulder, and was almost home, the gentlewoman saw her and suspected that something had happened to her and ran up to her, to learn where she had got the flour to make bread with. The poor woman innocently told her all.

The gentlewoman was envious and made up her mind that she, too, would go to see the young men. So, that night, when her husband and children were asleep, she slipped out of the house and took the road and went on till she found the tent where the twelve months were and greeted them.

And they said to her, "Greetings, mistress, how is it you have consented to visit us?"

"I am poor," she answered, "and I have come to you for help."

"Very good," said the young men, "and how are things where you come from?"

"They might be worse," she answered.

"Well, how do you get on with the months?" they asked next.

"How, indeed," she answered. "Each one is a sore trial. Just as we are getting used to the heat of August, straightway September, October, and November come along and chill us so that this one gets a cough and that one catches a cold. Then the winter months, December, January, and February, come in and freeze us, the roads fill with snow, and we cannot go out, and as for that lame-john of a February...!" (Poor February was listening.) "And then those accursed months March, April, and May! They don't consider themselves to be summer months, and all they want is to act like winter ones, so they make the winter last nine months. And we can never go out on the first of May and drink coffee with milk in it and sit on the new grass. Then come the months June, July, and August — they're the ones that are mad to stifle us with sweat by the heat they bring. Indeed, on the fifteenth of August, we are all in a fit of coughing and the bitter winds spoil our linen on the clothesline. What more can I say, lads? Our life with the months (may curses befall them) is a dog's life."

The young man said nothing but made a sign to him who sat in the middle of those bearing grapes.

And he got up and brought in a stoppered jar and gave it to the woman, and said, "Take this jar, and when you get home, lock yourself up in a room alone and empty it out. See that you do not open it on the way."

"I won't," said the woman.

She went and joyfully came home just before dawn. Then she locked herself in a room all alone and spread out a cloth and unstoppered the jar and emptied it out. And what came out of it? Nothing but snakes. They coiled themselves about her and devoured her alive; she left her children motherless, for it is wrong for one to accuse another. But the poor woman, with her true heart and her sweet tongue, went up in the world and became a great lady, and her children flourished. There! That's what they call a happy ending!

THE WITCHES WITH THE HORNS
(Ireland)

A wealthy woman was enjoying the quiet of the late evening, carding her wool while the family slept, when suddenly her peace was interrupted by a loud knock at the door.

"Who is there?" the woman asked. When she heard no answer, she assumed that one of the neighbors needed to borrow something or needed some help, and she opened the door.

To the woman's surprise in came a woman with a horn on her forehead. She carried a pair of wool carders and without a word sat by the fire and began to card the wool.

Suddenly the horned woman cried out, "Where are the women? They are late."

Just then the woman of the house heard a second knock on the door. The horned woman nodded to her and she felt compelled to open the door once again.

This time she was greeted by a woman who had two horns on her forehead. She carried in a spinning wheel, announcing that she was the witch of two horns, and she began to spin.

This ritual was repeated, and with each knock a woman entered with an increasing number of horns on her forehead until the last arrived with twelve horns. They made themselves busy carding, spinning, and weaving. They sang ancient rhymes while they worked, but never did they speak to the woman of the house. She felt their spell upon her, and try as she might she could not rise to call for help. She could only sit and watch in fear for her life and the lives of her family.

After some time, one of the horned women said to her, "Woman, take a sieve and bring water from the well. Then make us a cake to eat."

The woman took her sieve and went to the well, wondering how she would bring water in a sieve. She leaned over the well and spoke quietly, "Oh Spirit of the Well, I truly need your help. How am I to carry water in a sieve?"

Then she heard a voice from the well saying, "Use the clay and moss and cover the sieve with it. It will hold the water."

She used the clay and moss and the sieve held the water. Then she said, "Oh Spirit of the Well, I need your help once again. How am I to rid my house of these witches?"

The voice from the well said, "Go to the north side of the house and when you get there repeat three times, 'The Mountain of the Fenian Women and the sky about it is on fire.' "

The woman of the house summoned all her courage and returned quickly to the house. She went to the north side and cried out the message as the spirit had directed.

When the witches heard her, a great moan broke out among them. They screeched with anger as they rushed out of the house.

The woman of the house returned to the well to give her thanks, but the spirit told her she must return to the house and make ready for when the witches realized the ruse and returned. The spirit told her exactly what she must do.

Though she was weary with the events of the night, the woman hastened back to her house. She took the feet-water (water for washing her children's feet) and sprinkled it on the threshold and down the path. She found that while she was at the well, the witches had made a cake using the blood of her family, rendering them helpless. She broke the cake into bits and placed a piece in the mouth of each person and they were restored. She took the cloth they had woven and placed it in the chest. Finally she dropped the bar in place across the door so that they could not easily enter.

Soon she heard the witches at her door, screaming to be let in. "Open, feet-water! Open, feet-water!"

"I can't open," said the feet-water. "I have been scattered on the threshold and down the path."

"Open cake that we mixed with blood!" screeched the witches.

"I can't, for I am broken and on the lips of the family."

"Open door, open door!" cried the witches.

"I can't, for the bar is down and I cannot move," answered the door.

The witches swirled around the house three times, looking for an entrance, but they were defeated. Their curses filled the air as they departed, but their destruction was sure.

The woman hung up the cloth to show that she had conquered the witches, and they were never bothered by the horned women again.

ONE MORE CHILD
(India)

nce upon a time there was a lady who had lots of money. She was very very rich indeed. She had plenty of food, many beautiful clothes, and a very large house which was like a palace, but she had no children. She was very sad.

One day she asked a lady friend of hers what she could do to have one child at least, and her lady friend told her, "Go to that poor woman who lives at the end of your lane, for she has a dozen children and works hard to feed and clothe them. Her husband works hard to earn enough morsels of food for the children and I often have heard her groan and moan about her poverty and lack of food for her children. Go to her," said the lady friend, "for she will surely give one child to you who are so rich and who could feed the child much better."

The rich lady considered this advice and after a while she said, "But do you really think she would give away her child?"

The lady friend replied, "Why not? Take her a bag of gold and I'm sure she will hand you the child."

The following day the rich lady took a bag of gold and happily drove to the poor woman's hut. The poor woman could hardly believe her eyes when she saw such a rich lady condescending to step in her door. Nevertheless, she smiled in humble respect and offered the rich lady a little low stool. The lady sat down and made herself comfortable as best she could.

The children, who were sprawled about the hut, huddled close to their mother and cried for food. The mother rose, brought the pot of rice soup, and served the children, not in plates, not even on leaves (she was too poor to have even these), but in little shallow pits, scooped in the clay floor and polished smooth. There were twelve polished shallow pits, the shape of bowls, six in a row. The children began to eat while the poor mother looked on. After the children had eaten every grain, they rose. Then the mother went up to each pit in turn, scooped up the rice water with her hands and lapped it up with aching hunger. After she had lapped up the water left in the twelfth pit, she raised her eyes to heaven and sighed aloud. "Oh, God! if you had but given me one more child, I would have had one pit more with which to satisfy my hunger."

The rich lady looked on in silence, amazed to hear that poor woman wishing for still one more child. Would she then part with one child for adoption? No, never! Thinking thus, the rich lady rose, pushed the bag of gold toward the poor woman, and left the hut, going her way a sadder but wiser woman.

M·A·T·U·R·E W·O·M·E·N
Bold and Wise

THE POPPET CAUGHT A THIEF
(United States, Ozarks)

One time the people that was sleeping in a tavern all got robbed. It looked like somebody must have put powders in the liquor, and stole their stuff while they was asleep. There wasn't no banks in them days, so travelers had to carry their money in gold. They claimed there was three thousand dollars missing, besides four good watches and a snuffbox which the man says he wouldn't have took a hundred dollars for it. The fellow that run the tavern would not let nobody leave, neither. "Them valuables must be got back, or else I will wade knee-deep in blood," he says, "because the honor of my house has been throwed in jeopardy!"

The travelers was getting pretty mad, but just then an old woman come along and she says, "What is the matter?" The tavernkeeper he told her, and the old woman says, "My poppet can catch any thief in the world, and it won't take ten minutes." She pulled a little wooden doll out of her saddlebag, and rubbed some walnut-juice on it, and set it on a stand-table. "Them travelers can come in here one at a time," she says, "and the rest of us will set just outside the door. Every one of 'em must grab that there poppet and squeeze it. If the man's honest you won't hear a sound, but if he's a thief the poppet will holler like a stuck pig." The travelers says it is all foolishness, but they will try anything to get away from this lousy tavern. So they went in one after another, but the poppet didn't holler at all.

The old woman looked considerable set back. "Did you all pinch the poppet?" she asked. The travelers all says they squeezed it hard as they could. "Hold out your hands," says the old woman, and she studied each man's fingers mighty careful. Pretty soon she pointed at the traveler that done all the hollering about his snuffbox. "That's the thief," she says. The fellow tried to lie out of it, but when they got the rope around his neck he begun to holler. "If you turn me loose I will give everything back," says he. "But if you hang me you will never get a penny, because that gold is hid where you couldn't find it in a thousand years." Well, the tavernkeeper was unanimous for hanging him anyhow, but them travelers naturally wanted to get their money back. They promised to put the robber on a good horse and give him three hours' start. He made everybody swear with their right hand on the Book, and then he showed them where the stuff was hid under a woodpile. So pretty soon they turned the son-of-a-gun loose, and off he went down the road at a dead run. Nobody ever did catch up with him, neither.

Soon as the people got their money and watches, they begun to feel pretty good again. The tavernkeeper set up a big dinner, and everybody eat and drunk till they was full as a tick. Pretty soon they raffled off the robber's watch to pay for the dinner, and the man that won the watch give it to the old woman. Finally a fellow passed the old woman's bonnet around for a silver collection, and then he says, "You can have all this money, if you will tell us how you knowed which one was the thief."

The old woman just grinned at him. "Didn't you hear my poppet holler, when that scoundrel grabbed it?" she says. The fellow says of course not, and everybody knows a wooden doll can't holler. "A thief don't know nothing for sure," says the old woman. "Every one of you honest men squeezed that poppet. But the robber figured there might be a trick to it, so he never touched the poppet. All I done was to look for the fellow that didn't have no walnut juice on his hands."

THE WOMAN AND THE ROBBER
(United States, Ozarks)

Once upon a time, maybe it was in the War between the States, a woman was carrying gold and greenbacks under her clothes. She was taking it to some of her kinfolks up north, where things was not so disorderly. She had a good buggy at home, but it was better to keep off the main traveled road, so she come through on horseback, a-riding sidesaddle. She rode up to a house, and the man said he would show her a shortcut where she wanted to go. When they come out on a high bluff he pulled her off the horse and says, "Give me your money." She says the money is sewed under her dress and he must look the other way, as she is a decent woman. He kind of started to turn, and in that minute she out with a derringer and shot him in the guts, before he could throw down on her. Soon as he was dead, the woman took his wallet and pushed him over the edge, and then she went on down the road.

When she got to her kinfolks' place, she told them what happened. After the trouble blowed over they all come South again, and camped with their wagons on top of the big bluff. And next morning the boys went around by the path and found a lot of dead people at the bottom of the holler. They was folks that this man had robbed, and then throwed off the bluff so they couldn't tell nobody.

RACHEL
(United States, Northeast)

L‌ong ago there lived an old woman named Rachel. She lived in a town along the coast of Massachusetts. No one knew where she came from and she had no family. Her shelter was a mean hut near the rocks by the sea.

Though she was poor and raggedy, she was wise in the ways of the weather. She had little to do but wander the coast, day and night. Few people sought her company, but those who fished or traveled knew to ask her advice before they tried to leave the harbor.

Because of her knowledge of the sea, the fishermen had come to respect her and value her advice. Before departing to fish, they would respectfully seek her counsel, rewarding her upon their return by leaving a fish or two at her hut. Rachel survived by providing this service to the fishermen.

One day a ship put into the harbor. The sailors came ashore and soon heard stories of Rachel from the local fishermen. Having come from Boston, these sailors decided that these fishermen were simple and superstitious. They went to Rachel's hut and asked her for advice, but when she spoke to them they began to ridicule her. Rachel warned them against such foolhardy behavior, but they left, deriding her attempts at witchcraft.

Rachel grew more and more angry. She called to the departing sailors that there was a curse on the ship and that they should not sail off in her. But they continued into the town, ignoring her cries and planning their departure.

During the late hours of that night, one of the sailors slipped up to Rachel's hut and set it on fire. He dashed back to his ship as it made ready to depart. The local townspeople rushed to Rachel's hut to put out the fire and saw Rachel on a nearby rock, wrapped in an old sailcloth, looking toward the sea. Soon the departing ship passed the rock, and Rachel glared malevolently at the ship and crew.

Just outside the harbor the ship hit a reef and sank. The townspeople abandoned the hopeless fight against the fire and hurried to save the crew. All the sailors were saved except the one who had set fire to Rachel's hut. He drowned and his body was never recovered.

Later the people returned to Rachel's smoldering hut. They went to where she was sitting on the rock but found that she was dead. They buried her where her hut had once stood.

THE LITTLE OLD WOMAN WHO
WENT TO THE NORTH WIND
(Norway)

A little old woman wished to make a loaf of bread, so she went to the miller and bought a bowl of flour. She hurried home, eager to make her bread. Just as she neared her house, the North Wind whisked by, blowing her flour to the four corners of the world.

The little old woman was dismayed at this bit of bad luck, but she took a coin and returned to the miller and bought another bowl of flour. As she neared her house she held the bowl very carefully, but once again the North Wind blustered by, scattering her flour to the four corners of the world.

Once again the little old woman took a coin to the miller and bought a bowl of flour. Despite her care, the North Wind swept the contents of her bowl to the four corners of the world.

"I will go to the North Wind and demand that he give me back my three bowls of flour!" declared the little old woman.

She set out and walked a long way until she came to a mountaintop where she found the North Wind.

"How are you?" asked the little old woman.

"I am quite fine. What might I do for you, dear woman?" asked the North Wind.

"I would ask only that you return to me the three bowls of flour that you blew away," replied the little old woman.

"I am afraid I can not fulfill your request, for I have blown those bowls of flour to the four corners of the world. But I will give you something so that you will never be hungry again. Here is my magic tablecloth. Whenever you say to it, 'Cloth, spread yourself,' it will be covered with the finest of food and drink."

The little old woman thanked the North Wind for his kindness, took the magic tablecloth and started for her home. Having had no rest for some time, she stopped at an inn for the night, and feeling quite hungry, she spread out the cloth and said, "Cloth, spread yourself."

In a twinkling of an eye, the cloth was covered with a feast of such delicacies that the old woman hardly knew where to begin. As she ate, the innkeeper smelled her food and peeked in through the keyhole, and when he spied the tablecloth he decided to have it for himself.

When the little old woman went to sleep, the innkeeper sneaked into her room and took the tablecloth, hiding it in his cupboard.

The next morning, the little old woman was distraught at finding that her magic tablecloth was missing. She made her way back up the mountain, telling the North Wind that she feared it had been stolen.

"I will give you my magic staff," said the North Wind. "All you must do is return to the inn and say, 'Staff, dance.' The staff will dance on the toes of the thief."

The little old woman thanked the North Wind for his assistance once again and returned to the inn. There she found the innkeeper entertaining his guests with a magnificent feast provided by her magic tablecloth.

The little old woman wasted no time in saying, "Staff, dance."

The staff danced right over to the innkeeper, dancing on his toes. No matter what the innkeeper did, the staff continued to bounce up and down on his toes.

"Please stop this staff!" cried the innkeeper.

"Then return to me what is mine!" cried the little old woman.

The innkeeper gladly gave over the tablecloth and the little old woman left. The staff danced back to the North Wind and the little old woman returned to her home.

From that day forth, she was never hungry, for the magic tablecloth provided her with the most sumptuous meals until she died.

MARTHA, THE HOLY WOMAN

(France)

Night had fallen and stars shimmered softly on the gentle surface of the Mediterranean Sea off the southern coast of France. Quietly a large, long black shape with two gleaming, green eyes slithered through the water, making straight for the mouth of the Rhone River. It continued up the river, past towns and villages until it came to a forest. The creature crawled up the riverbank, disappearing into the trees.

In the nearby town of Nerluc a woodcutter made ready to go into the forest. He planned to chop down an oak tree and sell the wood to carpenters. He bade his wife goodbye, promising to be home for the evening meal. But he never returned.

Fearing an accident, his wife entreated two friends to go into the woods in search of him. The next morning they set out, confident they would come back with the carpenter. But they too never returned. The people of Nerluc became very frightened, reluctant to risk more lives.

It was not long before a group of people from a nearby town plodded along the path that led through the forest to Nerluc. They approached a particularly murky part of the forest, damp with vegetation and dark with the thick trees overhead.

As they uneasily worked their way along, they were suddenly confronted with two green, glowing eyes, a gaping mouth lined with dripping teeth, and a massive body covered with scales. It was a dragon! It had the advantage and quickly slaughtered all but one man, who fled toward Nerluc.

As he stumbled into the town, he gasped, "A dragon! It killed everyone but me!"

The town council met and advised people to avoid the forest. Through other routes messages were sent to nearby towns, warning of the danger. Hopefully the dragon would become hungry and leave.

Indeed the dragon became hungry, but rather than straying away from Nerluc, it silently slunk into town, crushed a house, devoured everyone inside, and returned to the forest.

The town council met again, and they decided to ask for volunteers who were willing to try to kill the dragon. Sixteen brave young men slipped into the forest, confident they could end the evil rampage. They found the dragon napping after his midnight repast, and they courageously attacked it with their swords and axes. But their weapons were useless, and the now enraged dragon killed half of the heroic men as the others fled into town.

The town council met again. The mayor led the discussion: "Somehow we must kill this beast, or we will all die. If only we had a magician who could assist us."

One of the councillors became excited. "Wait! We are forgetting about the holy woman, Martha. She is not far away, and I have heard that she can perform miracles. Perhaps she can help!"

Two of the councillors traveled at once, finding Martha sympathetic to their plight. "Ah," she said, "this sounds like the Tarasque, a vile creature indeed. I will return with you and try to help."

They returned to Nerluc, where they were met by many of the citizens and the mayor.

"Do you have a plan? Do you need any supplies or weapons? May we offer our assistance?" inquired the mayor.

"No," Martha replied. "I shall go alone into the forest, and when I find the beast I will decide what to do. I will take only my holy water and prayer book. I will leave now, before another person falls victim to the Tarasque."

The people followed her to the edge of the forest, marveling at her courage, watching uneasily as she disappeared into the woods.

Martha was uneasy as well, knowing that if the Tarasque saw her first she would be at a disadvantage. As she moved deeper into the forest, the birds stopped singing, and the silence became sinister. She nearly stumbled over human bones scattered through the underbrush, and she slowed her pace even more. She peered through the gloom and suddenly saw a broad scaly backside. Knowing it must be the Tarasque, she pulled the cork from her bottle of holy water.

Hearing her slight movement, the Tarasque turned its ugly head and stared at Martha. It opened its immense drooling mouth, ready to swallow Martha. Murmuring a desperate prayer, Martha threw the holy water into its mouth.

For a moment both Martha and the Tarasque seemed frozen. Then the Tarasque closed its mouth and dropped its head at Martha's feet. She turned toward the town and commanded the beast to follow. The enormous Tarasque obediently trudged behind her.

The people were awed when Martha and the dragon entered the town. She led it to the town square and ordered it to lie down. Then she turned to the people.

"The Tarasque can no longer kill, but it must be destroyed in punishment for those it has murdered. Your strongest man must use a club to hit it on the top of its head."

Martha then returned to her home, but her bravery and holiness were never forgotten by the town.

THE WOMAN IN THE MOON
(United States, Hawaii)

Long ago there lived a woman named Hina who had lived for many years. Day after day she made tapa cloths out of the bark of a tree by beating it with a mallet. Then she used the cloth to make clothing for her family. Her son and daughter had finally grown up and left home, leaving her with a husband who had become more embittered and demanding as he grew older. He offered her no help or companionship.

Each night when her cloth making was finished and the sun went down, she would fetch water with a gourd, fix the dinner, and pray for rest from her endless tasks. She would think about how she might escape from her weary existence and find peace. One day she was pounding out the tapa cloth and cried aloud, "If only I could go away and find some rest!"

The rainbow heard Hina's cry and set a rainbow in front of her. Hina decided she would follow the rainbow up to heaven and then to the sun where she would be forever at rest. She began her long journey up the rainbow, but when she passed through the clouds the sun's rays began to burn her. She pushed herself to continue, but the rays became too hot. The sun began to singe her hair and skin, and she felt her strength ebbing away. She let her body slide back down the rainbow, grieving at her failure.

When she had returned to earth, darkness had descended. As she came to her house she saw that her husband had fetched the water. He was grumbling about this chore, and when he saw her he reprimanded her for being gone from the house. His words strengthened her resolve to find quiet and rest. She noticed that the sun was gone, and as she stared at the quiet coolness of the moon she realized it would be a far better place to rest than the sun.

Before she left again, she entered the house and gathered up all the possessions that were dear to her and placed them in an empty gourd. As she left the house she saw that the rainbow had not deserted her, but had arched to the moon. Her husband followed her out and when he saw her with her belongings he knew she was not returning soon.

"Where are you going, my wife?" he asked brusquely.

"I am going to the moon where I can rest quietly," she answered.

She began to climb the rainbow, but her husband cried out in anger, grabbed her foot, and pulled her down. Hina felt the bones in her foot break as they fell together to earth, but she pulled herself up and started up the rainbow once again. Her husband was too stunned at her determination to try to stop her again.

Hina's lameness and the pain slowed her, but her heart filled with joy as she continued to climb up the rainbow. She climbed until she came to the stars and prayed they would guide her to the moon. The stars heard her prayer and led her onward.

Finally she came to the moon. It guided her to a place where she could keep her belongings and rest. Hina was overjoyed. She knew she would never leave this place of peace and quiet.

These days the people of Hawaii look up at the moon and see Hina there with her gourd of precious possessions at her side. Her foot is still lame, but her serenity and benevolence soothe all who take the time to look.

ST. DAVID'S FLOOD
(England)

St. David's Flood is a name for the spring tide which in the old days brought Christian saints to Somerset. They came up river on St. David's Flood. Later on there was a fishing hamlet down by the shore, and one day all the men were out fishing and a little herd boy came running back to the village in terror to say that six Danish galleys were sailing along and would come up the river on St. David's Flood. Well, the women and the children scampered away to the nearby village of Uphill, which could give them some safety, and they could warn the farming folk there. But one old granny was down by the riverside gathering gladdon for thatching her cottage, and as the long ships sailed by she crouched down among the rushes and watched the Danes landing and scattering to plunder. They had tied up their boats and left them without even a guard. St. David's Flood had brought them up, the very flood that had carried the saints up in olden days, but it was turning now, it was not waiting for the pirates to finish their work.

When they had gone the old woman crept out from her hiding place and watched the tide. It runs out very quickly there, and she saw that it was on the turn. So she undid the mooring of each of the galleys, and then she stood and watched them jostling against each other, going down river and out into the Severn Sea. In the meantime the men of Uphill had done their work well. They had ambushed the loaded pirates and driven them back toward their boats. But no boats were there, and not a *hurd-yed** survived that bloody day. And that, they say, is why the village is called Bleadon.

Hurd-yed means red-head, and it is supposed to mean either Danish or pixy blood in Somerset.

THE WHITE-HAIRED OLD WOMAN
(United States, Native American)

When Indian tribes were at war, homeless or wandering Indians were regarded with mistrust. Even women and children were subject to suspicion.

There was once an old, white-haired woman and her grandson who had been separated from their tribe. They traveled long distances in search of a tribe who would give them refuge. Again and again they were turned away. Wearily they continued, hoping that someone would take pity on them.

After many moons they came to the place of a tribe who had little to call their own; indeed they rarely had enough to eat. But they had compassion, and they offered to share what little they had with the old woman and the boy.

The chieftain came to them and told them they were welcome to stay, but that their lives would be hard, with starvation often threatening their existence. Game was scarce and hunters were forced to travel great distances to find small amounts of meat.

But the old woman was so grateful for their shelter that she offered to care for their children while the mothers tended to the chores and the fathers hunted.

One day all the adults had left the camp to hunt and gather food. The children were content to play, but they looked forward to the return of their parents and the arrival of the day's food. With the coming of the old woman, they found the days passed quickly thanks to her many stories of the earth and heavens.

But what made the days even more pleasant for the children was that they no longer had to wait for the return of their parents to be given a meal. Each day the old woman would disappear for a short time, returning with a large kettle of gruel.

"This is maize gruel," she told the children. "I will feed you every day that you behave well and obey me."

The children were delighted at having a midday meal and never gave the old woman a moment's trouble. Each day she would make them content and happy by bringing them their gruel. Each day they played and grew stronger.

Many moons passed and still the old woman cared for and fed the children. But her many years of hard work began to take their measure and she began to look quite fragile.

One morning she called her grandson to her and said, "My time to leave you grows near. But I am content to depart because I have finished my job. I have planted the maize grains near the camp. They have taken root. All that is left is for you and the children to water and tend them. In the spring you will see the sprouts, and with love and care there will be a harvest in the fall."

The old woman never left her bed and never spoke again. But each noon there would always be a kettle of maize gruel for the children. She lived on through the days of summer warmth until the day the golden maize was ready for harvest. Then she disappeared forever.

The chieftain called his tribe together, saying, "The old woman has repaid our hospitality manyfold. Never again will we be hungry if we tend the maize with the love she showed us."

Ever since the old woman with the white hair came to live with that tribe, the Indians remember her love when the corn shows its white hairs.

THE WISE WOMAN
(Algeria)

The people of a village in Algeria were under siege. Lack of food, water, and medical supplies had nearly reduced them to total destruction. Many had already died, and the remaining few were losing hope.

The mayor called a meeting and said, "My dear friends, the end is near. If we don't surrender immediately we will all die anyway. Perhaps our enemy will take pity on those of us who are still alive if we submit to them now."

The villagers listened with heavy hearts, bowing their heads with this latest burden. Then Aicha came forward. She was an ancient woman, but her eyes were still bright and she walked with dignity.

She turned to the people. "We must not give in just yet. I have an idea and if you will help me I believe we will be saved."

"What is your plan, Aicha?" the mayor asked.

"First I will need a calf!" said Aicha firmly.

The mayor was dismayed. "How can you request a calf? There has not been a calf in our village for months."

But Aicha insisted she needed a calf, and the villagers searched far and wide for one. And after some time they found a calf in the shed of a stingy old man who had hoped to sell it later for a healthy price. The villagers triumphantly brought the calf to Aicha, leaving the old man sputtering in anger at his loss.

"You have done well," praised Aicha when she saw the calf. "Now bring me some corn."

The villagers groaned upon hearing her request. But she entreated them to search everywhere. And soon they all returned with bits and pieces of corn until there was enough to fill a bucket. Aicha added some water to it and fed it to the calf.

"How can you feed that calf when children are crying for a bit to eat and people are dying of hunger each day?" asked the mayor.

But Aicha continued to feed the calf, stating, "Have faith, sir, and you will see that this will save our village."

323

The mayor resigned himself to giving in to her. When the calf had finished eating, Aicha led it to the city wall and told the sentry to open the gates. The mayor had followed and nodded to the sentry to do as she requested. When the gates were opened Aicha pushed out the calf which began to graze on the grass outside the gates.

The enemy was watching and wasted no time in capturing the cow and taking it in triumph to their leaders. The enemy king was stunned when he saw what they had brought.

"How can this be?" exclaimed the king. "I thought the villagers were starving and yet they have a calf that they can spare. They must be better prepared than we had assumed. However, let us not waste it. We shall feast tonight."

The men soon had slaughtered the cow and were shocked to find that the cow's stomach contained undigested corn. They took this news to the king who became even more concerned.

"If these villagers can feed corn to this calf they must have more food than we do. We cannot outlast them or we will be the ones who starve." The king's men agreed and the king gave the order to retreat.

The next morning the sentry ran to the mayor with the grand news. The mayor gathered the villagers and announced that as Aicha had promised, the enemy had departed. The villagers cheered Aicha and she lived the remainder of her days with honor and comfort.